CHAUMET

Parisian Jeweler Since 1780

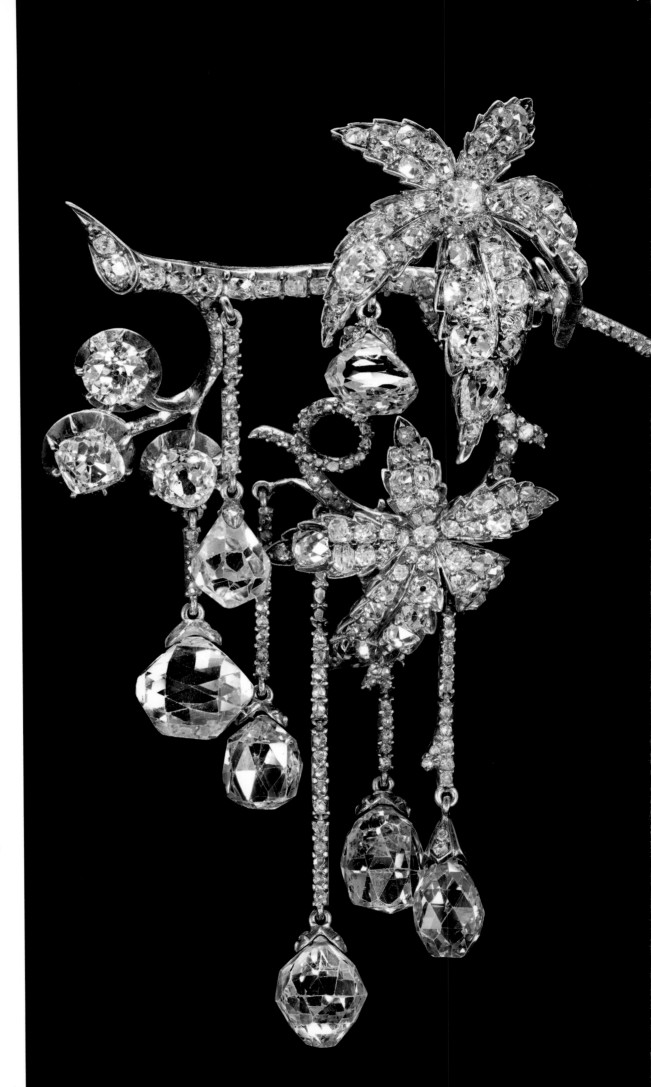

RIGHT
"Mancini" style hair ornament,
attributed to Fossin & Fils,
c. 1840.
Gold, diamonds,
H. 9.5; W. 5.6; D. 2 cm
Private Collection

PAGE 4
Chaumet workshop,
gold melt jets in a filing shovel

PAGE 5
Chaumet workshop,
jeweler's workbench

EXECUTIVE EDITOR
Suzanne Tise-Isoré
Style & Design Collection

EDITORIAL COORDINATION AT CHAUMET
Karine Huguenaud

EDITORIAL COORDINATION
Boris Guilbert

EDITORIAL ASSISTANCE
Inès Ferrand-Pérez
Pauline Garrone
Lara Lo Calzo

GRAPHIC DESIGN
Pitis e Associati, Paris

TRANSLATED FROM FRENCH BY
Deke Dusinberre
Alexandra Keens
Mot.tiff Unlimited Group, Paris

TYPESETTING
Joseph Tsai

PROOFREADING
Michael Thomas

PRODUCTION
Corinne Trovarelli

COLOR SEPARATION
Les Artisans du Regard, Paris

PRINTED BY
Musumeci S.p.A., Italy

Simultaneously published in French as
Chaumet Joaillier Parisien Depuis 1780
© Flammarion S.A., Paris, 2017

English-language edition
© Flammarion S.A., Paris, 2017

Flammarion S.A.
87, quai Panhard et Levassor
75647 Paris Cedex 13
France
editions.flammarion.com
styleetdesign-flammarion.com

17 18 19   3 2 1
ISBN: 978-2-08-020316-8
Legal Deposit: 04/2017

CHAUMET

Parisian Jeweler Since 1780

EDITORIAL DIRECTION BY

Henri Loyrette

FOREWORD BY

Jean-Marc Mansvelt

Flammarion

CONTENTS

CHAUMET: STANDING THE TEST OF TIME

Jean-Marc Mansvelt

CEO of Chaumet

The Hôtel Baudard de Sainte-James, entrance to Chaumet's historic salons

There is something special about running a company that has nearly 250 years of history. That's because, unlike many other firms, it cannot be summed up by a biography of its founder or founders. On the contrary, a house of jewelry that has been a renowned leader in its field for such a long time embodies a succession of names and talents, all of whom have endowed it with their own personal contribution, as well as the mark of their times. Few firms today can boast such a rich history, embracing numerous periods of artistic creativity and taste, resulting not in a single-minded career that reflects a lone founding figure but rather in multiple paths of expressiveness, representing the sum of those who contributed to it. Chaumet is one such house. Such a history requires both clear-sightedness and humility—clear-sightedness in seeing what really goes into a multi-faceted uniqueness, and humility in realizing that we are just custodians and trustees charged with enhancing and bequeathing a tradition.

In over two centuries of history, led by the artistic sensitivity of its various heads from Marie-Étienne Nitot to Joseph Chaumet, the house of Chaumet has explored almost all the styles and periods it has encountered, whether through its talent for reflecting the spirit of the times or through anticipation of its clients' tastes. Chaumet boasts a twin heritage—an exceptionally rich material heritage in the form of historic pieces and archival drawings, and the artistic heritage of a long tradition of tastes and visions that collectively comprise the unique "Chaumet spirit."

The multiplicity of periods and fashions has not, however, prevented the emergence of a coherent style. On the contrary, the apparent diversity of the Chaumet tradition is based on broad stylistic principles that each period must reconsider and reinterpret in its own way, based on two key themes: the first, related to the notion of power, is emblematic and highly structured, while the second, related to feelings, is poetic and naturalistic. These two main themes in fact converge more than they diverge, their special interrelationship being what gives Chaumet all its relevance and coherence today.

FIRST THEME: EMBLEMS OF POWER

This theme obviously includes not only the historic regalia for the coronation of Napoleon I but also a long tradition of grandeur, whether based on social rank or state power. It is embodied by tiaras—long a Chaumet specialty—as well as by royal and imperial symbols (crowns, eagles, fleurs-de-lis, coats of arms, and so on), not to mention an entire range of decorative motifs culturally related to the symbolic idiom of power: laurel leaves, ears of wheat, fasces, trophies, etc.

This emblematic repertoire certainly stems from the firm's start as one of the suppliers of regalia for Napoleon I's coronation. This ongoing link between Chaumet and history is still evident in the fact that we are the sole jeweler to have several pieces in the Louvre's permanent collection.

Logically extending from this first stylistic theme is an entire vocabulary directly related to classical architecture, such as friezes, foliage, scrollwork, palmettes, key patterns, fretwork, rosettes, and bowknots. All these motifs descend from the grand decorative tradition of the seventeenth and eighteenth centuries, as exemplified by the countless tiaras designed by Chaumet.

SECOND THEME: A FEELING FOR NATURE

The first theme—structured and emblematic—is matched by a second aesthetic principle that is equally crucial to Chaumet, for it evokes a sense of poetry through nature. This repertoire embraces an entire universe of plants, flowers, leaves, and bouquets, accompanied by a bucolic menagerie largely populated by birds and insects—not forgetting the wing motif, another of Chaumet's hallmarks. All these motifs are obviously combined in virtuoso designs.

This natural repertoire also includes wonderful allusions to water and ice, conveyed with unparalleled virtuosity, as well as to heavenly bodies such as the sun, moon, and stars. The virtuoso handling of natural motifs probably reached its peak under the aegis of Joseph Chaumet over a long period that lasted throughout the Belle Époque and beyond. Other jewelers shared this taste, of course, but with Chaumet it attained peerless refinement and artistry: certain details of flowers and insects were handled with a wonderful sense of naturalism, as witnessed by the many surviving drawings of plants that were subsequently used in designing jewelry. This naturalism perhaps reflected the fullest expression of an art of drawing and composition that Chaumet has always managed to transform into light, graceful, exquisitely delicate items.

This penchant for nature, by the way, has not been limited to noble motifs, for it also embraces humbler plants such as the fruit, wheat, and wild flowers gracing many tiaras still in the collection.

Another aspect of this same repertoire concerns the sensitive, poetic items known as "jewels of sentiment." As a leading jeweler among grand rivals prior to 1850, Chaumet can boast that it furnished such items not only to the French royal and imperial courts, but also throughout the Romantic era, a very special period in the history of jewelry in the

"Apollonian Firmament" necklace, La Nature de Chaumet Collection, 2016. Gold, sapphires, diamonds, moonstones Chaumet Paris

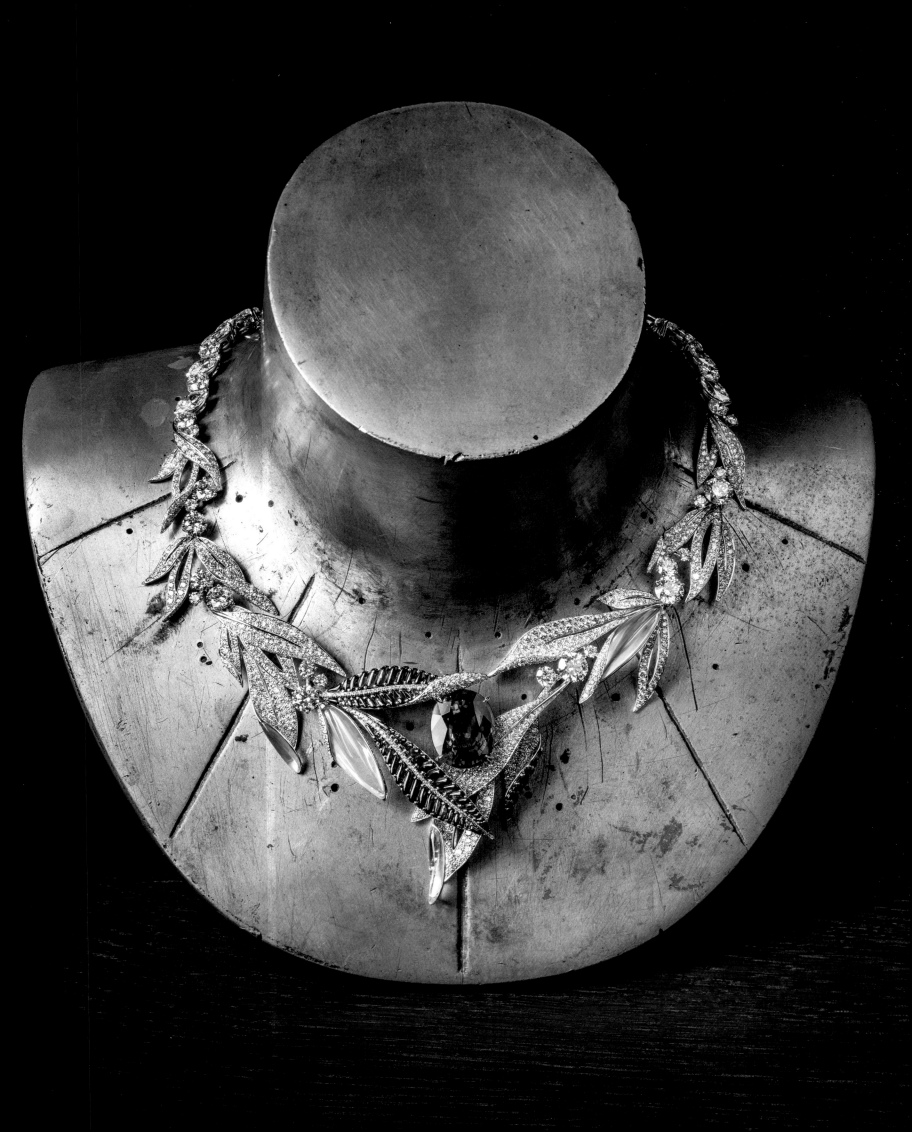

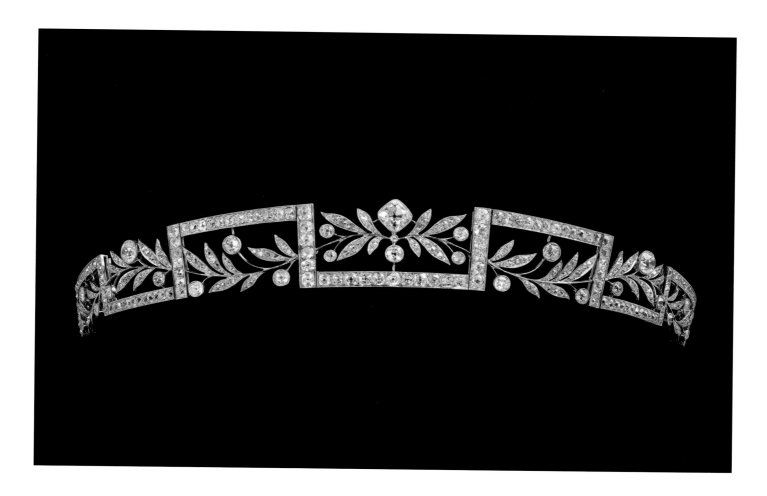

way it built on an eighteenth-century tradition to develop a coded, sentimental vocabulary. At that time, the most brilliant minds of the day were familiar with the firm, as revealed in the books of various Romantic authors such as Balzac, Musset, Théophile Gautier, and Alexandre Dumas. The repertoire of jewelry obviously includes famous acrostic bracelets—such as those ordered by Emperor Napoleon and his wife Joséphine—not to mention an entire series of crowned hearts, dates, mottos, etc. Such signs of love are still a priority at Chaumet, whether via engagement and wedding rings or through its line of *Liens* ("Links"), an emblematic yet modern expression of jewelry of sentiment.

TWO INTERSECTING PRINCIPLES

Far from being contradictory, these two themes share numerous features. One, already mentioned, is the artistry of drawing and design. Yet also worth stressing is the strong link that both themes have with symbolism: whether alluding to emblems of power or signs of feeling, whether coded in the language of flowers or acrostics, Chaumet displays unerring skill in transforming symbols into jewels. Few jewelers have been able to master the "language of jewelry" to the same extent because Chaumet has benefited not only from its own talent but also—and perhaps above all—from the input of great clients whose sense of distinction was expressed through the subtle coordination of symbols. Take a Chaumet ring that contained a sentimental lock of hair and was also adorned with the coronet of a marquess, which a character in an Alfred de Musset novel had to decipher. This double stylistic heritage is certainly reinforced not only by Chaumet's skill in arraying symbols but also in its clientele's skill in employing and interpreting them.

LEFT

Design for the "Scottish bowknot" brooch, 1907.
Graphite pencil, gouache, ink wash, and white gouache highlights,
H. 10.6; W. 9.5 cm
Chaumet Paris Collection

FACING PAGE

"Scottish bowknot" brooch, Joseph Chaumet (1852–1928), 1907.
Platinum, gold, diamonds, and colored gemstones,
H. 9; W. 6 cm
Private Collection

Chaumet's image encompasses this double heritage. Unlike firms whose heritage is expressed in the singular, Chaumet's is conjugated in the plural. Its vocabulary plays on the link, or tension, between two rich and complementary dimensions, the former playing on symbols of power, the second on signs of feeling (whether for nature or romance). Chaumet forges a unity from grandeur and subtlety, history and poetry, and a relationship between emblematic and bucolic motifs that have survived through the generations, as respectively embodied today in the emblematic *Joséphine* and bucolic *Hortensia* (Hydrangea) lines, not to mention countless designs of exclusive jewelry.

In the end, it might be said that the link between these two themes goes back to the couple who first launched the firm on the path to greatness: Napoleon and Joséphine. Emperor Napoleon understood the importance of symbols in affirming the legitimacy of his power, while Joséphine, his first wife and the love of his life, had a sense of beauty that left a lasting mark on the taste of her day. Their very special love story, at the summit of the nation, is documented not only in the letters they exchanged throughout their lives but also in the many jewels of sentiment that Napoleon ordered for Joséphine. Joséphine's elevation to the rank of empress as immortalized in the painting by Jacques-Louis David, which depicts the tiaras and regalia made by the firm, indeed celebrates the marriage of power and feeling that remains at Chaumet's stylistic heart.

It seems as though this founding act is still central to the firm, as though the grandeur of the symbols of power wielded by Emperor Napoleon was matched by his love of the empress and her passion for nature. This stylistic heritage halfway between strength and sentiment, between symbolism and naturalism, perfectly reflects the era in which the firm was founded, when the "grand French style" inherited from the classical age was subtly wedded to a sensitivity to nature and feelings typical of the Romantic era. Ultimately, this combination is very specific to Paris, where Chaumet was born, the city that Balzac—one of the firm's famous clients—compared to an ocean where, however fully explored, "there will always be lonely and unexplored regions in its depths, caverns unknown, flowers and pearls … overlooked or forgotten by the divers of literature."

LEFT
"Apollonian Firmament"
necklace, La Nature de
Chaumet Collection, 2016.
Gold, sapphires,
diamonds, moonstones
Chaumet Paris

FACING PAGE
"Carnation" tiara ordered
by Monsieur de Wendel,
Joseph Chaumet
(1852–1928), 1907.
Platinum and diamonds,
H. 7; W. 19 cm
Private Collection,
Courtesy of Albion Art
Jewellery Institute

"THIS RADIATING WORLD OF GOLD AND STONES"

Henri Loyrette

Steeped in republican asceticism, Pliny the Elder wrote that, "the worst crime against mankind was committed by him who was the first to put a ring upon his fingers." Tradition does not name the culprit, but Pliny mentions Prometheus, who wore on his finger a fragment of Caucasian stone set on an iron ring, "such being the first ring and the first jewel known." After having catalogued all the registers of nature, the Roman author devoted the final book of his *The Natural History* to what we call "gemstones." He explained this conclusion, or apotheosis, as follows:

> That nothing may be wanting to the work which I have undertaken, it still remains for me to speak of precious stones: a subject in which the majestic might of Nature presents itself to us, contracted within a very limited space, though, in the opinion of many, nowhere displayed in a more admirable form. So great is the value that men attach to the multiplied varieties of these gems, their numerous colors, their constituent parts, and their singular beauty, that, in the case of some of them, it is looked upon as no less than sacrilege to engrave them, for signets even, the very purpose for which, in reality, they were made. Others, again, are regarded as beyond all price, and could not be valued at any known amount of human wealth; so much so that, in the case of many, it is quite sufficient to have some single gem or other before the eyes, there to behold the supreme and absolute perfection of Nature's work.[1]

A gemstone, according to Pliny, is a valuable compendium of the universe (condensing and explaining it) and an object of contemplation and meditation, and yet a gem—like the gold in which it is set—is the product of an impious act: in order to extract it, men must rummage in the bowels of our planet—"our sacred parent"—following every vein to the end, hollowing the earth so much that it has become "undermined … beneath our feet."

[1] Pliny the Elder, *The Natural History*, trans. John Bostock and H.T. Riley (London: Taylor and Francis, 1855), respectively XXXIII: 4, XXXVII: 1, XXXVII:1, and (subsequent passage) XXXIII: 1

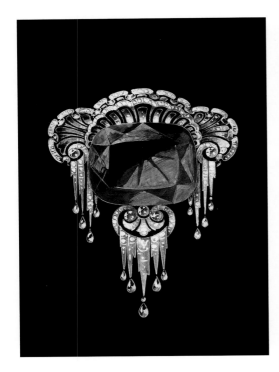

Thus in the late first century, Pliny simultaneously admired nature's wonders, worried about the way they were mined, waxed enthusiastic over human ingenuity in transforming them, and stigmatized their tendency to induce cupidity and an immoderate taste for luxury. This ambivalent attitude would mark subsequent centuries. Long sought after and desired, patiently and artistically assembled yet easily taken apart, the regalia of gems—by which we mean precious stones and the sundry objects and jewelry made from them—were among the most costly and symbolic items in the treasury of a church or state. But they also underwent vicissitudes. In a sad echo of the Revolutionary vandalism a century earlier, in 1887 France's "crown jewels" were sold. True, the virtuous young French republic was seeking to eradicate everything that reminded it of the monarchy, but it despoiled a heritage in which it saw no artistic interest, merely material value. Paradoxically, nothing is more volatile than anything connected with these hard stones; companions in exile, they vanish with life's ill fortune; cut and set, re-cut and re-set, they follow the twists and turns of history, the caprices of fashion and, on a domestic level, the joys and misfortunes of a family. The *Régent* diamond, for example, first adorned the monarchy's coronation sword, then briefly graced the imperial sword, only to be reduced today to the nudity of its many carats and wonderful sparkle in an armored display case in the Louvre's Apollo Gallery; a chatelaine worn by the Duchess of Luynes and exhibited at the Universal Exposition of 1855 was simplified in the late nineteenth century into a pendant watch; and part of the lavish set of jewelry belonging to the Duchess of Trévise was reset as a tiara in 1904. The examples could go on and on. The value of the stones, often much greater than the setting, made the latter seem secondary and makeshift, designed only to serve the gems it supports and enhances. That is what largely explains the marginal presence of jewelry in museums and its limited treatment by art historians. Despite the pioneering work of Henri Vever, jewelry still represents the most glaring absence in the history of the decorative arts.

Strangely, the same is true of literature, where usually vague, discreet allusions do little more than name the stones. Balzac and Proust, so attentive to garments, barely mentioned jewelry. Maupassant, in two short stories, played on the difference between real and fake, first on the level of farce *(The Jewelry)* then of tragedy *(The Necklace)*. Jewelry

nevertheless glittered with striking charm for the champions of art for art's sake during the Romantic and Symbolist periods. Already in his preface to *Albertus* (1831–32) Théophile Gautier, whom Théodore de Banville dubbed "the prince among these jewelers," compared literature that served no cause to purely superfluous, "strangely chased gems." Later, glossing the title of his latest volume of poetry, *Enamels and Cameos*, he wrote, "The title, *Enamels and Cameos*, indicates my intention to treat slight subjects within a restricted space, sometimes with the brilliant colors of enamel upon a plate of gold or copper, sometimes by using the cutter's wheel upon gems such as agate, cornelian, or onyx. Every poem was to be a medallion fit to be set in the cover of a casket, or a seal to be worn on the finger— something recalling the copies of antique medals one sees in the studios of painters or sculptors."[2] Poets, like jewelers, favor clean lines, show a concern for shapes, and employ various materials and colors. Both professions entail precision work. So it is not surprising to discover that some of the most pertinent comments on jewelry were made by Mallarmé. It was the subject of his first column for a fashion magazine called *La Dernière Mode*, dated August 1, 1874. He first of all stressed Paris's pre-eminence in the art of jewelry, given the skill of its artisans and their ability to "comprise the universe…. Nothing so strange but [Paris] will accept it; nothing exquisite that it cannot offer." That is because Paris jewelers look elsewhere, to "spun-glass bracelets from India" and to "cut-paper earrings from China." They also look to the past, every past, "the heavy clusters of jewels of long-forgotten centuries," treasures of "the classic and the barbaric." Attentive to discoveries in distant lands as well as to recent archaeological finds, Paris jewelers drew inspiration from the Campana Collection in the Louvre and the display cases of the Musée de Cluny, not forgetting "the Paris shopcounters of Japanese or Algerian traders." If jewelry occasionally strays into facile "wit" or, as in London, "strange and massive" pieces, that is because the jeweler has forgotten that he is firstly an ornamentist. "Decoration! Everything is in that word; and I would advise a lady, hesitating whom to apply to, to design a particular piece of jewelry, to ask the architect who built her town house, rather than the famous dress designer who created her festal gown. Such, in a word, is the art of the Jewel."[3] In other words, jewelry is not an accessory but an autonomous work related to architecture and the decorative arts; it must proceed in the same way, through attentive study of old examples and exotic models, via indispensible recourse to drawing and design. Drawing—trial by design, what Degas and Cézanne called the "probity of drawing"—is the basis of the jeweler's art, as Chaumet's ample archives demonstrate. Countless drawings covering the company's two centuries of history—many published here for the first time—are sketches of the works that followed, whose existence they record like a photograph. At the same time, they also encouraged experimentation, functioning like a laboratory, exploring unknown terrain even if, as Philippe Thiébaut shows, the drawings were often more impulsive, capricious, and bolder—more sensitive to the fashion of the day—than the item that was actually executed. They constitute inexhaustible documentation, a *museo cartaceo* or "paper

2   Théophile Gautier, *Enamels and Cameos*, trans.
    Agnes Lee, from F.C. de Sumichrast (ed.), *The Works
    of Théophile Gautier* (Cambridge, Mass: The Jenson
    Society, 1906), vol. 24, pp. 31–32.

3   P.N. Furbank and A.M. Cain (trans. and eds.),
    *Mallarmé on Fashion: A Translation of the Fashion
    Magazine* La Dernière Mode (Oxford: Berg, 2004),
    pp. 21–22.

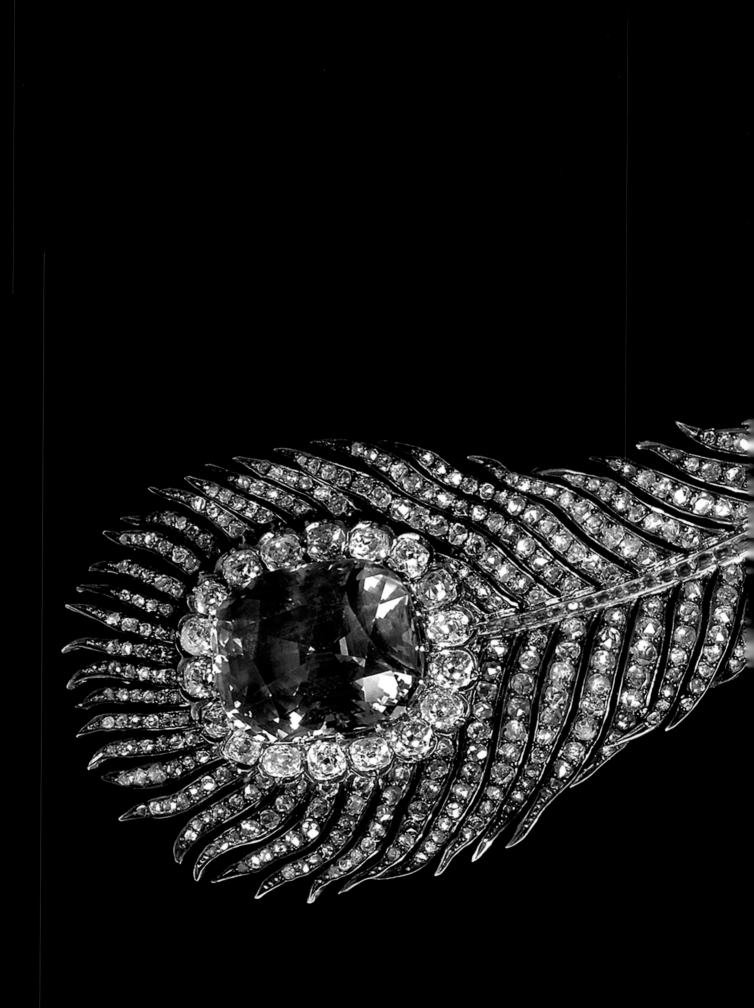

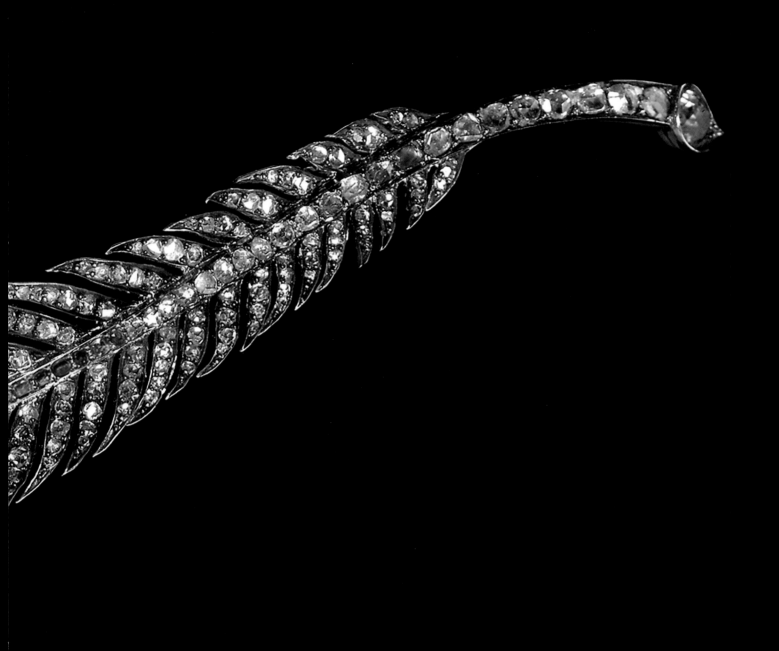

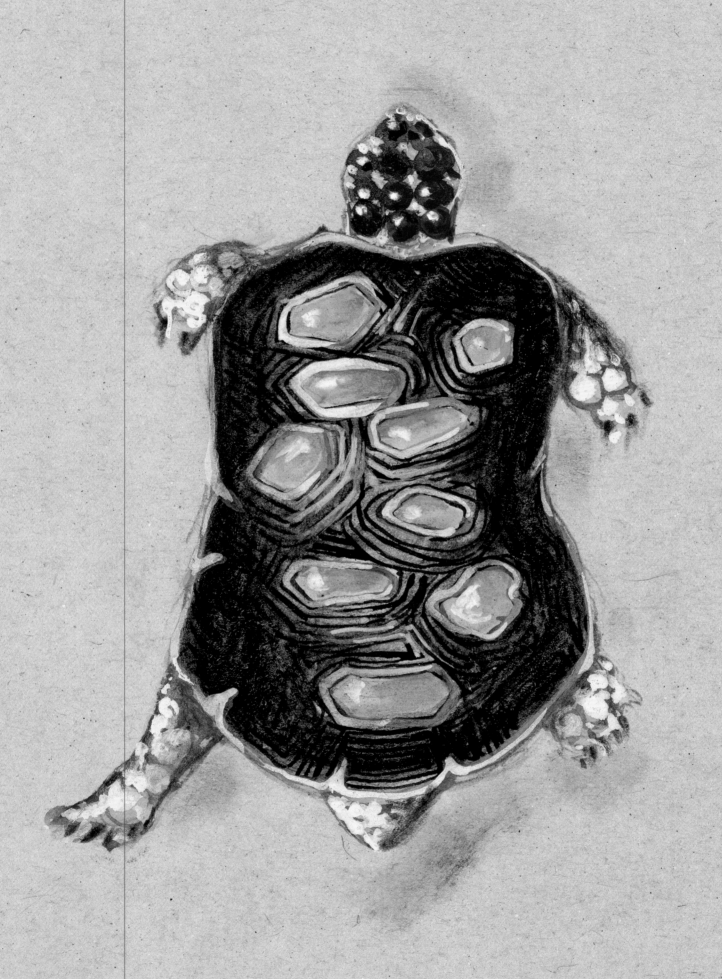

museum," which acts not only as Chaumet's memory but is above all a constantly consulted source of inspiration for today's designs, offering an antidote to sterile amnesia. It is a recollection of roots, a reminder of rules.

When Des Esseintes, the protagonist of Huysmann's *Against the Grain* (1884), had his turtle glazed with gold, he was dissatisfied with the "Visigothic" shield that he had envisaged as a "gigantic jewel," for it was only "half finished." It would only be truly complete once he incrusted it with rare stones. He selected a design from a collection of Japanese curios representing "a bunch of flowers springing from a thin stalk," and took it to the jeweler to have every leaf and petal of every flower set in precious stones and mounted on the turtle's actual scales. If Huysmans turned a live animal into a jewel—as did Théophile Gautier's daughter, Judith, and Robert de Montesquiou—that was because it moved, imparting a shifting sparkle to the stones, constantly altering the pattern of the shell, "throwing its flashing rays over the carpet."[4] Once again, we confront the difficulties in displaying jewelry, the obstacle to making it suitable only for a museum display: jewels are made to be worn (or to be used, in the case of snuffboxes and tea services), that is to say they should accentuate the movements of the body, shimmering with a varied, fleeting sparkle, never appearing in quite the same light. Chaumet's wonderful and highly skillful *tremblant* technique (or "tremored setting") introduces an airy breeze into a world of solidity (the hardness of stones, the rigidity of settings), imparting life to diamonds, sapphires, and emeralds. The art of jewelry is a kinetic one.

Baudelaire claims that it is also musical: "My dearest one was nude, her resonating jewelry all she wore." It is this familiar resonance that lends erotic charge to his poem.

> *Quand il jette en dansant son bruit vif et moqueur,*
> *Ce monde rayonnant de métal et de pierres*
> *Me ravit en extase, et j'aime à la fureur*
> *Les choses où le son se mêle à la lumière.*
> [When dancing, ringing out its mockeries,
> This radiating world of gold and stones
> Ravishes me to lovers' ecstasies
> Over the interplay of lights and tones.][5]

Even as it sparkles with countless flashes, jewelry resonates with endless jingling, clinking, tintinnabulations, clashing, and rustling—jewels are often indiscreet. The light clatter of a bracelet or necklace, once associated with the woman wearing it, becomes a sign as distinctive as the sound of her voice or the fall of her footstep. Worn regularly, often in contact with the skin, a jewel—family heirloom or sentimental item—lives its owner's life. It bears the imprint of its owner, even after her death, seemingly outliving her. In a short story by Villiers de l'Isle Adam, Count Athol still mourned his wife Vera one year after her death.

Design for a "turtle" brooch in tortoiseshell, yellow gold, blue chalcedony, and amethysts, Béatrice de Plinval for Chaumet, 1972. Graphite pencil, gouache, colored pencils, H. 21; W. 14 cm Chaumet Paris Collection

4 Joris-Karl Huysmans, *Against the Grain*, trans. anonymous (New York: Dover, 1969).

5 Charles Baudelaire "Les Bijoux," *The Flowers of Evil*, trans. James McGowan (Oxford: Oxford University Press, 1993), p. 47.

LEFT
Two studies of swallows,
c. 1890.
Graphite pencil, ink wash,
white gouache highlights,
H. 9.7 and 7.7 cm;
W. 13.1 and 10.9 cm
Chaumet Paris Collection

FACING PAGE
Series of six swallows,
Joseph Chaumet
(1852–1928), 1890.
Diamonds,
H. from 6.5 to 3 cm;
W. from 4 to 1.1 cm
Lalique Museum, Wingen-
sur-Moder, courtesy of Shai
Bandmann and Ronald Ooi

He took up a bracelet of pearls in a goblet and gazed at them attentively. Vera had taken the pearls from her arm (had she not?) just a little time ago, before disrobing, and the pearls were still warm, and their water softened, as by the warmth of her flesh. And here was the opal of that Siberian necklace; so well did it love Vera's fair bosom that, when sometimes she forgot it for awhile, it would grow pale in its golden network, as if sick and languishing. (For that, in days gone by, the Countess used to love her devoted trinket!) And now this evening, the opal was gleaming as if it had just been left off, as if it were still infused with the rare magnetism of the dead beauty.[6]

Yes, stones are faithful: more than any other lifeless object, jewelry has a soul.

So wherein lies Chaumet's soul? Why do we detect—from 1780 to the present, beyond the variety of styles and constant twists in the history of taste—a single continuity of melodic line? Prior to settling at Place Vendôme, the company wandered across Paris, and prior to being Chaumet it was called Nitot, Fossin, and Morel; the firm delved into every resource of history, from classical antiquity to the Middle Ages and Renaissance up through eighteenth-century Rococo and Neoclassicism, and also called at exotic shores in India, China, and Japan. And yet from the incunabulum of the little Marquise of Lawoestine box to the latest items, we can hear the same basso continuo that underpins the house style, setting it apart. Philippe Thiébaut, compiling the compliments addressed to Chaumet in the late nineteenth century, listed beauty of stones, finesse of cut, deftness of setting, refinement of skills, perfection of finish, purity of style, and novelty of design. In other words, it entailed not only impeccable skills but stylistic curiosity and a taste for innovation. Chaumet has obviously always been sensitive to fashions, but often adopts them in a measured way, after they have proven that they are not fleeting, but will become a true style, a period of art. The firm's relationship to Art Nouveau is enlightening in this respect, for it was characterized by a late—and very measured—assimilation into house jewelry. A fascinating report prepared by the house designer Wibaille in 1899 was as circumspect as it was open-minded. This never-published document, explicitly titled "Report prepared for Monsieur Chaumet on the Subject of the Various Developments in Jewelry and Precious Metalwork in Recent Years, and on the Course of Action to be Taken," advised against slavishly imitating Lalique, that pioneer whose misunderstood audacity had paved a new path. Rather, the report suggested adopting the "many flattering arrangements [that are] unrelated to any specific style, of a boldness that never excludes good taste."[7] In other words, after an attentive look at a movement that had become part of the artistic landscape, Chaumet should adopt only what was compatible with the house style and with its restrained, acceptable development. This sense of moderation primarily reflects a concern to be part of a tradition, to meditate on its own history, to remain faithful to the characteristics of its style, in short everything

6   Auguste de Villiers de l'Isle Adam, "Vera," in *Sardonic*   *Bijouterie & Orfèvrerie depuis quelques années et*
     Tales, trans. Hamish Miles, New York: Alfred Knopf, 1927.   *du parti qu'il y aurait lieu d'en tirer*, dated July 12, 1899,

7   Wibaille, *Rapport adressé à monsieur Chaumet au sujet*   Paris, p. 6. Chaumet Archives.
     des différentes phases traversées par la Joaillerie,

that embodies the Chaumet name. But as Marcel Proust pointed out, "in order to describe moderation in an entirely convincing way, moderation will not suffice, and some of the qualities of authorship which presuppose a quite immoderate exaltation are required."[8] Such "immoderate exaltation" is evident in a great number of pieces of precious metalwork that Chaumet made in the nineteenth and early twentieth century. Jean-Valentin Morel's *Hope Cup* (1853–55) was set with multicolored enamel figures recalling the eccentricity of German rococo, incrusting the thin, blood-red jasper bowl like shells on an object that had sunk to the bottom of the sea. Later—in 1900—the *Via Vitae* and *Christus Vincit* would far outstrip local religious artifacts of the day to become original, baroque works of art. Compared to these showy masterpieces—caprices for a Universal Exposition, clear manifestations of Joseph Chaumet's faith during a period of troubled times for the Catholic Church in France—jewelry displayed more restraint. Not that it was devoid of extravagance, as strikingly illustrated by orders placed by Sir Valentine Abdy for his wedding (1970), but it was constrained by the value of the gems, a concern for investment and legacy, and the simple need to be "wearable." The taste and desires of the client also mattered because the client often inspires, suggests, and orders, selecting stones and patterns, seeking to express a feeling via the gift to be made. Indeed, jewelry also functions as "canting arms," to borrow a term from heraldry. So Princess Bagration, Countess Le Hon, the Duke of Luynes, and Anatole Demidov, all mentioned in Isabelle Lucas's chapter on romantic jewelry, like the American clients discussed by Philippe Thiebault, should be seen as active participants who played a crucial role in Chaumet's development.

That is how the world of Chaumet is elaborated and defined: through the use of a consistent vocabulary in infinite, ever-renewed variations on a theme. The Chaumet line has grown from this shared repertoire. There is clear continuity from Queen Hortense's hydrangea brooch, Empress Joséphine's ears of wheat, the diamond flowers and leaves of the Bedford tiara, and the most recent jewels. This continuity reveals the designs (for, once again, design is a key element in that continuity) behind the world of Chaumet.

This volume maps that world. Coming after Diana Scarisbrick's pioneering book in 1995, it explores for the first time the incomparable wealth of the company archives: drawings, photographs, ledgers of various kinds, and correspondence—breeding grounds for many of the pieces that followed. It also documents the Chaumet jewelry collection, recently enhanced by remarkable additions. For four decades now, Béatrice de Plinval has preserved these archives and built the collection. It was her work that has made this book possible. Jean-Marc Mansvelt, the Chief Executive Officer of Chaumet, wanted to see it published not only as a defense and illustration of the firm he heads but also to stress the fact that Chaumet's future rests on faithfulness to its past, on an enlightened awareness of earlier designs, on a *total* vision that contributes to the constant revitalization of this unique, wonderful universe of ribbons, water, flowers, birds, wings, and feathers, as glimpsed in the rain, under frost, beneath the snow, or in the light of twinkling stars. *Totally* Chaumet.

"Waterfall" tiara with diamond stalactites ordered by the Marquis of Lubersac, 1904. Print from gelatin silver bromide glass negative, H. 30; W. 40 cm Chaumet Paris Collection

8   Marcel Proust, *Remembrance of Things Past— The Guermantes Way*, trans. C.K. Scott Moncrieff and Terence Kilmartin (New York: Vintage, 1982), p. 189.

THE FOUNDERS: MARIE-ÉTIENNE NITOT AND HIS SON FRANÇOIS-REGNAULT

Anne Dion

The social and artistic rise of the Nitot family is absolutely exemplary. Nothing predestined Marie-Étienne Nitot to become a jeweler to the French imperial court. His father, Claude-Antoine Nitot (1714–before 1791), from Chézy near Chateau-Thierry in the Champagne region, was orphaned at an early age and moved to Quai des Ormes in Paris, where he became a "wholesale fish merchant for provisioning Paris." Claude-Antoine's fish came from ponds in Champagne,[1] but he ran into financial difficulties between 1755 and 1760, ultimately declaring bankruptcy in December 1760.[2]

FAMILY BACKGROUND: FOUR JEWELER BROTHERS

In addition to two girls, Claude-Antoine and his wife Marie-Aimée-Apolline Girard (Chassy sur Yonne, 1716–Paris, 1795) had five sons, four of whom went into the jewelry trade. Only Antoine-Claude became a decorative painter of interiors, moving to Versailles, where he died prior to the Revolution. The reason for the Nitot brothers' penchant for jewelry escapes us. The eldest, Claude-Régnault, born around 1748–49, paved the way. He became a master goldsmith on July 28, 1781, sponsored by the jeweler Pierre Pension, who lived on Rue du Harlay in Paris, as did Claude-Régnault.[3] Marie-Étienne Nitot (Paris, April 2, 1750–Paris, September 9, 1809), born shortly after Claude-Régnault, became a master goldsmith in turn, on February 22, 1783, sponsored by Jean-François Gombault.[4] All we know of his early years is that he studied at the *École Royale Gratuite*

1 Archives Nationales, Paris, MC, étude LXXXIV/441, lease of the pond of Margary, February 1, 1751.

2 Archives de Paris, Paris, D4B5 22, no. 1110, backruptcy statement dated December 11, 1760.

3 Henry Nocq, *Le Poinçon de Paris* (Paris, H. Floury, 1928), p.282. Claude-Régnault and Marie-Étienne were already described as jewelers in 1779 at the baptism of François Régnault on February 25, 1779. Archives de Paris.

4 Nocq, *Le Poinçon de Paris*. Paris: H. Floury, 1928, t.III, p. 282.

"Dressed" cameo featuring a portrait of Napoleon (front and back), cameo by Nicola Morelli (1771–1838), mounting attributed to Nitot, after 1805. Yellow gold, diamonds, lapis lazuli, and cameo mounted as a brooch, H. 5.8; W. 3.5 cm Private Collection

de Dessin (Royal Free School of Art).[5] He lived at Place Dauphine, at the corner of Place Henri IV (later Place du Pont Neuf), which was sometimes given as his address. He had a maker's punch made, featuring an ear of wheat. The two younger brothers, Jean-Pierre (born circa 1756) and Jean-Rose (circa 1761), also became jewelers, although never admitted as masters.[6] The brothers, despite a certain mobility once their respective children were born, remained within the former parish of Saint-Barthélemy around Place Dauphine on Île de la Cité (the traditional goldsmiths' district), or Rue Saint-Louis. The brothers give the impression of great personal and professional cohesiveness.

In 1778 Marie-Étienne married Marie-Catherine Endiger.[7] After he died, Marie-Catherine demonstrated her ability to manage his property, and she must have provided solid support during her husband's career. Their eldest son, François-Régnault (1779–January 19, 1853) was born on February 25, 1779. Three other sons followed in 1784, 1787, and 1792. The choice of godparents suggests full admission into the circle of jewelers and clockmakers (such as Joseph-Simon Cousin, clockmaker to the Count of Artois).

Little is known of the Nitots' business during the ancien régime. The ledger of Ange-Joseph Aubert (1736–1785), jeweler to the king and keeper of the royal gems from 1773 onward, nevertheless confirms connections asserted by family tradition. On March 15, 1783, Aubert listed "The jeweler Nitot, advance on work he has done for me, 480

5   Ulrich Leben has collated various sources to compile a list of artists who studied at this school. See Ulrich Leben, *L'école royale gratuite de dessin de Paris (1967–1815)* (Saint-Remy-en-l'Eau: Éditions Monelle Hayot, 2005), p. 98.

6   This information is drawn from Paris municipal registries and identity cards issued in 1793.

7   Declaration made by Marie-Étienne Nitot on 2 Messidor VI (June 20, 1798). There was no marriage contract

involved. Archives Nationales, Paris, Min. centr. XXVIII/588. An unverified family tradition says that the bride came from Dusseldorf.

8   Aubert's business ledger, 1781–85, fol. 65 (March 15, 1783), and fol. 80 (June 23, 1783). Archives Nationales, Paris, T*299/8.

9   Ibid., fol. 114 (April 10, 1784).

10   Ibid,. fol. 137 (December 11, 1784).

[livres]."[8] The balance of 573 livres was paid on June 23 of that year. The name of Nitot was mentioned more regularly after February 1784. The first mention in March 1783, just when Marie-Étienne was inducted as a master, leaves little doubt that it referred to him, the second son, who apparently soon outstripped his elder brother. In April 1784 Nitot made for Aubert a ring adorned with the monogram B (for a certain Monsieur Bertrand) in rose-cut diamonds on a blue composition flanked by brilliants,[9] which prefigured similar rings later delivered to Napoleon. Nitot also supplied items to Madame de Bougainville in September 1784.[10] The pieces are not usually described in detail. Aubert supplied the court—notably Marie-Antoinette and Madame Élisabeth—with parures (matching sets of jewelry), as well as objects mounted with semiprecious stones, agate, sard, and so on.[11] Nitot also bought brilliants from Aubert, and the sums exchanged between them could approach 18,000 livres.[12] Aubert's death in 1785 put an end to this connection, and we lack sufficient documentation to account for Nitot's business in the final years of the ancien régime.

FROM REVOLUTION TO EMPIRE: AN EXPERT IN GEMS AND PRECIOUS STONES

In 1790 Marie-Étienne Nitot was sought as an expert, alongside a mineralogist called Sage, during an inventory of the crown gems and jewelry. More precisely, this inventory was a revision, with new estimates, of an inventory that Ville-d'Avray had commissioned in 1784. The estimates were pitched low, since the most precious items "could be assigned only an arbitrary value, given their extreme rarity." The inventory was published in the revolutionary year of 1791, following the inventory of the crown diamonds and gems done at the request of the Assemblée Nationale with a view to establishing a civil list.[13] In November 1793 Nitot drew up a memorandum for the Comité d'Instruction Publique on "the reasons that should induce the Nation to assemble and preserve the diamonds, pearls, and rare or precious stones now in demesne."[14] In February 1794 Nitot was appointed to the natural history committee of a temporary commission on the arts.[15] In September 1794, the Comité du Salut Public asked him to inventory the gems in the cupboards of the jewelry room in the *Garde-Meuble National* (national furniture repository), specifying that he was needed for "his thorough knowledge of said precious articles."[16] These events indicate not just Nitot's cordial relationship with the revolutionary authorities but his reputation as a connoisseur of gems and semiprecious stones.

Marie-Étienne Nitot does not seem to have suffered financially during the Revolution, since he was able to invest in real estate at the end of the Convention period. On May 16, 1795, he and his wife bought a large town house in Chaillot, with courtyard, stable, sheds, orangery, and garden, plus two other adjoining houses; then on June 23 he bought a house on Rue Saint-Martin in Paris for 190,000 livres,[17] which he resold in February 1801.[18] Just prior to the Consulate period, he seems to have been the only one of the brothers still

11   Vincent Bastien, "L'orfèvre-joaillier Ange-Joseph Aubert (1736–1785), fournisseur de la reine Marie-Antoinette," *Versalia*, n° 16, 2013, pp. 31–46.

12   Ibid., fols. 104, 117, 124, 130, 138, and 146. 13 *Inventaire des diamants de la Couronne*, 1791, p. 3.

14   5 Frimaire II (November 25, 1793). Archives Nationales, Paris, D XXXVIII/2.

15   He was named by a decree dated 18 Pluviôse II (February 6, 1794). See Tutey 1912, vol. I, pp. xxxv and xlii.

16   Report on the inventory, 23–25 Fructidor II (September 9–11, 1794. Archives Nationales, Paris, O² 470.

17   The purchase of the Chaillot property, done before the notary Maître Boursier, was mentioned in Marie-Étienne Nitot's posthumous estate inventory; for acquisition of the house on Rue Saint-Martin on 5 Messidor II (June 23, 1795) see Archives Nationales, Paris, Min. centr. LXIX/841.

18   The Rue Saint-Martin house was sold on 13 Pluviôse IX (February 2, 1801). Archives Nationales, Paris, Min. centr. I/677.

LEFT
Antoine-Jean Gros
(1771–1835), *Bonaparte,
First Consul*, 1802.
Oil on canvas,
H. 205; W. 127 cm
Musée national de la
Légion d'honneur et des
ordres de chevalerie, Paris

FACING PAGE
Robert Lefèvre (1755–
1830), *Empress Joséphine
with a Herbarium*, 1805.
Oil on canvas,
H. 216; W. 175 cm
Museo Napoleonico, Rome

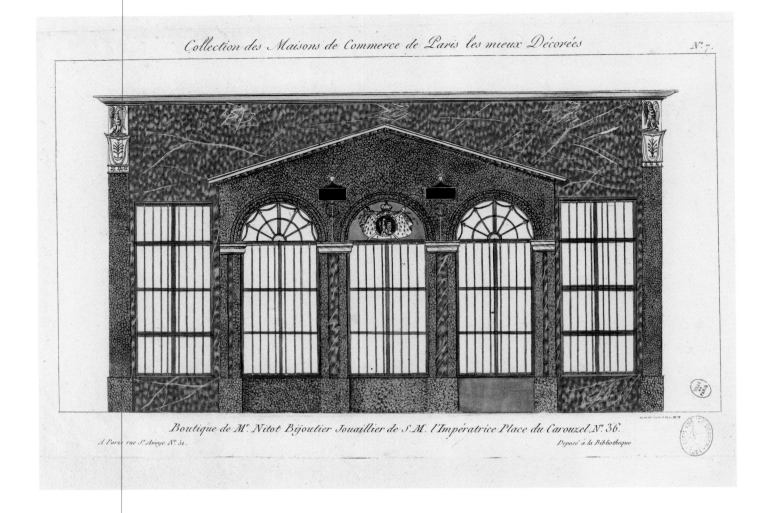

Collection des Maisons de Commerce de Paris les mieux Décorées   N.º 7.

Boutique de Mr. Nitot Bijoutier Jouaillier de S.M. l'Impératrice Place du Carouzel N.º 36.

A Paris rue S.ᵗ Avoye N.º 51.   Déposé à la Bibliothèque

in the jewelry business in Paris. The business directory for 1799–1800 mentions a female Citizen Nitot on Rue du Harlay (still present in 1802 as Widow Nitot on Place Dauphine), probably referring to Madeleine Thierry, the widow of Claude-Régnault, Marie-Étienne's older brother. Jean-Pierre had probably died, and Jean-Rose no longer worked.[19]

      Strangely enough, when new legislation on hallmarks was passed, Marie-Étienne Nitot failed to have a maker's punch made. Neither he nor his son ever used a mark, so their works are identifiable only when signed or when orders are documented. In the 1806 Douet repertoire of goldsmiths, Marie-Étienne was included in the short list of "merchant goldsmiths and jewelers … with no maker's mark."[20]

      During the Consulate period, Nitot's expertise was once again requested when selecting the twenty most beautiful gems in the government's Cabinet de Minéralogie.[21] Most important of all, Marie-Étienne was involved in producing a sword ordered by First Consul Napoleon Bonaparte, and thus had a chance to make his talent known, although a more decisive event occurred when he and goldsmith Henri Auguste made a tiara that

19   In December 1800 Jean-Rose divorced Marie-Geneviève Langlois, daughter of the cutler to the king; they had married in 1791, but already in 1798 Marie-Étienne and his wife had taken in the couple's daughter (their goddaughter), whom they raised until she married in 1811. Jean-Rose was subsequently declared "absent" (see a power of attorney dated November 28, 1811, Archives Nationales, Paris, Min. centr. XCIII/326), even though he was still alive in 1825.

20   Simon-Pierre Douet, *Tableau des symboles de l'orfèvrerie de Paris* (Paris: self-published, 1806), p. 78.

21   Ernest Théodore Hamy, "L'émeraude du pape Jules II au Musée d'histoire naturelle (1798–1805)," *Bulletin du Musée d'histoire naturelle,* t. II, 1896, p. 50.

22   Ibid., pp. 111–12.

23   See the above-mentioned posthumous estate inventory of 1809; the owner of the building was Charles Dehyonne, also mentioned in the property owners'

Napoleon gave to the pope. Marie-Étienne's son, François-Régnault Nitot, was charged with taking it to Rome, and along the way he stopped in Milan to show it—along with other jewelry—to Napoleon and Joséphine. He managed to convince Joséphine of the excellence of their work. From that moment onward, we learn from Joséphine's lady's maid, Mademoiselle Avrillion, that "Monsieur Nitot was admitted to the Empress as a jeweler; later he received the [imperial] warrant and accompanied her on several voyages."[22] Father and son were thereafter awarded the title of "Official Jeweler." The backing of Joséphine, whose passion for jewelry was notorious, provided striking publicity. Their business was truly launched.

NITOT & FILS, OFFICIAL JEWELER TO THE EMPRESS

François-Régnault's trip to Italy therefore constituted a turning point in the history of the family firm. That same year of 1805, Marie-Étienne moved from Place du Pont-Neuf to 36, Place du Carrousel, near the Tuileries. Subsequent to architect Pierre Fontaine's work on Place du Carrousel and Rue de Rivoli, the address changed to 2, Rue de Rivoli, the building occupied by the Nitots being on the corner of Rue Saint-Nicaise and Rue de Rivoli, where the storefront stood.[23]

Money was spent on the installation of the store and the purchase of furnishings in 1805.[24] The façade of the boutique, for that matter, was judged sufficiently elegant to be included in a set of an engravings of "the best decorated stores" by Pierre de La Mésangère, titled *Collection des maisons de commerce de Paris les mieux décorées*.[25] A triangular pediment struck with the imperial arms capped a central avant-corps with three arched windows of large panes of clear glass, protected by iron bars. Flanking the façade were pilasters topped by capitals with the imperial eagle, again recalling the title of jeweler to the empress. Inside, the oak-paneled boutique was furnished with a mahogany desk and chairs upholstered in hazelnut kerseymere. On the black, columned mantelpiece stood a clock by Leroy depicting Theseus and Hippolyte. The jewelry was probably stored in an oak cupboard containing an iron-lined safe.[26]

Marie-Étienne's eldest son, François-Régnault, seems to have joined the business in early March 1806. The first business ledger, headed "Étienne Nitot and Son, jewelers to Her Imperial Majesty and Queen," began on March 1, 1806, while the correspondence register started on March 5.[27] It is known that François-Régnault held a one-third interest in this first company. Their partnership clearly brought new dynamism to the firm.

The company participated in the exposition of industrial products hosted in Paris in 1806. Its presentation read, "The workshop conducts a very broad trade, combining skilled craft in diamonds with that of colored stones. The selections by which Their Imperial Majesties have honored it render unnecessary any praise of the products it is presenting at the exposition."[28] The firm did not win an award, however.

---

ledger. Archives de Paris, DQ[18] 208. But the first mention of a tenant dates from 1812, just after the Nitots moved out. The building was expropriated on August 13, 1853 and subsequently demolished.

24 The costs ran to 3,886.66 francs according to the corporate liquidation statement, April 12–May 5, 1810. Archives Nationales, Paris, Min. centr. XCIII/310.

25 La Mésangère, no. 7. The engraving was advertised in the *Journal de Paris*, June 8, 1806.

26 Posthumous estate inventory dated September 14, 1809. Archives Nationales, Paris, Min. centr. XXCIII/305.

27 Posthumous estate inventory of 1809.

28 Champagny, *Notice sur les objets envoyés à l'exposition des produits de l'industrie rédigées et imprimées sur ordre de M. de Champagny, ministre de l'Intérieur, an 1806* (Paris: Imprimerie nationale, 1806), p. 278.

In March 1809, François-Régnault married Jeanne-Agathe Irisson.[29] He brought to the marriage settlement his share of company assets, namely 230,000 francs, which indicates that business was flourishing at that time. And the witnesses of the event testify to the glamorous patrons the Nitots enjoyed: Empress Joséphine, Hortense de Beauharnais, Talleyrand, General Duroc, and Count of Lavalette. At the time of the wedding, the verbal clauses governing the company of Nitot & Fils were modified and set for two years: François-Régnault henceforth held a half, rather than one-third, share. It is probable that Marie-Étienne, then aged fifty-nine, was preparing to retire, but fate would dictate differently, for he died several months later, in September 1809, still at work.

NITOT'S CLIENTELE

In addition to the title of official jeweler to the empress, in 1809 the Nitots became jeweler to the king and queen of Westphalia. They subsequently styled themselves "jewelers to Their Majesties the Emperor and Empress and to the King and Queen of Westphalia." In exchange for the warrant of official supplier to the court of Westphalia, the king's master of the wardrobe, Marinville, persuaded the Nitots to send an agent named Bocquet to Kassel in 1809.[30] King Jérôme wished to develop a business locally, which might have been a kind of branch of the Nitot company, but the Paris jewelers did not fulfill this wish. In September 1810 Marinville reproached them for not allotting sufficient resources to Bocquet.[31] The king wanted the jeweler to have a store well-stocked with items of jewelry, and with enough craftsmen to execute commissions, whereas Bocquet was alone and without resources. Marinville further complained of delays in delivery by the Nitots. Although the jewelers retained their title, commissions from the court of Westphalia slowed and then stopped in 1812.

LEFT
*Napoleon's tie pin
containing a lock of
the King of Rome's hair,*
attributed to
François-Régnault Nitot
(1779–1853), c. 1812.
Gold, silver, diamonds, and
rubies, H. 2.6; W. 2.8 cm
Private Collection

FACING PAGE
*Badge of the Order
of the Iron Crown
belonging to Napoleon I,*
François-Régnault Nitot
(1779–1853), 1810.
Gold, silver, diamonds,
rubies, sapphires, enamel,
H. 5.5; W. 3.3 cm
Musée de l'Armée, Paris

29   Marriage contract dated March 18, 1809. Archives
      Nationales, Paris, Min. centr. XCVII/654.

30   All information here on the Nitots' relationship with
      King Jérôme via Marinville is based on Marinville's
      correspondence in the Masson Collection, Bibliothèque
      Thiers, Fondation Dosne-Thiers, Paris. My thanks to

      Guillaume Nicoud for sharing the results of his research
      with me.

31   Letter from Marinville to Nitot dated September 24,
      1810. Masson Collection, Bibliothèque Thiers, Fondation
      Dosne-Thiers, Paris, Ms 40, pp. 58–59. Bocquet would be
      named royal jeweler and groom of the chamber.

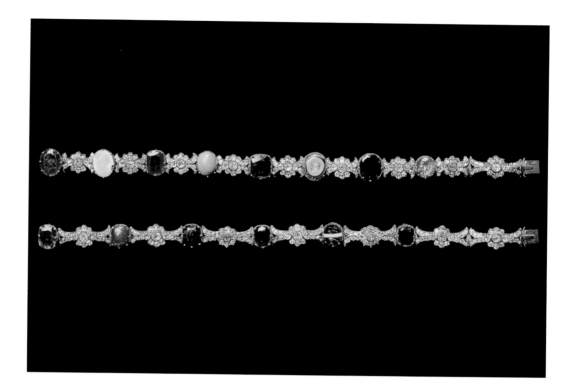

The Nitots were not the only suppliers to the empress. And they also worked for the emperor's household, in an almost exclusive fashion, in fact, from 1810 onward. The jeweler Bernard-Armand Marguerite had the title of jeweler to the emperor, which meant he was keeper of crown gems under the authority of the royal treasurer, whereas the Nitots supplied and set the stones. Thanks to their knowledge of diamonds and other gemstones, they considerably increased the crown's collection of diamonds.

The posthumous estate inventory and liquidation proceedings for Marie-Étienne Nitot & Fils in 1810 tell us much about the firm's clientele. The extended imperial family was obviously well represented: in addition to Napoleon, Empress Joséphine, and the King of Westphalia (37,822 francs), clients included the Queen of Holland (39,212 francs), Princess Stéphanie of Baden (11,973 francs), Eugène de Beauharnais (11,200 francs), and Caroline Murat (3,687 francs). Officers of the crown were also mentioned, such as Talleyrand (921 francs) and especially his wife (7,211 francs), and the imperial chamberlain, Auguste de Rémusat (5,127 francs).

The custom of the Queen of Holland (Hortense de Beauharnais) is confirmed by her ledger of expenditures, kept by Mademoiselle Cochelet. Nitot is listed there in October 1807 as having received an advance of 12,000 francs.[32] Large sums were regularly paid to him, although details of the purchases are not given.

Parisian Jewelers Who Worked for the Nitots

We might have expected the posthumous estate inventory to include a description of the workshop and a list of jewelry-making tools—nothing of the sort. The shop itself and

32 Ledger of expenditures kept by Mademoiselle Cochelet
for Queen Hortense starting in the month of Floréal XIII

(April 1805). Masson Collection, Bibliothèque Thiers,
Fondation Dosne-Thiers, Paris, Ms 65.

the stocks of jewels and gems are indeed enumerated but, somewhat troublingly, not a single tool is listed. It should be recalled that the Nitots never had a maker's punch made. However, two subtenant jewelers, Jean-Baptiste Leblond and François-Louis Guinegagne, are included among the creditors, and thus surely worked for the Nitots. We know that the regalia for the King of Bavaria, ordered from Nitot, bears Leblond's maker's mark.[33] Meanwhile, Guinegagne (1769–?) was the son-in-law of Nicolas-Toussaint Bingant (1741–1813), who was expressly identified as working for Nitot father and son as early as 1806.[34] In 1807 Bingant and Guinegagne were both living at 1, Rue Saint-Nicaise when they formalized—before a notary—the corporate partnership they had begun fourteen years earlier (which would terminate the following year, probably due to the age of the father-in-law).[35] When the Nitots moved to Place Vendôme, Guinegagne went with them.[36]

Creditors listed in 1809 included "Fossin & Fils" for the significant sum of 7,616 francs, tending to prove that even before Jean-Baptiste Fossin (1786–1848) became directly involved in the Nitot business, his father, the jeweler Jean-François Fossin (Charleville, 1761–Nemours, 1845) had worked for the Nitots.[37] Furthermore, Marie-Étienne Nitot seems to have taken an interest in Jean-Baptiste's start in life: in 1807 the young Fossin married the daughter of Nitot's friend and neighbor in Chaillot, François Ribadeau Duclos.[38]

The inventory listed other subcontractors among the creditors, such as stone workers like Langlois, Sénécal, and Peichenot, and jewelers like Blerzy and Nicolas-François Demoget. The demands of the imperial household in terms of quantity of items and dates of delivery clearly obliged the Nitots to subcontract work to other Parisian jewelers. Sometimes the imperial household directly paid a goldsmith or miniaturist for a snuffbox delivered along with others by Nitot; such was the case with Poulain, a jeweler based at Palais-Royal since the turn of the century, and with the jeweler Picard.

Finally, the presence of the maker's marks of other goldsmiths on items signed by Nitot provides the names of certain subcontractors. The mark of Étienne-Lucien Blerzy (circa 1771–1806) appears on several snuffboxes, with either portrait or monogram.[39] The mark of Adrien Vachette occurs even more often. Adrien-Jean-Maximilien Vachette (1753–1839), who became a master in 1779, was the same generation as Marie-Étienne Nitot, whom he must have known as a neighbor in the early days on Place Dauphine near the Pont Neuf. Then there is the mark of Antoine-Pierre Chanat on a matching set of mosaic-work jewelry made for Marie-Louise and on a very similar set composed of engraved gems set with oak leaves, given to the daughter of the mayor of Reims in 1809. Chanat, located at 23, Rue Saint-Jacques la Boucherie, was using his own maker's mark by 1802–3, and specialized in parures.

The Regent's imperial sword created by Nitot in 1812. Anne-Louis Girodet de Roussy-Trioson (1767–1824), Studies for the Portrait of Napoleon I in His Coronation Costume. Black stone, white highlights, H. 48.7; W. 35 cm Musée du Louvre, Paris

33 The business directory for 1810 lists his address as 1, Rue Saint-Nicaise, the secondary entrance to the Nitot building.
34 Douet, *Tableau des symboles...*, p. 18.
35 Incorporation dated May 11, 1807. Archives Nationales, Paris, Min. centr. LXXXVII/1333); dissolution dated June 15, 1808. Archives de Paris D^{32}U^5 3. Note that they owned their tools (anvils, rolling mills, etc.).
36 Guinegagne was living at 15, Place Vendôme when he reported the death of his father-in-law Bingant in October 1813.
37 In contrast, in 1816 it was "Fossin the elder, formerly jeweler," who owed over 4,000 francs to the Nitots. Archives Nationales, Paris, Min. centr. XLVIII/537.
38 Marie-Étienne Nitot was an official witness at the wedding on August 11, 1807. Paris municipal registers.
39 His mark was probably used by his widow, Veuve Boizot, until 1808, when she had her own punch made.

Épée du Sacre de Napoléon 1er

THE NITOT FIRM AT ITS PEAK

After Marie-Étienne died, the incorporation that bound father and son for two years was extended between François-Régnault and his mother Marie-Catherine Endiger,[40] who expressed the desire that her elder son take as partners his two jeweler brothers, Joseph-Étienne-Auguste (1784–1816) and François-André-Théodore (1787–1824), who were already working in the family business. The reorganization of the house of Nitot coincided with Napoleon's marriage to Marie-Louise, followed by the birth of their son, styled the King of Rome, which led to an abundance of orders. The Nitot company was at its peak.

In March 1811, François-Régnault bought the three houses in Chaillot from his mother, enabling her to buy the townhouse known as the hôtel de Gramont at 15, Place Vendôme.[41] The entire family then moved into this spacious mansion with courtyard, garden, stables, and outbuildings, which also became the headquarters of the Nitot firm. The trading company incorporated between mother and son was wound up on October 1, 1812, when François-Régnault formed a new company with his younger brother, Joseph-Étienne-Auguste, known as Auguste, who held one quarter of the capital.[42]

There is no documentation on how the business was organized on Place Vendôme. We know that Guinegagne moved there, but did Leblond go, too? Furthermore, it should be recalled that when Jean-Baptiste Fossin succeeded François-Régnault at the helm, he described himself as the Nitots' former pupil and head of workshop.

The fate of the Nitot firm was closely linked to the fate of Napoleon's empire. On October 30, 1814, the existing partnership between François-Régnault and his brother Auguste was dissolved and the assets were shared.[43] Right from the first Bourbon restoration the Nitots lost their prerogatives, and the Duchess of Angoulême (King Louis XVIII's niece) immediately called on jewelers Gibert and Menière to alter some of the crown jewels. François-Régnault obviously remained faithful to Napoleon to the end, delivering for the last time a few portrait-decorated snuffboxes and some rings as potential, if modest, gifts, on June 15, 1815, just two days before the emperor set off on his final, fateful campaign.[44] The once-imperial jeweler who owed his career to the patronage of Empress Joséphine then chose to retire early—he was still only thirty-five—and to lead the life of a gentleman. Nitot's remarkable early retirement is worth stressing—other suppliers to the imperial court, such as Jacob-Desmalter and even Biennais, who owed everything to Napoleon, continued to do business for several more years. François-Régnault Nitot subsequently divided his time between Paris and an estate in Échardon, south of Paris, that he bought in December 1816; he served as the mayor of Échardon from 1825 to 1837.

40   In addition to the notarized declaration of liquidation cited above (Archives Nationales, Paris, Min. centr. XCIII/310), see also the declaration of incorporation dated April 26, 1810. Archives de Paris D³²U³ 5.

41   For the sale of March 31, 1811, see Archives Nationales, Paris, Min. centr. XCIII/319. For the purchase of the Place Vendôme property from Jacques-Marie Chapelin de Brosseron for 301,000 francs, see Archives Nationales, Paris, Min. centr. LXXXVII/1363. See also the municipal property registers, Archives de Paris, DQ¹⁸ 6. After Marie-Catherine Endiger died, François-Régnault became the sole owner of the property, which his sons sold on May 18, 1853 to the Société Général du Crédit Mobilier. Archives Nationales, Paris, Min. centr. VIII/1658.

42   The liquidation was a private agreement, and the new company formed by oral arrangement; these clauses were mentioned in Auguste Nitot's posthumous estate inventory on April 4, 1816. Archives Nationales, Paris, Min. centr. XLCVIII/537.

43   See Auguste Nitot's posthumous estate inventory, dated April 4, 1816. Archives Nationales, Paris, Min. centr. XLCVIII/537.

44   Archives Nationales, Paris, O² 32.

The Earliest Known Work: The Marquise of Lawoestine Box

Karine Huguenaud

The oldest known example of Marie-Étienne Nitot's work is a small precious object: an oval box of gold, tortoiseshell, and enamel delivered in 1789 to Charles-Alexis Brûlart, Count of Genlis and Marquis de Sillery (1737–1793), who in 1763 had married Félicité du Crest de Saint-Aubin (1746–1830), famously known as Madame de Genlis, governess to the children of the Duke of Orléans (including the future king, Louis-Philippe). The portrait of the young woman adorning the box is their eldest daughter, the Marquise of Lawoestine (1765–1786), who died in childbirth at age twenty-one.

Snuffboxes and other little boxes were highly popular in the eighteenth century. Objects of precious metalwork, they would be adorned with gemstones, enamels, or porcelain and—depending on the whim of the maker or client—enlivened with miniature paintings of mythological scenes illustrating the loves of the gods or, more often, little portraits painted in gouache on paper or ivory. Marie-Étienne Nitot, who became a master goldsmith in 1783, made such boxes on behalf of Aubert, jeweler to the king. Soberly signed *Étienne NITOT à Paris*, this commemorative box also bears the mark of Adrien-Jean-Maximilen Vachette, a goldsmith with whom Nitot would continue to work during the Empire period in order to fill the numerous official orders for boxes to be given as diplomatic gifts by Napoleon I.

This earliest known work by Nitot—extending the history of the house all the way back to the ancien régime and the court of Versailles—was therefore a sentimental item designed to recall a loved one, namely Caroline de Genlis, who in 1779 married a Belgian gentleman named Bevalaer, Marquis of Lawoestine. The marquise, "of startling beauty, delightful talents, and highly refined mind," was described by Queen Marie-Antoinette herself as having "the face of Venus and the waist of Diana."[1]

The death of the young woman a few days after giving birth to a son was a tragedy that Madame de Genlis described in her memoirs, notably recording the reaction of King Louis XVI. "I shall never forget that the king himself was sorely afflicted; he clapped his hands over his eyes and cried, 'How dreadful.'"[2] The decoration of the box commissioned by the bereaved father thus conveys all the sorrow of his loss. Framed by two shell cameos of putti, the miniature portrait by an unknown artist shows a young woman whose very evanescence suggests absence. Wrapping herself in a veil, meditative and melancholic, she stands before a cloudy sky, while a shaft of divine light can be glimpsed in the heavens above. Other decorative motifs and inscriptions employ a neoclassical repertoire to convey sorrow and mourning. On the back, a mother and her child mourn before an ancient-style tomb flanked by cypress trees, a scene ringed by four medallions bearing the letters W/ES/TI/NE. Below is the Latin inscription *CECIDIT UT FLOS* ("She fell like a flower") and on the right are the letters *D[is] M[anibus]* ("To the divine shades"). Along the edge are the poignant lines: *Ton père infortuné te regarde sans cesse, te joindre bientôt il attend le moment. Ah, quand on a perdu l'objet de sa tendresse, la douleur est un siècle et la mort un instant.* (Upon your face dwells a wretched father's gaze, awaiting our reunion's blessed moment. Ah! once a beloved soul has passed away, sorrow lasts for ages—death, a mere instant.)

1   Madame de Genlis, *Mémoires inédits de Madame la comtesse de Genlis, sur le dix-huitième siècle et la Révolution française, depuis 1756 jusqu'à nos jours* (Brussels: P. J. de Mat, 1825), vol. 3, p. 182.

2   Ibid., p. 183.

FACING PAGE

The commemorative Marquise of Lawoestine box, Marie-Étienne Nitot and Adrien Vachette, master goldsmiths, 1789. Gold, tortoiseshell, shell cameos, enamel, gouache, H. 2.7; W. 10.1; D. 7.4 cm Fondation Napoléon, Paris, Lapeyre donation

Nitot & Fils:
Place Vendôme's First Jeweler

Karine Huguenaud

In March 1811, Marie-Étienne Nitot's widow, Marie-Catherine Endiger, who along with their three sons inherited the jewelry business he founded, paid 301,000 francs for the townhouse known as the hôtel de Gramont, at 15, Place Vendôme. It was sold by Jacques-Marie Chapelain de Brosseron, whom Napoleon had elevated to the rank of baron that very year.[1] The purchase of a mansion at such a glamorous address—the very square chosen to host the Column of the Grand Army, topped by a statue of Napoleon himself—is indisputable proof of Nitot's brilliance as jeweler to the empress.

In 1811 and 1812, the annual Paris business directory, *Almanach du Commerce de Paris*, was still listing "Nitot & Fils, jewelers to the Empress, and the King and Queen of Westphalia," as located at 2, Rue de Rivoli. The laying out of the new Rue de Rivoli—named after a victorious battle during Napoleon's first Italian campaign—meant that this address was in fact the same as the former 36, Place du Carrousel, where Marie-Étienne Nitot had opened his boutique in 1806. The move to Place Vendôme therefore probably took place sometime during the year 1812. Indeed, the *Registre de l'Intendance Générale de la Couronne*,

which recorded details of the gems supplied to Nitot for the making of the imperial sword, clearly indicated his address as 15, Place Vendôme on November 16, 1812.[2] And in 1813, the *Almanach du Commerce*, in its section on jewelers, indicated a new address for "Nitot (M.-Ét.) & Fils, jewelers to Their Majesties the Emperor and Empress, and to the King and Queen of Westphalia," namely 15, Place Vendôme.[3] It is therefore accurate to assert, at that date, that the house of Nitot was the first jeweler to set up on Place Vendôme.

We lack precise information on how the business was organized within the hôtel de Gramont, but an 1822 novel by Madame de Sartory, *Petit Tableau de Paris*, includes in its fresco of Paris an account of the Nitot boutique on Place Vendôme. Sartory described a store with several rooms, crowded with "many customers," where the jewelry was displayed on counters.[4]

Remaining loyal to Napoleon, François-Regnault retired when the empire fell in 1815. On February 7, 1825, his widow died. In a probate document dated August 13, the value of the building was estimated at 360,000 francs—two-thirds of it was to go to her son François-Regnault, who was living there, while

1   Fernand de Saint-Simon, *La place Vendôme* (Paris: Éditions Vendôme, 1982), p. 268.

2   O² 32, Archives Nationales, Paris.

3   *Almanach du Commerce de Paris, des départements de l'Empire français et des principales villes du monde* (Paris: J. de la Tynna, 1813), p. 155.

4   Madame de Sartory, *Petit Tableau de Paris pour 1821* (Paris: Boucher, 1822), pp. 36–37. The writer and translator Madame de Sartory, née Joséphine von Wimpffen (1770–1823?), published this three-volume novel from 1818 to 1822. Its protagonists were the Countess of Bagneux and her sister Olympia, Lady Sommerset, who left London for Paris when her husband died. The Nitot reference is set early in 1821: "One morning, Madame de Bagneux suggested

to her sister that they do some shopping. Passing by Place Vendôme, the countess wanted to stop at the boutique of Nitot the jeweler. There were many customers in the shop…. From a counter she picked up a fine, artistically worked gold chain, and seemed to examine it attentively, draping it over her fingers and arm; she even put it around her neck, as though verifying it was the right length. "The crowd slowly thinned. Madame de Bagneux lost track of time while bargaining over emerald earrings in a nearby room. The only people left in the store were Lady Sommerset and two men."
In 1821 François-Regnault Nitot had already retired from the business several years earlier—the author was probably unconcerned by the accuracy of dates.

one-third went to her grandson, François-Adolphe Nitot. Subsequent to a court decision on October 10, 1825, François-Renault Nitot became the sole owner of the mansion, valued at 602,873 francs.[5] He lived there until his death on January 18, 1853, entertaining many leading figures in what became a hotbed of Bonapartists, including Prince Napoleon, Minister Jules Baroche, and Comte Achille Treilhard (who in 1846 married the jeweler's daughter, Estelle Nitot).[6] Louis-Napoleon Bonaparte—the future Napoleon III—while imprisoned in the fort of Ham following a coup attempt in Boulogne, wrote in late 1844 to journalist Arsène Peaugier, who was charged with finding new supporters: "Try to make the acquaintance of Mr. Nitot, the emperor's former jeweler. I don't know him but I know he has remained a Napoleonist [sic]."[7]

The will of January 19, 1853, named five Nitots as heirs. On May 18, they sold the townhouse for one million francs to the bank, Société Générale du Crédit Mobilier, which on July 13, 1896, sold it for 1,700,000 francs to the Ritz Hotel Syndicate, Ltd.[8]

5   Saint-Simon, *La Place Vendôme*, p. 268.
6   Roseline Hurel and Diana Scarisbricke, *Chaumet Paris: Two Centuries of Fine Jewellery*, trans. Charles Penwarden (Paris: Paris-Musées, 1998), pp. 9–19.
7   Letter dated December 11, 1844, from Louis-Napoléon Bonaparte to Arsène Peaugier. Quoted in *La nouvelle Revue* (1894), p. 668.
8   Saint-Simon, *La Place Vendôme*, p. 268.

ABOVE, LEFT
Louis Léopold Boilly
(1761–1845), *François-Régnault Nitot*, c. 1810.
Oil on canvas,
H. 22; W. 16.5 cm

ABOVE, RIGHT
*Invoice from Nitot & Fils,
Jewelers of Her Majesty,
15, Place Vendôme, Paris,
June 29, 1813.*
Chaumet Archives

FACING PAGE
*Comb from the
"oak leaves" set with
cornelian intaglios,*
Nitot & Fils, Antoine-Pierre
Chanat's stamp, c. 1809.
Gold, enamel, cornelian.
Private Collection

AU
COMTE
DE
PARIS
SA
VILLE
NATALE
24
AOUT
1838

THE SUCCESSORS: FROM FOSSIN TO MOREL

Anne Dion

In 1815, Jean-Baptiste Fossin (1786–1849) took over the business from François-Regnault Nitot. As recounted above, Fossin father and son were closely linked to the Nitot family. Jean-François Fossin, the elder, was born in Charleville in 1761 and had his own maker's punch made (JFF with an imperial crown) in Paris in 1804. At the time he was working out of 21, Rue de Savoie, which he left the following year for Rue Saint-Germain l'Auxerrois.[1] A maker of fine and costume jewelry, he was probably one of Nitot's subcontractors.

It was certainly Marie-Étienne Nitot who arranged the 1807 marriage between the young Jean-Baptiste Fossin and Alexandrine, the daughter of widow Ribadeau Duclos, his neighbor on Rue Chaillot.[2] When Alexandrine's health declined in 1827 she drew up a will that designated François-Regnault Nitot as executor. Four years her elder, François-Regnault was described as her "oldest and best friend," and she asked him to show her son the same friendship he had displayed to her since childhood.[3]

At the time of the wedding Jean-François Fossin took his son Jean-Baptiste as a partner "in the business whose purpose is the manufacture of all things related to jewelry, for a period of three years beginning with the day of the marriage," namely August 11, 1807. The bride's dowry of five thousand francs in cash was the groom's still-modest investment in the firm.[4] When Marie-Étienne Nitot died in September 1809, the Fossin business was owed 7,916 francs,[5] a notable sum that demonstrates the importance of the Fossins' work for

1   Catherine Arminjon, *Dictionnaire des poinçons de fabricants d'ouvrages d'or et d'argent de Paris et de la Seine*, 1798–1838, with James Beaupuis and Michèle Bilimoff, Cahiers de l'Inventaire 25, 1991, n° 1785, p. 194.
2   Marie-Cécile-Maurice Helbau, whose husband, surgeon François Ribadeau Duclos, died in 1792, lived at 11, Rue Chaillot; in 1795 Marie-Étienne Nitot bought numbers

13 and 15 on that street. Nitot served as witness for the marriage contract and the wedding itself.
3   Handwritten will signed and dated October 4, 1827. Archives Nationales, Paris, Min. centr. LXXXVII/1454.
4   Marriage contract dated July 21, 1807. Archives Nationales, Paris, Min. centr. LXXXVII/1334.
5   XCII/305. Archives Nationales, Paris

the Nitots. We do not know exactly when the Fossin company, established in 1807 for three years, was dissolved. We simply learn later that the company had been dissolved verbally and that the liquidation took place amicably, perhaps at the end of the three years initially stipulated. In 1810, the Fossin firm was mentioned as working at 10, Rue de Richelieu, the street to which Jean-Baptiste and his son Jules would later remain faithful, but by 1812 the young Fossin-Duclos couple was living with the Nitots on Place Vendôme. Upon taking over from Nitot and transferring the business to 78, Rue de Richelieu, Jean-Baptiste presented himself not only as Nitot's successor but also as his former pupil and head of workshop. Since nothing is known of Jean-Baptiste's training, we are reduced to hypotheses. It can be safely supposed that his early apprenticeship in the trade took place in his father's workshop, and perhaps later continued at Nitot's. It is also possible to speculate that he attended the *École Royale Gratuite de Dessin* (Royal Free School of Art) once we consider Fossin's mastery at drawing and sculpting, which later prompted him to show his work at the Salon. This asset was noted by the *Bazar parisien* in 1821: "J.-B. Fossin's love of painting, which he does for relaxation, has endowed him with an ease of composition and execution that places him at an advantage over his colleagues."[6] Jean-Baptiste's reputation for this talent survived into the early twentieth century, as reported by Henri Vever: "A true and admirably gifted artist, Jean-Baptiste Fossin drew as fluently as he spoke. He apparently found it fun to draw charming compositions before amazed clients even as he chatted."[7]

Although he won no prize at the industrial products exhibition of 1819—the only one he entered—Jean-Baptiste's work received much notice. His display included a bouquet of brilliants set in silver with gold stems, which won high praise in the jury report. "The way in which the diamonds are set, the arrangement of each flower, their differences and similarities, the accuracy of shapes, and finally the value of the materials, presented in varied ways in the best of taste, demonstrate great talent on the part of the maker, who merits our congratulations for the masterpiece he exhibited."[8] Jean-Gabriel-Victor Moléon waxed ecstatic over this bouquet, which would look truly natural with the right colors—and he therefore published an engraving based on Fossin's drawing and recorded the price of the jewel: 45,000 francs.[9] Thus right from the start naturalism was a characteristic of Fossin's art. Even though naturalism had not entirely vanished during the Empire—we notably think of Nitot's decorative ears of wheat—Fossin redeveloped that tendency, which had been alive at the end of the ancien régime but was stifled by the Empire period's penchant for stylization. Fossin's bouquet was not dissimilar to a corsage ornament in the form of a bouquet of eglantine made by Georges-Frédéric Bapst for Queen Marie-Antoinette at the end of the ancien régime.

Sèvres Manufactory, Jean-Charles Develly (1785–1849), *Preparatory Design for a Plate from the Industrial Arts Service: the Jeweler's Workshop*, 1825. Ink, ink wash, and gouache Manufacture de Sèvres Archives

6   *Bazar parisien ou Annuaire raisonné de l'industrie des premiers artistes et fabricans de Paris*, 1821, p. 202.

7   Henri Vever, *La bijouterie française au XIXe siècle (1800–1900)* (Paris: H. Floury, 1906), vol. 1, pp. 217–18.

8   Louis Héricart de Thury, *Rapport du jury d'admission des produits de l'industrie du département de la Seine à l'exposition du Louvre* (Paris: C. Ballard, 1819).

9   Jean-Gabriel-Victor Moléon, *Description des expositions des produits de l'industrie française, faites à Paris depuis leur origine jusqu'à celle de 1819 inclusivement, servant d'introduction aux Annales de l'industrie...* (Paris: 1824), vol. 2, pp. 273–74 and pl. 32

FACING PAGE

*Tiara convertible into a
brooch, known as the
"Leuchtenberg" tiara,*
attributed to Fossin,
c. 1830–40.
Gold, silver, emeralds,
diamonds, H. 9; W. 14 cm
Chaumet Paris Collection

RIGHT

Jean-Baptiste Paulin
Guérin known as Paulin
Guérin (1783–1855),
*Marie-Caroline,
Princess of Bourbon-Sicile,
Duchess of Berry,* c. 1825.
Oil on canvas,
H. 69; W. 54 cm
Musée national du
Château de Versailles

Fossin obviously lost the status of supplier to the court, which Nitot father and son had enjoyed during the Empire. The title of jeweler to the Bourbon crown went first to Paul-Nicolas Menière (1746–1826), the last pre-revolutionary jeweler to the Bourbons, then to his son-in-law, Jacques-Evrard Bapst (1771–1842). Fossin's talent nevertheless earned him the custom of the Duchess of Berry. The young woman was partial to novelty and particularly liked the Gothic-style jewelry designed by Fossin, such as a Gothic necklace of colored stones, a drawing of which, dated 1822, is still in the archives of the Chaumet Collection. The duchess's purchases were nevertheless eclectic—a desk seal adorned with amethysts and a mother-of-pearl handle, a bracelet of plaques forming the name of Henri, the young Duke of Bordeaux, and a matching set comprising a bracelet, earrings, and a *sévigné* (bow brooch worn between the breasts).[10] In another sign of her trust in Fossin, in late 1824 she accorded him the title of jeweler to the royal children,[11] which he proudly displayed on his letter-headed paper. Shortly after, on January 17, 1825, Jean-Baptiste Fossin had a maker's punch made (JF, pear-shaped pearl above, star below), whereas Nitot, it should be recalled, never had a maker's mark after the Revolution.

10   Archives originally from the Château de Rosny, now
      Archives Nationales, Paris, AP 371/21.

11   *Moniteur universel,* December 25, 1824, p. 1652.

The settlement of the estate following the death of Jean-Baptiste's wife in December 1830 shows that business prospered during the Restoration. Items of fancy and fine jewelry were valued at 380,367 francs, while pieces of precious metalwork were estimated at 25,491 francs, and gemstones at 137,968, for a total of 543,826 francs.[12]

Jean-Baptiste always honored the wish expressed by his wife in her will that he not lumber their only son Jules with "a step-mother." Shortly afterward, in April 1832, he took Jules on as a partner when the young man married.[13] The twenty-four-year-old Jules—officially named Jean-François, like his grandfather—was born in 1808 and grew up with the Nitot family on Place Vendôme. Marie-Catherine Endiger, François-Regnault Nitot's mother, seems to have been very fond of the boy, whom she called "my dear little Jules Fossin" when bequeathing him a jabot pin adorned with two brilliants.[14] Jules thus trained in the family workshop, and like his father he was a highly talented draftsman. The Fossin & Fils company was established for a period of fifteen years, but was dissolved slightly before that span on June 1, 1845.[15] The father retained sole right of company signature for the first three years, except when Jules was traveling on company business. Both father and son brought the sum of 200,000 francs to the company, which indicates how far they had come since Jean-Baptiste first joined his own father's business. The new partnership lent a

Necklace part of a "bunch of grapes" set (detail), attributed to Jean-Valentin Morel (1794–1860), c. 1850. Mauve pearls, emeralds, gold, enamel, L. 40 cm Private Collection

12   Liquidation of estate, February 21, 1831. Archives Nationales, Paris, Min. centr. LXXXVII/1454. No inventory is attached.

13   Act of incorporation, April 4, 1832 (Min. Centr. LXXXVII/1460), registered at the Tribunal de Commerce (Archives

de Paris, D31U3 51, no. 1179). Jules' marriage contract with Gabrielle Delalande is dated the same day (XV/1804).

14   Handwritten testament signed and dated February 1825. Archives Nationales, Paris, Min. centr. XCVIII/447.

15   Archives de Paris, D31U3 129, no. 8.

new dynamism to the firm, which for that matter was closer to the court during the July Monarchy (1830–48) than it had been under the Bourbon Restoration (1814–30).

Bapst retained the title of jeweler to the crown awarded by the Bourbons, but Fossin became jeweler to the new king, Louis-Philippe, on September 7, 1832. He therefore regularly supplied the royal family with jewels and precious metalwork. Especially during the early years of the July Monarchy, he notably recovered Nitot's previous role of maker of presents distributed by the king, even if he shared that privilege with Mellerio, Ouizille & Lemoine, and Martial Bernard. This policy of spreading commissions around was typical of Louis-Philippe.

In December 1831, for the baptism of Maria Amélia of Braganza—daughter of deposed Brazilian emperor Dom Pedro I, Duke of Braganza, then in exile in Paris— Fossin supplied the queen with two portrait bracelets set with brilliants and pearls, plus two small parures (or matching sets) for the Duchess of Braganza's lady-in-waiting and the little princess's governess.[16] In 1834, Louis-Philippe purchased a Gothic-style quatrefoil vase highlighted with garnets, *pietra-dura* inlay, and enameled foliage, to be given as a gift to Marshal Étienne Gérard (now in the Hessisches Landesmuseum, Darmstadt).[17]

Other orders were related to family events. Fossin delivered several items of jewelry for the marriage of Princess Marie: a chased, enameled gold bangle bracelet, a so-called slave bracelet with large Gothic links and a ruby, a riding whip adorned with two turquoise-studded snakes, and a pin-tray made of a shell set on a dolphin.[18] And for the wedding of Helen of Mecklenburg-Schwerin with the Duke of Orléans, the firm supplied a desk set.[19]

Fossin furthermore profited from regular purchases by the Duke of Orléans (heir to the throne) and his wife. In 1835, under the supervision of the crown prince's architect, Questel, Fossin designed a binding of precious metalwork for a missal (*Le Paroissien dédié aux dames*); it was decorated with niello plaques of Christ and the Virgin on the boards, and the four symbols of the evangelists on the spine. There was then a revival in the fashion for medieval-style bindings of precious metalwork.[20] That same year Fossin also supplied the prince with a so-called Venetian vase with cover, highlighted with arabesques of blue enamel, garnets, and emeralds, crowned by a seated putto made by the Marrel brothers (whom the Fossins occasionally employed).[21] The Gothic-revival taste can also be seen in a silver-gilt and malachite box flanked by pinnacles housing knights and topped by a statuette of a woman reading, given by the Duchess of Orléans to her husband in 1835 (now Hessisches Landesmuseum, Darmstadt).[22] Fossin's elegant little items of precious metalwork were enthusiastically offered as gifts to friends and family: in 1838 there was a paperweight set with stones and a rock crystal flacon with gold mount, while in 1841 the Duchess of Orléans ordered an incense burner featuring an old enamel painting by Mailly. Fossin

16 Invoice for 7,000 francs, dated December 31, 1831. Archives Nationales, Paris, O⁴ 1394.

17 Daniel Alcouffe, *Un âge d'or des arts décoratifs* (Paris: RMN, 1991), pp. 309–10, no. 161.

18 Invoice for 1,800 francs, dated November 20, 1837. Archives Nationales, Paris, O⁴ 1725.

19 *Annuaire historique universel pour 1837* (1838), p. 181.

20 Invoice for 1,420 francs, dated April 20, 1835. Archives Nationales, Paris, 300 AP I 2417.

21 The vase was priced at 2,000 francs. Ibid.

22 Alcouffe, *Un âge d'or...*, p. 331, no. 177.

jewelry was also appreciated, for in 1838 the firm delivered a large lizard bracelet of gold set with emeralds and brilliants, a serpent ring, and a bowknot ring, followed in 1839 by a *sévigné* and a brooch given to Rachel, in 1841 by a matching set of jewelry for Monsieur Asselineau, the principal private secretary, and in 1842 by Gothic- and Renaissance-style bracelets and a bow brooch.[23]

When the Duke of Orléans's oldest son, styled the Count of Paris, was baptized, the City of Paris commissioned Fossin to make the hilt and chape of a sword whose blade and scabbard were made by the weaponsmith Lepage (now Musée Carnavalet).[24] Based on a design by sculptor Jules Klagmann, the sword was executed by a number of craftsmen. The gold repoussé work was done by Jean-Valentin Morel, Fossin's head of workshop. Yet Froment-Meurice, the City of Paris jeweler charged with supervising the execution of this important commission, was keen to record the truth about Fossin's personal participation. "True, it is the work of Morel, but *it is also the work of Fossin*, who supervised the making from start to finish…. We should not overlook, as we are perhaps wont to do, the role of the person who, nominally in charge of this important business, effectively supervised, led, and drew it to a successful conclusion."[25]

Other princes and princesses of the Orléans family were also Fossin clients. The Duke of Nemours gave Victoria of Saxe-Coburg an acrostic bracelet for their wedding anniversary. Louise, Queen of Belgium, often placed orders. As a general rule, the cream of Paris society paraded through the company ledgers, from the nobility of the ancien régime and empire to manufacturers, bankers, senior civil servants, and diplomats. In their wake came the leading figures of the English, German, Russian, and Polish aristocracies then populating Parisian salons. Count Anatole Demidov was particularly prodigious, draping his wife Princess Mathilde in jewelry even as he ordered himself a sword, based on a design by Triqueti, of silver-gilt and *pietra-dura* inlay, with a bas-relief of Saint George, not to mention silver-gilt dishes enriched with commemorative medallions of Tsars Nicolas and Alexander.[26] For the widow of Paul Demidov, Anatole's brother, Fossin set the Sancy diamond on a necklace—twice! Thus Balzac's comment to Countess Hanska begins to make better sense: "Before the sublime Fossin deigned to abandon tiaras and princely crowns in order to set the pebbles collected by your daughter, I had to do much begging and beseeching, often leaving my retreat where I am trying to set wretched sentences."[27]

It might be recalled that Nitot supplied crowns and a scepter to King Maximilian of Bavaria; Fossin in turn was commissioned to make the scepter and crown of Maximilian's grandson, Otto I, elected king of Greece in 1832 and crowned on coming of age on June 1, 1835. Before sending the regalia to Greece, Fossin showed them to Louis-Philippe, who responded with "the most flattering praise."[28]

The Fossins' growing success under the July Monarchy can be detected in the press. Allusions became more frequent, notably in the *Petit courrier des dames* and the *Journal*

23 Archives Nationales, Paris, 300 AP I 2418 to 2421.

24 *Chaumet* exhibtion, 1998, no. 74.

25 Letter from Froment-Meurice to the Duke of Luynes, quoted in Philippe Burty, *F.-D. Froment-Meurice, argentier de la Ville, 1802–55* (Paris: 1883), p. 14.

26 Auction of the San Donato Collection, Paris, April 6 and 14, 1870, nos. 648, 1222, and 1223.

27 Letter from Balzac to Countess Ewelina Hanska, dated November 13, 1833. Spoelberch-Lavenjoul Collection, Bibliothèque de l'Institut de France, Paris.

28 *Moniteur universel*, May 14, 1835, p. 1155.

des dames et des modes.[29] The Fossins were also innovators on the technical level, and they adapted to the requirements of fashion, which called for multiple colors. In 1835 they filed two successive patents: one, in January, lasting fifteen years, for a method of creating mosaics with inlaid gems set in gold wire; and the other, in June, lasting five years, for a method of enameling silver-gilt, at a time when enameling was enjoying revived interest and spurring several goldsmiths to carry out research. The Fossins claimed to match "the elegance of the models of the Florentine school."[30] That same year they were accepted into the Société d'Encouragment à l'Industrie Nationale, and they exhibited various items of chased gold jewelry inlaid with semiprecious stones.[31]

In October 1838, Jean-Baptiste Fossin was awarded the rank of Knight of the Legion of Honor, shortly after having been summoned to the bench of the *Tribunal de Commerce* (commercial court) in Paris. "Very few of the works sold by Monsieur Fossin's firm have not been designed by him. It is for his twin merits of inspired artist and skillful manufacturer that he has made his reputation in France and Europe."[32]

The Fossin house on Rue de Richelieu was therefore one of the most eminent in Paris. The shop, preceded by an antechamber, was located on the second floor. Furnished in mahogany, with a desk, counter, sets of drawers, paper cabinet, pier table, and chairs, it also contained iron safes.[33]

The account ledgers and correspondence—preserved from roughly the moment that Jean-Baptiste and Jules Fossin became partners—offer valuable information on the way the firm functioned, on its workshops, and on its suppliers. Élie Fauveau served as an efficient assistant until his death in June 1848. The fine jewelry workshop, headed by Émile Darras, employed some twenty craftsmen on third-floor premises at 62, Rue de Richelieu.

29 Aurélia Moulin, *Le bijou au XIXe siècle dans le périodique de mode 1820-1870*, PhD dissertation, 2016

30 Database of nineteenth-century patents, Institut National de la Propriété Industrielle.

31 *Bulletin de la Société d'encouragement à l'industrie nationale* 34 (1835), pp. 291 and 608.

32 *Moniteur universel* October 3, 1838, p. 2273.

33 See the posthumous estate inventory of Gabrielle Delalande Fossin, April 12, 1850. Archives Nationales, Paris, Min. centr. LXXXVII/1557.

The workshop for precious metalwork and decorative objects, headed by Jean-Valentin Morel from 1834 onward,[34] kept some fifteen craftsmen busy on the Île de la Cité. While the costume jewelry mostly came from J.-L. Crouzet's workshop on Rue Coquillière, the borders between the workshops were not hermetic, and Morel, whose professional background made him familiar with every kind of jewelry, regularly supplied costume jewelry as well.

Gems, pearls, and diamonds were bought from Salomon Halphen in Paris, from Hope in Amsterdam, or from Rothschild in London. The Fossin firm was also supplied by the finest Paris craft workshops: Potefer for cases, Bréguet for watches, Picard and Caillot for mosaics and coral, not forgetting Jules Chaise, Dutreih, Marchand Père & Fils, Philippi, Robin, Louis-François Cartier, Alexis Falize, and Eugène Fontenay. Abroad, sales were handled by agents: Borgnis (who had already worked with Nitot during the First Empire) in Frankfurt, Bertedano in Madrid, and J.-J. Billois in London. Furthermore, Jules Fossin himself would travel, notably to London.

Jean-Baptiste Fossin retired in 1845. Like François-Regnault Nitot before him, he was comfortably wealthy and invested in real estate, owning a house on Rue de Cléry in Paris and the Château de Vauboyen in Bièvres, outside Paris. In the final three years of his life he devoted himself to sculpture and painting, exhibiting his work at the Salons (e.g., a sculpture titled *Le Miroir* in 1847).

THE LONDON OPERATION

Jules Fossin was thereafter sole master of the Rue de Richelieu firm, a job for which he had already demonstrated his abilities. He had often traveled to promote the family business, notably to London, which is perhaps why he seized the opportunity to open a branch when Morel, his former workshop manager, moved there.

Jean-Valentin Morel (1794–1860) was a goldsmith with multiple talents. Son of a stonecutter from Piedmont, he was trained in cutting hardstones before he continued his apprenticeship with Andrien Vachette, a maker of snuffboxes who supplied Nitot. Morel began by producing small objects of wood, tortoiseshell, or mother-of-pearl, inlaid with gold, silver, or platinum, which curiosity shops would sell as old items. After briefly working with the jeweler Betmon, in 1827 Morel started his own business on Rue de la Calandre on the Île de la Cité in Paris, having his own maker's punch made (MV with a compass). But by 1828 he moved out to Château-Thierry to devote himself to stonecutting. On returning to Paris he teamed up with Jean-François Veyrat in 1833, then in 1834 was hired by Fossin to head a workshop. He kept his own workshop on Rue de la Vieille-Draperie, for which the Fossins paid the rent, and made items of decorative art and stonework for them. Morel nevertheless regained his independence in 1840, and in 1842 went into partnership with architect and interior decorator Henri Duponchel, trading under the name of Morel &

34   On Jean-Valentin Morel, see Isabel Lucas, *Vie et œuvre de Jean-Valentin Morel (1794–1860), orfèvre-joaillier*, dissertation, École du Louvre, 1999.

Attributed to Eugène Lami
(1800–1890), *View of the
Jean-Valentin Morel
Booth at the London
World's Fair of 1851*, 1851.
Watercolor,
H. 21.3; W. 32.5 cm
Chaumet Paris Collection

Compagnie. Despite winning a gold medal at the exhibition of industrial products in 1844, dissension between the two men led to a lawsuit and dissolution of the company in favor of Duponchel. Morel, who was thereafter prohibited from working in Paris, moved to London in 1848, as did for that matter a certain number of French craftsmen after the revolution of 1848. There Morel founded a new company, financed by Edmond Joly de Bammevile, an art lover descended from a family of Saint Quentin mill owners.

Morel went to London accompanied by his wife, Louise-Angélique-Fanny Laurent, and also his son, Prosper, and his new daughter-in-law, Blanche Prévost. The young couple in fact gave birth to two daughters in London. The store was located in the center of town, at 7 Burlington Street, near the main shopping district of Regent Street. Morel staffed his workshop with trusted French craftsmen such as Édouard Marchand (workshop manager), Constant Sevin (decorator), and Désiré Attarge (chaser). Others, such as Foudinois and the enameler Lefournier, worked for him on a more occasional basis.

Jules Fossin backed the undertaking by opening an outlet at Morel's place. Business was hardly booming in Paris following the revolutionary events of February 1848, and Fossin was probably seeking new markets. The Fossin operation simultaneously reinforced the investment made by Joly de Bammeville. Merchandise was shipped by train and the daily mail boats that crossed the English Channel, thanks to forwarding agents (Lalouette in Boulogne-sur-Mer and Faulker in Folkestone). Every time a craftsman or employee made the trip another shipment could be made, and Jules himself regularly crossed the channel. A swift response to a client's desires had to become the rule.

The stock of jewelry destined for the London branch was managed separately from the strictly Paris inventory. In 1850, when Jules's wife died, that stock was valued at

91,673 francs, roughly one-third of total inventory.[35] Lavish items of jewelry were rare, although a bandeau of rubies, pearls, and brilliants adorned with pendeloques was valued at 22,000 francs. Most abundant was enameled jewelry—as Morel commented, the English liked sturdy and brightly colored things, garnets, "showy enamels" (notably turquoise blue), and small sentimental gifts. Fossin therefore sent rings, necklaces, lady's chains, vest chains, sautoirs, key-seals, medallions, clasps, lorgnettes, men's pins, desk sets, pocketknives, mechanical pencils, and so on. Although not of great material value, these items had to be highly fashionable. The Fossin branch in London was managed by Prosper Morel.

Fossin's role was not limited to supplying jewelry.[36] His regular correspondence with Morel, and sometimes even with Joly de Bammeville, shows that he was a skilful adviser to Morel, rigorous when it came to management but deft in human relations. When things became tense between the various partners, Fossin sought to resolve the conflicts. Furthermore, he served as Morel's go-between with French suppliers, patiently monitoring their work. Finally, his reputation helped to draw English customers to Morel's shop.

Morel received support from the Orléans family, exiled to Claremont in Surrey following the overthrow of the July Monarchy. Louise d'Orléans, whose husband, Leopold

Thomas Couture
(1815–1879), *Study for the
"Christening of the
Imperial Prince,"* 1856.
Princess Mathilde wearing
the crown and the tiara
with the Imperial eagle
supplied by Fossin.
Oil on canvas,
H. 92; W. 73 cm
Musée national du Palais
de Compiègne

35   Posthumous estate inventory dated April 12, 1850.
      Archives Nationales, Paris, Min. centr. LXXXVII/1557.
36   See Lucas, *Vie et œuvre de Jean-Valentin Morel....*

of Saxe-Coburg, was King of Belgium and related to Queen Victoria and Prince Albert, was so good as to introduce Morel to Victoria. On March 22, 1849, she suggested that he present a selection of jewelry in a drawing room where she was expecting to receive a visit from the queen. The operation paid off because Victoria subsequently made several purchases from Morel, including two costly pieces of jewelry: a bow brooch of rubies, brilliants, and gray pearl (given to Princess Marie Alexandrine of Saxe-Weimar) and a diamond-and-pearl bandeau. In February 1852 he obtained a warrant as official supplier to the queen without difficulty.

At London's Great Exhibition of 1851, Morel scored a victory by winning the highest award, a Council Medal. In the category of jewelry, particularly admired was Morel's large corsage ornament of rubies and diamonds in a *tremblant* (quivering) setting that represented a bouquet of roses, tulips, and morning glories; the bouquet could be dismantled to form a hair ornament and several brooches.[37] In addition to his specialty of objects set with hardstones, Morel also exhibited an equestrian statue of Queen Elizabeth I with silver repoussé work of great skill.

Yet despite royal patronage and critical acclaim, business stagnated. Furthermore, Morel's relationship with his backer, Joly de Bammevile, deteriorated to the point where he decided to close the store and return to France in late 1852. Jules Fossin recovered his merchandise. Morel, still prohibited from working in Paris, moved to Sèvres, just outside the capital. He continued to receive orders from Fossin for enameled jewels adorned with pearls or diamonds, as well as other items of finery set with bloodstone or lapis lazuli. His final masterpiece, a large ceremonial cup of bloodstone on an enameled gold mount illustrating the myth of Perseus and Andromeda, ordered by Henry Thomas Hope, won Morel a grand medal of honor at the Universal Exposition held in Paris in 1855.

The advent of the Second Empire restored an atmosphere conducive to the sale of all kinds of jewelry in France. The fact that the Countess of Montijo (mother of the new French empress, Eugénie) and her sister the Duchess of Alba were among Fossin's clients was most auspicious. For the imperial wedding, celebrated on January 29, 1853, the press reported that Fossin "specially worked on the crown jewels" to which the jeweler made "felicitous changes."[38] As noted above, Louis-Philippe had not wanted to use the crown jewels, but Napoleon III intended to add sparkle to his court, as his uncle Napoleon I had done. Fossin apparently recomposed strands of pearls left by the Duchess of Angoulême into one eight-strand necklace, another four-strand necklace, and two one-strand necklaces (of which one had a ruby clasp). Furthermore, Fossin supplied bracelets and shoulder and corsage brooches for the wedding. Despite this promising start, and after supplying a dagger-shaped pendant of emeralds and diamonds, Fossin was neglected by the empress after 1854.[39] According to Vever, Empress Eugénie offered Fossin the title of official supplier, but he demurred out of loyalty to the house of Orléans. The empress then awarded the glamorous warrant to Kramer, Fossin's former manager.

37   *Illustrated London News*, July 26, 1851, p. 125; *Official Illustrated Catalogue of the 1851 Exhibition*; Luynes 1844, p. 206.

38   A. R. de Beauvoir (Mademoiselle Doze), "Toilette de l'Impératrice," *Le Constitutionnel*, January 29, 1853.

39   Diana Scarisbrick, *Chaumet: Master Jewelers Since 1780* (Paris: Alain de Gourcuff, 1955), p. 122

Fossin nevertheless benefited from the custom of other members of the court, such as Princess Mathilde, whose jewelry already came from Fossin in the days of her marriage to Anatole Demidov. For the imperial wedding celebrated at Notre Dame Cathedral, Mathilde gave the empress a precious binding for her missal. Adorned with scrolling foliage and birds, the binding won the admiration of critics. "The book is covered in white velvet with chased silver. On one side is an eagle on a field of gules surmounted by an imperial crown studded with diamonds; on the other side are Her Majesty's initials, also on a field of gules and surmounted, like the eagle, by an imperial crown of diamonds. The manuscript, although modern, is admirable."[40] In addition, Fossin supplied Mathilde with an eagle pavé-set with diamonds, sometimes worn as a tiara ornament and sometimes as a corsage ornament.

Fossin's fame can also be assessed through various signs of recognition. Like his father, Jules was named a judge of the commercial court, on which he sat from 1849 to 1856. He was a committee secretary for the Universal Exposition of 1855, a member of the admissions jury for the London Exhibition of 1862, and chair of the jewelry jury for the Exposition of 1867, serving as co-secretary with Baugrand.

Jules Fossin progressively arranged to retire from the business. The London experience had shown him the qualities of Morel's son, Jean-Prosper Morel (Paris, 1825–Saint-Pryvé-Saint Mesmin, 1908). Trained in his father's workshop, the young Morel mastered the various aspects of the trade. In 1854 Fossin first hired him as a manager, then in 1862 handed the business to him. Prosper then ordered his own maker's mark (PM, a strawberry-shaped pearl above a star). Morel & Compagnie was incorporated on April 14, 1862.[41] Jules Fossin, with an investment of 300,000 francs, was a silent partner for fifteen years. Prosper ran the company. He brought his wife and his "industry" to the business. Fossin was the sole creditor, but his name was not to appear. The Morels received a monthly income of 1,200 francs plus 80% of the profits. It was stipulated that they would become owners of the business after fifteen years and repayment of the silent partner's investment, or earlier if full repayment was completed.

Thanks to his skills, Prosper Morel managed to maintain the reputation of the business he inherited from Fossin. Quality remained high, and Morel knew how to move with fashion, offering the Greek-revival jewelry fashionable in the 1860s along with items of Egyptian, Oriental, and Japanese inspiration. Revival styles remained popular, spurring the design of Renaissance, Louis XV, and Louis XVI jewelry. Like Fossin, Prosper Morel called on the best craftsmen in Paris, including Robin, Ogez, Tetéger, Picart, Philippi, Eugène Fontenay, Jules Wièse, Alexis Falize, Charles Duron, and Oscar Massin.

In 1875 Morel took on his son-in-law, Joseph Chaumet, who had married his daughter Blanche-Marie and to whom he would sell the business in 1885.

Chatelaine and watch with monogram "MS", ordered by the Prince Kotchoubey, Jean-Valentin Morel (1794–1860), c. 1850. Gold, sanguine jasper, diamonds, rubies, silver, pearls, H. 11,5; W. 3 cm Chaumet Paris Collection

40   *L'art en France sous le Second Empire*, catalogue of the exhibition, 1979, no. 96, Private Collection; Roselyne Hurel and Diana Scarisbricke, *Chaumet: Two Centuries of Fine Jewellery* (Paris: Paris-Musées, 1998), p. 78, no. 101

41   Act of incorporation dated April 14, 1862. Archives de Paris D31U3 2131; see Jacqueline Viruega, *La bijouterie parisienne du Second Empire à la Première Guerre mondiale* (Paris: L'Harmattan, 2004), pp. 96–97 and 376.

Morel & Compagnie and Queen Victoria

Romain Condamine

In the fields of fashion, feminine finery, and the decorative arts more broadly, French products were the most appreciated in mid-nineteenth-century Europe.[1] This rule applied not only to wealthy art lovers and elegant ladies, but also among nobility. In this specific context of the history of taste, the house of Morel & Compagnie managed to forge a close link with Queen Victoria. Subsequent to the republican uprising in February 1848 that disrupted the French luxury trades, the queen acknowledged that "there is no end to the jewelers and artists arriving from Paris, half ruined and with beautiful and tempting things, some of which one cannot resist buying."[2] The branch of the business opened by Jean-Valentin Morel at 7 New Burlington Street in the fashionable Mayfair neighborhood also benefited from the general British infatuation with Parisian jewelry.[3] Approaching the queen, however, was no easy matter.

In March 1849, Louise d'Orléans—whose family had long been a major company client—arranged to have the jeweler's work presented to Queen Victoria. The encounter took place at Claremont House in Surrey, where the exiled French king, Louis-Philippe d'Orléans, was living with his family. Louise—who was queen of Belgium—suggested that Morel display some of his jewelry in one of the drawing rooms in the house.[4] On March 16, 1849, Morel rejoiced. "The queen of Belgium kept her promise … we literally took our entire stock and displayed it in the drawing room … where the Queen of England and Prince Albert would later retire."[5] Working through various go-betweens, such as the ladies-in-waiting and Her Majesty's cautious but shrewd principal dresser, Miss Marianne Skerrett, other feelers were made. Skerrett, charged with getting Morel "into the wealthiest aristocratic homes" in London,[6] instructed him several months later to go personally to Windsor Castle for a true interview with the queen. It was agreed that he would show her "fine things, but not too expensive," and above all no "very costly objects."[7] Morel had to present himself to Miss Dittweiler, another dresser, who would announce him to the queen. The day following the interview Morel sent Fossin an enthusiastic letter in which he said he had been "very well received" at Windsor Castle by Queen Victoria, and that during the meeting "Her Majesty promised to buy many things for Christmas."[8]

A "list of items sold" by the London shop thus included two diamond-and-pearl brooches, an emerald brooch with rubies, brilliants, and a large black pearl, a small enamel-and-pearl cross, and a charm, all delivered to the queen for 165 pounds.

1   Oliver Gabet, "Une histoire de goût: regards croisés sur les arts décoratifs français et anglais autour de l'Exposition universelle de 1855," *Napoléon III et la reine Victoria* (Paris: RMN, 2008), p. 134.

2   Queen Victoria's journal of July 5, 1848, quoted in Diana Scarisbrick, *Chaumet: Master Jewelers Since 1780* (Paris: Alain de Gourcuff, 1995), p. 110.

3   Shirley Bury, *Jewellery 1789–1910* (London: ACC, 1991), p. 26, quoted in Isabelle Lucas, *Vie et œuvre de Jean-Valentin Morel (1794–1860), orfèvre-joailler*, dissertation supervised by Daniel Alcouffe, École du Louvre, 1999, vol. 1. p. 115.

4   Scarisbrick, *Chaumet...*, p. 112.

5   Lucas, *Vie et œuvre...*, vol. 1, p. 130.

6   Letter from Morel to Fossin, December 2, 1848, Chaumet Archives, quoted in Lucas, *Vie et œuvre*, vol. 1, p. 129.

7   Unnumbered, undated, unsigned document in the Chaumet Archives.

8   Letter from Morel to Fossin, November 22, 1849, Chaumet Archives.

FACING PAGE

Franz Xaver Winterhalter (1805–1873), *Portrait of Queen Victoria (1819–1901)*, 1842. Oil on canvas, H. 132; W. 97 cm Musée national du Château de Versailles

Also identifiable are several orders placed by His Royal Highness Prince Albert, notably three "dendritic agate brooches."[9] In 1849, three days after the death of Dowager Queen Adelaide, the widow of King William IV, Victoria commissioned Morel to make four mourning medallions to commemorate her dear aunt.[10] Such items confirm the royal couple's particular penchant for "jewels of sentiment."[11] Yet Morel also supplied the Queen of England with objets d'art of major significance, such as a paperweight of silver, silver-gilt, and alabaster depicting animal sculptor Antoine-Louis Barye's famous *Lion with Snake*.[12]

Finally, there is evidence of true closeness in Morel & Compagnie's relation to Queen Victoria. The Chaumet Archive contains a small ink drawing in the queen's own hand depicting a pin, part of a precious note given to Jean-Valentin Morel on May 3, 1851, when he was present in the Crystal Palace for the Great Exhibition. These various contacts, plus the Queen's satisfaction, resulted in the granting of a royal warrant to Morel & Compagnie as jeweler to the queen in February 1852. As Victoria herself noted with alacrity, "request made the day before yesterday, warrant accorded last night."[13]

9   List of articles sold, March 16–23, 1849, Chaumet Archives.

10 Letter from Morel to Fossin, December 5, 1849, Chaumet Archives.

11 Charlotte Gere, "Love and Art: Queen Victoria's Personal Jewelry," paper given at the symposium on *Victoria and Albert, Art and Love*, National Gallery, London, June 5–6, 2010.

12 Isabelle Lucas, *Vie et œuvre...*, vol. 2, cat. 89.

13 Diana Scarisbrick, *Chaumet...*, p. 114.

FACING PAGE
Attributed to Eugène Lami (1800–1890), *View of Jean-Valentin Morel's Booth at the London World's Fair of 1851* (detail), 1851.
Watercolor,
H. 21.3; W. 32.5 cm
Chaumet Paris Collection

ABOVE
Sketches of Queen Victoria's hand for a pin, "Exhibition May 1, 1851," 1851.
H. 5.7; W. 11.2 cm
Chaumet Archives

JOSEPH CHAUMET, MASTER JEWELER OF THE BELLE ÉPOQUE

Karine Huguenaud

Born in Bordeaux on August 15, 1852, Jean-Baptiste Chaumet—called Joseph Chaumet (1852–1928)—was the son of sea captain Théodore Chaumet and Marie Ducot. His mother was from a Bordeaux family that had acquired a goldsmith and jewelry business.[1] The young Chaumet began his apprenticeship in the family firm in 1868 and then joined Morel in 1875 (through a Madame Savard, a friend of his parents).[2]

The picture he later painted of the Paris jeweler at that time was mixed, describing a weakened business in search of new blood.[3] Prosper Morel granted Chaumet the hand of his daughter, Marie Morel (1851–1929), and the marriage took place on June 17, 1875. Little by little, Morel acquainted Chaumet with the firm's heritage, rich as it was with the skills of several generations of glamorous jewelers and a unique artistic and creative history. "I was only twenty-three at the time, but from the age of sixteen my parents had striven to train me in the business, including me in all the acts involved in managing their company…. An employee of Monsieur Morel from 1875 to 1885, I was official director from 1885 to 1899 and since that time have been the owner."[4]

1   Gustave Babin, *Une pléiade de maîtres-joailliers*, 1780–1930 (Paris: Imprimerie de Frazier Soye, 1930), p. 81.

2   Roselyne Hurel and Diana Scarisbrick, *Chaumet: Two Centuries of Fine Jewellery*, trans. Charles Penwarden (Paris: Paris-Musées, 1998), p. 17, notes 36 and 37.

3   "Exposition universelle de 1900. Classe 95, Joaillerie & Bijouterie: Notice sur L'organisation actuelle de la Maison J. Chaumet Successeur de Morel & Compagnie présentée à Messieurs les Membres du Jury," n.p., folder 12, *Rapports sur Expositions*. Chaumet Archives.

4   Ibid.

Chaumet's modeling and sculpture workshop, 1905. Print from gelatin silver bromide glass negative Chaumet Paris Collection

RUNNING A GRAND JEWELRY COMPANY WITH A FIRM HAND

In taking over the running of the company when his father-in-law retired in 1885, Joseph Chaumet provided a new thrust that took the business to new heights. Right away he imposed his style and ambitions, giving his own name to the firm in 1889 (although that name was followed by "Successor to Morel & Compagnie" until the time of World War II). In 1890 he had his own maker's punch made, featuring his initials, JC, a crescent moon, and a star. Thanks to his thorough knowledge of the art of jewelry, Chaumet was able to monitor every phase of creative design, from preparatory sketch to finished drawing in watercolor or gouache, to choice and size of stones, to full-fledged model and final execution. He was attentive not only to the harmony of line and shape, but even more to the choice and setting of gemstones. In order to fulfill a desire to reconnect with the fundamental principles of jewelry, Chaumet endowed the firm with resources that "might seem daring to veterans of the profession, but whose rapid success proved them to be perfectly appropriate."[5] Thus in

5   Babin, *Une pléiade...*, p. 82.

TOP

Chaumet's diamond-cutting workshop,
c. 1900–1905.
Print from gelatin silver bromide glass negative
Chaumet Paris Collection

BOTTOM

Chaumet's colored stones-cutting workshop,
c. 1900–1905.
Print from gelatin silver bromide glass negative
Chaumet Paris Collection

TOP

Chaumet's jewelry workshop,
c. 1900–1905.
Print from gelatin silver bromide glass negative
Chaumet Paris Collection

BOTTOM

Chaumet's jewelry workshop, view of the draw bench, 1900–1905.
This tool used to stretch metal wires is still in use at Chaumet's workshop today.
Print from gelatin silver bromide glass negative
Chaumet Paris Collection

an attempt to lower the cost price of gemstones, he displayed initiative by setting up his own diamond-cutting operations. In a document addressed to the members of the jury of the 1900 Universal Exposition held in Paris, he wrote, "The company's current organization enables it to produce goods almost entirely through its own resources. The changes that led to this outcome were implemented progressively: our first experiment in diamond-cutting dates back to 1877, but it was only in 1894, after several tests that were not always felicitous, that we resolutely adopted this path by limiting ourselves to stones of large size."[6]

A diamond-cutting workshop was thus set up in Auteuil in 1894, numbering forty cutting benches and ten employees by 1900. Although he continued to buy rough diamonds from Antwerp, in 1903 Chaumet studied the feasibility of buying diamond mines in Brazil through an intermediary, Rodolphe Silva, who sent him a list of potentially attractive mines.[7]

In addition to the diamond workshop, Chaumet set up facilities for cutting colored stones. Up to 1918 all cutting operations were managed by Paul Bernard, assisted by great workshop heads such as Charles Jamin and Clavier Père.[8]

Company operations were rigorously reviewed and expanded. Advocating collaboration between the various branches of the jewelry trade because he was convinced that "their cooperation on work together results in constant progress for all," Chaumet constantly encouraged a competitive spirit between the various workshops at 62, Rue de Richelieu (and, later, at 12, Place Vendôme). The design workshop, where Édouard Wibaille stood out, having worked there for sixteen years and having won a gold medal for the firm at the Universal Exposition of 1900, was matched by a sculpture studio headed by Henri Delaspre (himself a designer) and staffed by carvers such as Lindener and sculptors such as Castex. Furthermore, a goldsmith workshop headed by Rocher included casters, founders, and chasers, not to mention an electroplating unit for preserving certain designs in metal. These four workshops employed over twenty people. As to the jewelry workshop, it numbered some sixty-five craftsmen overseen by three heads. Chaponnet, Colin, Rigaux, and Roussel were a few of the leading jewelers who guaranteed Chaumet's success during the Belle Époque. Roussel, who was head of the guild as well as the workshop, was awarded a gold medal at the 1900 Universal Exposition.[9]

This organizational structure was complemented by a machine shop devoted to perfecting tools, by another workshop that made jewelry cases, and finally by a photo studio that made a visual record of all jewelry and stones consigned to the firm, as well as of all the jewels made or altered there. Having benefited from the rich heritage of the company that henceforth bore his name, Joseph Chaumet laid down the broad lines of a policy of conservation and transmission of skills based on the methodical classification of drawings and photographs of designs, plus the presentation of volume models of tiaras, necklaces, and corsage ornaments in what became the *Salle des Modèles* (design showroom).

6 "Exposition universelle de 1900. Classe 95, Joaillerie & Bijouterie...." n.p.

7 Letter sent by Rodolphe Silva from Biribiry on July 2, 1903, to Joseph Chaumet. Folder 50, Chaumet Archives.

The letter included a sample diamond from a mine in Brazil.

8 Folder 112, Chaumet Archives.

9 *Rapports sur Expositions*, file 12, Chaumet Archives.

View of Chaumet,
12, Place Vendôme, 1907.
Print from gelatin silver
bromide glass negative
Chaumet Paris Collection

As a true businessman, Joseph Chaumet was a demanding yet benevolent leader, present everywhere. In addition to its workshops, the company employed a substantial sales and administrative staff of over 180 people. Chaumet went beyond simple paternalism by setting up employee policies for the well-being of his staff and their families, financing insurance to cover accidents at work, setting up vacation homes, and pensioning widows and their children. Loyalty was de rigueur at Chaumet, as embodied by the brothers Valentin and Maxime Vigier, two salesmen who worked there for forty and thirty-six years, respectively. During annual business assessments on December 31, the longest-serving employees were awarded service medals.

Joseph Chaumet notably distinguished himself in late 1903, when a strike by the Paris jewelers' union led to a walkout by 2,500 workers who demanded a reduction of the working day from ten to nine hours with no loss of pay. The strike started at Le Saché, then spread to other companies. A newspaper called *L'Intransigeant* reported that on December 3 Chaumet addressed the employers' association, which had rejected the strikers' claims, and that he "demonstrated, using high-level economic arguments, that the jewelry workers were right to demand a nine-hour working day, as long practiced in other major industrial nations; and he urged his colleagues to accept their claims."[10] In a statement to the union dated December 23, 1903, the unionized jewelers working for Chaumet made the unusual declaration that they would resume work the following day:

10   *L'Intransigeant,* December 9, 1903. Folder 346 (*Grèves*
      1903–1906), Chaumet Archives.

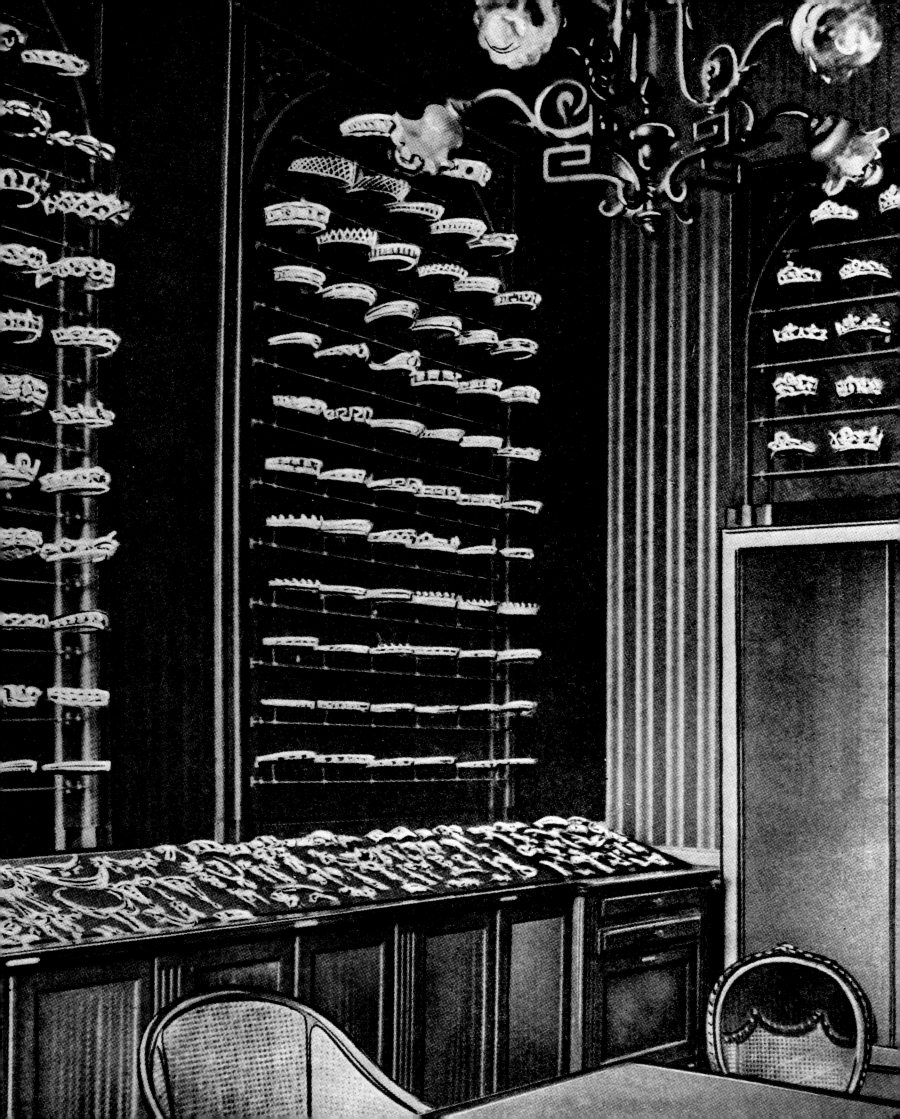

We did not hesitate to down tools, thereby sustaining a loss with no hope of gain, since in fact we demand nothing of our employer. As we have stated, he has long accorded us benefits that go far beyond the current demands…. He has always recognized and respected the workers' right to unionize, to strike, or to work.

He has thereby demonstrated the greatest respect for our individual liberty, just as he also always shown concern for our best interests…. We know that he is disposed to pursue in the future, as he has in the past, the improvement of our situation as far as circumstances allow.

Given the attitude our employer has shown and continues to show toward us, we believe that it would besmirch our honor and dignity as free men, if we were the last ones to return to work when we are the first in our union to be so well treated by an employer.[11]

In April 1906, another strike led to the acceptance of an eight-hour working day for the entire union.

RETURN TO PLACE VENDÔME AND AN INTERNATIONAL CLIENTELE

View of the Model Room in the present Tiara Room, 1907. Print from gelatin silver bromide glass negative Chaumet Paris Collection

The last—yet hardly the least—organizational decision made by Joseph Chaumet occurred in 1907 when he moved the company to its historic location on Place Vendôme, at number 12 in the splendid former townhouse known as the Hôtel Baudard de Sainte-James. Across the square at number 15 was the hôtel de Gramont, home and boutique of the son of François-Regnault Nitot, the firm's founder and official jeweler to Napoleon. Transformed into the Ritz Hotel in 1898, the mansion thereafter hosted the cosmopolitan aristocracy that frequented the jewelers and luxury houses around the Opéra and Rue de la Paix in the late nineteenth century. New commercial considerations required a boutique at a glamorous address—selling from rooms at 62, Rue de Richelieu was no longer appropriate. So in late 1905 Joseph Chaumet negotiated a lease for the premises at 12, Place Vendôme from its owners, Prince Amédée de Broglie and his wife Marie-Charlotte Constance Say, both major clients of the firm.[12] In 1907 Chaumet moved back to Place Vendôme, even if installing all the activities of a large jewelry firm there was not without its drawbacks. In 1909 another company housed in the building, Wagner & Compagnie, sued for 100,000 francs of damages for noise generated by the jewelry workshops. Chaumet won the case, however.[13]

11 Ibid., statement by the unionized jewelers working for Chaumet.

12 The areas designated by the lease for 12, Place Vendôme were: ground floor and mezzanine to the left of the main door; the cellar and basement allocated to that ground floor and mezzanine; the entire second flior overlooking Place Vendôme; the cellars and basement allocated to that second floor; the third floor (the one above the mezzanine) of the wing overlooking the main courtyard. The Prince de Broglie and his wife Marie-Charlotte

Constance Say formally agreed to "for nine or eighteen full and consecutive years, at the same rent, maintenance charges, clauses and conditions, the lease granted this day to Monsieur Jean-Baptiste (called Joseph) Chaumet and to his wife Madame Blanceh-Marie Morel, residing at 62, Rue de Richelieu, Paris, by act notorized before Maître Panhard, Notary Public at Paris, on April Eleventh in the year Nineteen Hundred and Six." Folder 18, Chaumet Archives.

13 Folder 90, Chaumet Archives.

Chaumet's new location in the heart of glamorous Paris in the Belle Époque reflected the firm's quest for an international clientele. Thanks to a loyal aristocratic following built up in the nineteenth century under the successive ownerships of the Nitots, Fossins, and Morel, Joseph Chaumet elaborated an ambitious policy of conquest at the dawn of the twentieth century, developing a strategy in keeping with the times. Reflecting the changes and evolution in high society, Chaumet's clientele grew to include financial, industrial, and commercial circles, plus the international, cosmopolitan elite that was drawn to Paris.[14] Chaumet prospected intensely. Between 1905 and 1907 lists of potential clients staying in various hotels in Paris were sent to him by the Institut International de Renseignements Commerciaux (a Weiss & Compagnie limited partnership). The Chaumet Archives contain one file on North Americans and another on South and Central Americans.[15] In 1911, Chaumet negotiated exclusive access to the list of names and nationalities of rich foreigners staying in the grand hotels in Paris, including the special list of South Americans.[16] In 1913, he obtained a list of Argentineans and Brazilians.[17]

Prospecting extended beyond France. Imitating Fossin's effort, in 1903 Chaumet opened a London branch at 154 New Bond Street, managed by Reuben Astley.[18] Joseph Chaumet presented himself as official supplier to the court of Saint James and to the queen mother of Italy, as well as a supplier to the Spanish court. He attempted to open branches in Berlin in 1910 and New York in 1911.[19] As early as the summer of 1894 he had sent feelers to Constantinople and, that same year, to Russia, the goal being to appeal to the young imperial couple of Tsar Nicholas II and Alexandra Feodorovna, who wed on November 26, 1894. Right up to the Bolshevik revolution of 1917, Russia provided the firm with

TOP, LEFT
"Hummingbird" aigrette transformable into a brooch, Joseph Chaumet (1852–1928), c. 1890. Gold, silver, rubies, diamonds, garnets, H. 4; W. 4 cm Chaumet Paris Collection

TOP, RIGHT
Félix Tournachon known as Nadar (1820–1910), *Princess of Ligne Wearing an Aigrette with Emeralds and Diamonds by Chaumet,* 1886.

14   For a good picture of Chaumet's clientele during the Belle Époque, see Diana Scarisbrick, *Chaumet: Master Jewelers since 1780* (Paris: Alain de Gourcouff, 1995), pp. 155–80.

15   Folder 161, Chaumet Archives.

16   Contract between J. Chaumet and A Constant, April 25, 1911. Paris. Folder 129, Chaumet Archives.

17   List dated March 13, 191, folder 111, Chaumet Archives.

18   Folder 3, Chaumet Archives.

19   Folders 164 (Berlin) and 136 (New York), Chaumet Archives.

major clients, including Grand Duchess Maria Pavlovna (wife of Grand Duke Vladimir, the brother of Tsar Alexander III and uncle of Nicholas II) and Prince Felix Yusupov. The latter, for his marriage in February 1914 to Princess Irina Alexandrovna Romanov (1895–1970, niece of Nicholas II), placed one of the most glamorous orders of the day with Chaumet, commissioning five matching sets of jewelry made from family stones including the famous Polar Star diamond.

In December 1910 Joseph Chaumet looked further afield, dispatching a team to India to examine the collection of gems owned by the Gaekwad of Baroda (now Vadodara in the state of Gujurat), as part of a consultation on the resetting of these old gems. This mission—composed of Joseph's son, Georges Chaumet, Paul Bernard (a great expert in stones who headed the firm's stone-cutting operations), and Henri Delaspre (a house designer and carver)—testifies to the jeweler's visionary instincts and his desire to win over the new clientele constituted by Indian maharajas. The maharajas of Jaipur, Bikaner, Gwalior, and Hyderabad were approached by the team, which stayed in India until late 1911, and those of Baroda and Indore remained faithful clients into the 1930s.[20]

This international quest was matched by participation in major exhibitions, a crucial aspect of recognition in the world of jewelry and among the general public. Such participation spurred the creation of exceptional pieces. Chaumet was awarded a gold medal at the 1900 Universal Exposition in Paris, the imperial Russian Order of Saint Anne at the International Red Cross Exhibition in Saint Petersburg in 1901, a grand prize at the 1904 World's Fair in Saint Louis, a grand prize and the Order of Leopold of Belgium at the Liège Exposition in 1905, and a grand prize at the International Exposition in Milan in 1906.[21] The reorganization undertaken by Joseph Chaumet and his demanding standards of excellence with respect to the jewelry it made clearly bore fruit.

JOSEPH CHAUMET AND GEMOLOGY

In the 1890s, the jeweler of the cream of Paris society followed in the tradition of his illustrious predecessors by producing items of a religious nature. Like Fossin & Fils and Prosper Morel, who made rosaries, crosses, and enameled bindings for missals, Chaumet sought to develop this aspect of the company's business. The faith of this devout Catholic verged on mysticism, and he spent a major part of his income on charitable works, even participating in a project to build a church in Brussels.[22] Given the tense political context of the separation of church and state in France, epitomized by clauses in a law of 1901 and another law of 1905, Joseph Chaumet asserted his values by making devotional objects and masterpieces of religious art: *Christus Vincit* won a gold medal at the 1900 Universal Exposition while the *Via Vitae* of 1904, a monumental sculpture representing the spiritual path of Christians, required ten years of work under the supervision of both Chaumet and

20 *Voyages aux Indes 1910–1911*, folder 110, Chaumet Archives, Paris.

21 *Rapports sur Expositions*, folder 12, Chaumet Archives, Paris.

22 Folder 331, Chaumet Archives.

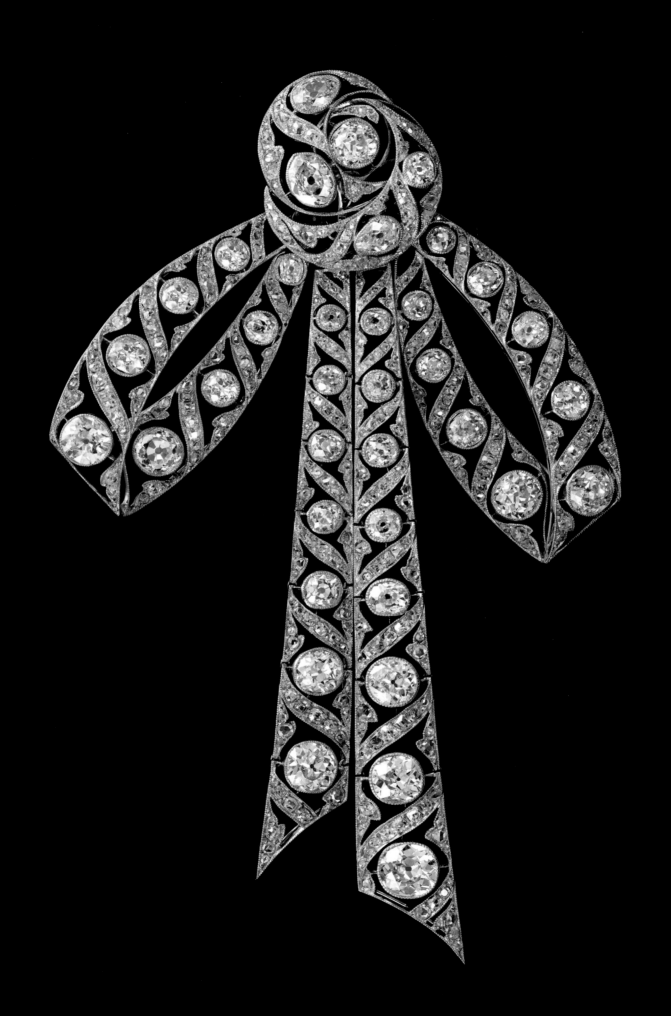

his head of the sculpture workshop, Delaspre. Chaumet's religious convictions were matched by his patriotism. World War I inspired him to make special jewels featuring the French flag, helmets, the Gallic rooster, the cross of Lorraine, and images of Joan of Arc. During the war he gave his daughter, a nurse with the Red Cross, a medal with the three colors of the French flag. Other items were made with aluminum recovered from the trenches, or stones from Verdun. Various accessories in steel were designed in the shape of cannon shells, such as a mechanical pencil bought in 1916 by the King of Belgium, Albert I, engraved with his famous declaration of August 4, 1914, refusing to allow the German army to cross his neutral nation at the outbreak of conflict: "I have faith in our destinies; a country which is defending itself conquers the respect of all; such a country does not perish! God will be on our side in this just cause. Long live an independent Belgium."[23]

Joseph Chaumet applied his mastery of the jeweler's art to every field of creativity. In a constant quest for perfection that included incessant technical research, he exploited the innovations of his day, starting with platinum settings called *fil de couteau* (knife-edge); platinum's strength made it possible to thin and lighten settings until they became lace-like. Roughly ten patents were filed in Chaumet's name between 1904 and 1912, including no fewer than three for techniques for setting gemstones.[24] This scientific approach contributed to advances in gemology. His research lab, set up in the 1890s to verify stones and pearls, employed radiography, microphotography, and spectroscopy for analyses and evaluations that not only revealed imperfections but also fraud. Since the first synthetic colored stones were beginning to appear, in 1902 Joseph Chaumet developed a scientific method for distinguishing a natural stone from a synthetic one. A lecture he gave that year on "the action of light on gemstones" described the importance of the fluorescence of violet light.[25] On June 21, 1904, he delivered another major lecture, this time on rubies, to the combined federations of diamond merchants, stonecutters, and jewelers. Revealing the results of his research into natural and artificial rubies, he argued that once a jeweler accepted "the responsibility of receiving a considerable sum of money in exchange for natural semiprecious stones whose rare qualities justify their cost," that jeweler should provide a certificate of authenticity.[26] Chaumet described the ideal form such a certificate should take and the information it should contain, and urged his colleagues to adopt the practice with their clients.

The man who can take credit for elevating the Maison Chaumet to its commanding position summed up his life-long fascination with and respect for gemstones as follows: "Let us treat natural pearls and gemstones with the deference that these fine products of nature deserve. They delight the eye, they take the mind off sorrows, and they come to us in the tributes that we render to everything we recognize as superior to ourselves, whether among our fellow men or above them."[27]

"Articulated knot" brooch,
Joseph Chaumet
(1852–1928), c. 1915.
Platinum and diamonds,
H. 12; W. 8.5; D. 1 cm
Private Collection

23   Glass-plate negative no. 6741, February 12, 1916, Chaumet Archives.

24   Patent 345,614 (October 21, 1904) *Mode de montage des pierres destinées à la fabrication des bijoux ou joyaux de toute nature*; Patent 401,217 (July 12, 1909) *Mode de montage des pierres précieuses*; Patent 416,863 (August 17, 1910) *Dispositif de montage des pierres employées en joaillerie*. Folder 7, Chaumet Archives.

25   Report delivered to the Académie des Sciences on May 20, 1902. Folder 87, Chaumet Archives.

26   "Rubies," folder 93, Chaumet Archives.

27   *Discours de Monsieur Chaumet le 7 Juin 1922 concernant les pierres précieuses et les perles fines ainsi que les pierres fabriquées et les perles cultivées*, folder 196, Chaumet Archives.

Chaumet and Russia

Karine Huguenaud

Thanks to a Franco–Russian alliance established in 1892, the rapprochement between France and Russia sparked a stream of Belle Époque travelers, not just to Paris but also to fashionable vacation spots, resorts, and the Riviera. High society in Russia was heavily Francophile, and saw French luxury goods as the model for a lifestyle inspired by the Russian imperial family and nobility. Joseph Chaumet's jewelry participated in that quest for an aristocratic lifestyle, and his clientele grew significantly at the turn of the century. Even prior to that peak, leading Russians had shown their trust in the Paris jeweler, including Princess Catherine Bagration (1783–1857). The grand niece of Prince Potemkin and the widow of General Pyotr Bagration (a hero of the battle of Borodino), Catherine was a famous and somewhat scandalous beauty who charmed the cosmopolitan society of Restoration Paris. She remained loyal to Fossin's jewelry all her life. Another important client was Count Anatole Demidov (1812–1870), Prince of San Donato. An art lover from a powerful Russian family, Demidov had a strong penchant for jewels, lavishing them first on his mistress, Valentine de Sainte-Aldegonde, Duchess of Dino, and then, after 1840, his wife, Princess Mathilde, daughter of Napoleon's brother, Jérôme Bonaparte, the former king of Westphalia. In 1841 Demidov ordered for Mathilde—niece of Napoleon I and cousin of the future Napoleon III—a bracelet containing locks of hair of Napoleon and his son, followed in 1842 by a diamond eagle to be worn as a corsage ornament or placed on a tiara.[1] Also in 1841 Anatole's brother, Count Paul Demidov, commissioned Fossin to set the Sancy diamond, a 55.23-carat gem having belonged to the crown jewels—but pawned in 1796 and never redeemed—which he gave to wife Aurora as a "morning gift" the day after their wedding.

Even during the Second Empire, despite the Crimean War opposing France and Russia, Russian aristocrats continued to order jewelry from Fossin, and then from his successor, Morel.

In the late nineteenth century, Grand Duchess Maria Pavlovna (1847–1920), wife of Grand Duke Vladimir (brother of Tsar Alexander III and uncle of Tsar Nicholas II), was indisputably the Russian client most earnestly wooed by Joseph Chaumet. Her first major purchase, on July 28, 1899, was a "waterfall" tiara typical of the jeweler's designs of the day: three clusters ended in dangling briolette-cut diamonds that gave the illusion of drops of water about to fall.[2] Maria Pavlovna made many other purchases up to 1914, including corsage ornaments, necklaces, chokers, tiaras, and other head ornaments, even commissioning the jeweler to reproduce the Kremlin bells in marble, chased silver, and rubies.[3]

Thanks to support from the Grand Duchess, Joseph Chaumet was a star at the International Red Cross Exposition hosted in Saint Petersburg in 1901, earning him induction into the imperial Russian Order of Saint Anne. The Chaumet display, valued at five million francs, included masterpieces previously exhibited in Paris in 1900, such as the *Christus Vincit* and jewels such as a corsage ornament with the Russian coat of arms. The reinterpretation of Russian motifs played an important role in the pieces Chaumet devised for this demanding clientele, and he also maintained several agents in Saint Petersburg and Kiev.[4] The custom of exchanging gifts, so valued in imperial Russian society,

1   Diana Scarisbrick, *Chaumet…*, p. 79.
2   Invoice ledger H (1897–99), p. 472, Chaumet Archives.
3   Glass-plate negative no. 5381, December 16, 1911,
     photo collection, Chaumet Archives.
4   Folders 20, 88, and 142, Chaumet Archives.

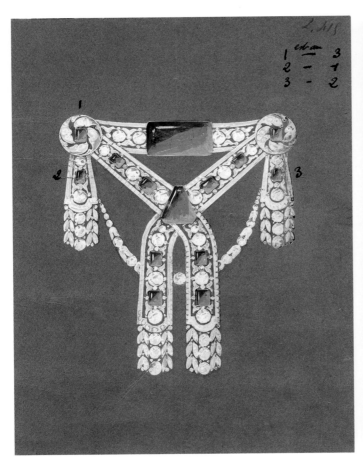

favored the purchase of special little jewels in the form of an egg or a bell, traditionally given at Easter (some of them bore the initials XB, for Christ Resurrected). In April 1911, the list of items that Chaumet dispatched to Saint Petersburg for sale at Easter reveals that 268 of the total of 603 jewels were eggs, while 33 were bells.[5]

Chaumet's clients also included other Russian nobles, as well as friends and family of Duchess Maria Pavlovna. It was for Irina Alexandrovna Romanov (1895–1970), a niece of Tsar Nicholas II,

that Chaumet filled some of the firm's largest Russian orders. For Irina's marriage in February 1914 to Prince Felix Yusupov, Chaumet reset old family jewels and delivered five parures of diamonds, pearls, rubies, emeralds, and sapphires, "each more beautiful than the other," according to the memoirs of the prince, who noted that they "were greatly admired."[6]

War put a brake on business. And once the 1917 revolution overturned the Russian regime, a world came to an end. Aristocratic Russian clients slowly vanished from the company's ledgers.[7]

ABOVE, LEFT
Design for an emerald and diamond corsage ornament with ribbon and swag motif belonging to Princess Yusupov, 1914. Graphite pencil, white pencil, gouache, ink wash and highlights, black ink, H. 26.4; W. 20.4 cm Chaumet Paris Collection

ABOVE, RIGHT
Design for a ruby and diamond corsage ornament with ribbon and swag motif for Princess Yusupov, 1914.

Graphite pencil, gouache, ink wash and highlights, H. 22.6; W. 17.1 cm Chaumet Paris Collection

FACING PAGE, TOP
After their discovery in a cache of the Yusupov Palace in Moscow, Princess Irina's gems were appraised and scattered by order of the Soviet government in 1925. Some of the Chaumet pieces are recognizable here: in the foreground, the "baguette" diamond necklace; to the right, the ribbon and swag

corsage ornament from the emerald set (the tiara from the same set is also to be found on the table); in the center, the triple-sun tiara (see p. 331).

FACING PAGE, BOTTOM
Corsage ornament with ribbon and swag motif, neckclace and earrings from Princess Yusupov's emerald and diamond set, 1914. Print from gelatin silver bromide glass negative, H. 30; W. 40 cm Chaumet Paris Collection

5   Folder 20, Chaumet Archives.

6   Felix Yusupov, *Mémoires* (Paris: V & O Editions, 1990).

7   In 1918 Russians owed the firm 748,271.70 francs. See folder 205, Chaumet Archives.

Joseph Chaumet and Religious Art

Maylis Roqueplo

The personality of Jean-Baptiste ("Joseph") Chaumet steadily emerges from study of the archives of the house of Chaumet. That personality could be summed up by referring to the three theological virtues of faith, hope, and charity. A man of convictions, Chaumet placed his artistic talent not only at the service of feminine beauty but also at the service of God. This ideal prompted him to seek good in everything, with unflagging effort. Chaumet expressed his devout beliefs through artworks of a religious nature. Three pieces characterize that output—the *Via Vitae, Christus Vincit*, and *France Victorieuse*. All three made a big splash in the society of his day.

The *Via Vitae* (1894–1904) was a monumental piece, nearly ten feet high, to which Chaumet devoted ten years of his life. This startling artwork, which testifies to a profound spiritual vision, combines precious metalwork, jewelry, and sculpture with true virtuosity. Everything in the choice of materials—gold, ivory, alabaster, diamonds, and rock crystal—helps to magnify the effect and to encourage theological reflection. Gold and ivory were used for the 138 figurines depicting scenes from the life of Christ from birth to resurrection. The Trinity, meanwhile, is composed of silver-gilt and rock crystal set in a majestic aureole. Platinum, diamonds, and rubies were used for the Eucharist, while marble of various colors, alabaster, onyx, and gilt-bronze went into the base and the setting for each scene. According to Chaumet, the *Via Vitae* is the path that every Christian must take, guided by the words of Christ: "I am the way, and the truth, and the life."[1] Twenty-eight replicas of the scene of Jesus praying in the Garden of Gethsemane were made, two of which Chaumet gave to Pope Pius XI.

In *Christus Vincit*, exhibited at the Universal Expositions in Paris (1900) and Liège (1905), Chaumet sought to convey the influence of Christ and his teachings on civilization through a symbolism evoked through the choice of stones, cut of stones, and chased metal.[2] In the upper part, for example, the Trinity is embodied by a triangular sapphire set in a majestic, diamond-studded aureole, topped by a crucifixion on a cloud of jade.[3] The central section features a globe of agate ringed by the apostles, supported by Saint Michael slaying a demon. The lower part alludes to the theological virtues. Silver-gilt replicas of *Christus Vincit* were made for some of Chaumet's major clients, such as the Duke of Orléans, King Alfonso XIII of Spain (in 1905), and the South American industrialist Simón Iturri Patiño (in 1918).[4]

Thanks to his artistic genius and innate sense of balance and aesthetics, Chaumet was able to express his deepest convictions while giving a new impetus to religious art through original, startling, and largely symbolic pieces. In addition to these major works, he also produced numerous liturgical items such as monstrances,[5] chalices,[6] pectoral crosses, and episcopal rings. The house archives contain three drawings of crowns of stars and a cross done at the request of the Carmelite nuns at Lisieux.[7] An abbé named Malijay had a silver chalice repaired in 1922, whereas Abbé Bailleul, a priest at Agon Coutainville in northern France, ordered a statue of the Sacred Heart in 1923. When repairing or mending statues, Chaumet often donated liturgical objects to churches. The firm also delivered monstrances to Orvieto Cathedral in 1927 and the Institut Pédagogique de Montréal in 1955, as well as a reliquary for Saint Louis to the Basilica of Saint-Denis in 1956.

---

1   Book of John, 14: 6.

2   Booklet on *Christus Vincit*, Chaumet Archives.

3   *Divines Joailleries: L'Art de Joseph Chaumet (1852–1928)*, p. 18. The *Via Vitae* is now held by the Musée du Hiéron in Paray-le-Monial, France.

4   Glass plate negative no. 7065 (30 x 40 cm), Chaumet Archives.

5   Glass plate negatives nos. 316, 317, 485, 486, 487, 1979, 1980 (18 x 24 cm), Chaumet Archives.

6   Glass plate negative no. 1782 (30 x 40 cm), Chaumet Archives.

7   Folder 307 (Lisieux, 1922–23), Chaumet Archives.

FACING PAGE

Via Vitae,
Joseph Chaumet
(1852–1928).
Musée du Hiéron,
Paray-le-Monial

FROM MARCEL CHAUMET TO THE PRESENT

Karine Huguenaud

After the slowdown caused by worldwide war in 1914–18, the luxury trades returned to prosperity during the great social swirl of the 1920s. At the dawn of that new era, Chaumet, having retained the loyalty of its pre-war clientele, swiftly recovered thanks to its solid reputation. A transition was in the offing, yet the change in management occurred in stages. Joseph Chaumet, who had run the company for thirty-three years, agreed in 1922 to delegate his responsibilities to various colleagues, including his younger son, Marcel Chaumet (1886–1964), who then took over the reins upon Joseph's death in 1928.[1]

Marcel Chaumet had been trained in the family business and knew how it operated. Respecting the solid organization built by his father, he followed the line laid down by that master jeweler of the Belle Époque even as he modernized things. "Continuing the furrow he plowed, perpetuating his work in every sphere, such is my goal, to which I will devote all my effort," declared Marcel in a speech delivered at this father's funeral in 1928.[2] In 1920 Marcel had married Henriette Monnet, sister of Jean Monnet, one of the founding fathers of the European Union; Marcel remained very close to his brother-in-law throughout his life.

1   Folder 288 (*Pouvoirs divers*, 1922–24), Chaumet Archives, Paris.
2   Chaumet Archives.

LEFT

Deauville in the Roaring Twenties: the Dolly Sisters on the beach, Josephine Baker walking her leopard, promenade on the boardwalk. Present in the fashionable seaside resorts—Biarritz, Cannes, and Deauville— Chaumet offers a selection of its finest creations, as evidenced by the stock archival photographs.

FACING PAGE

The Cannes store's stock, 1929. Print from gelatin silver bromide glass negative, H. 30; W. 40 cm Chaumet Paris Collection

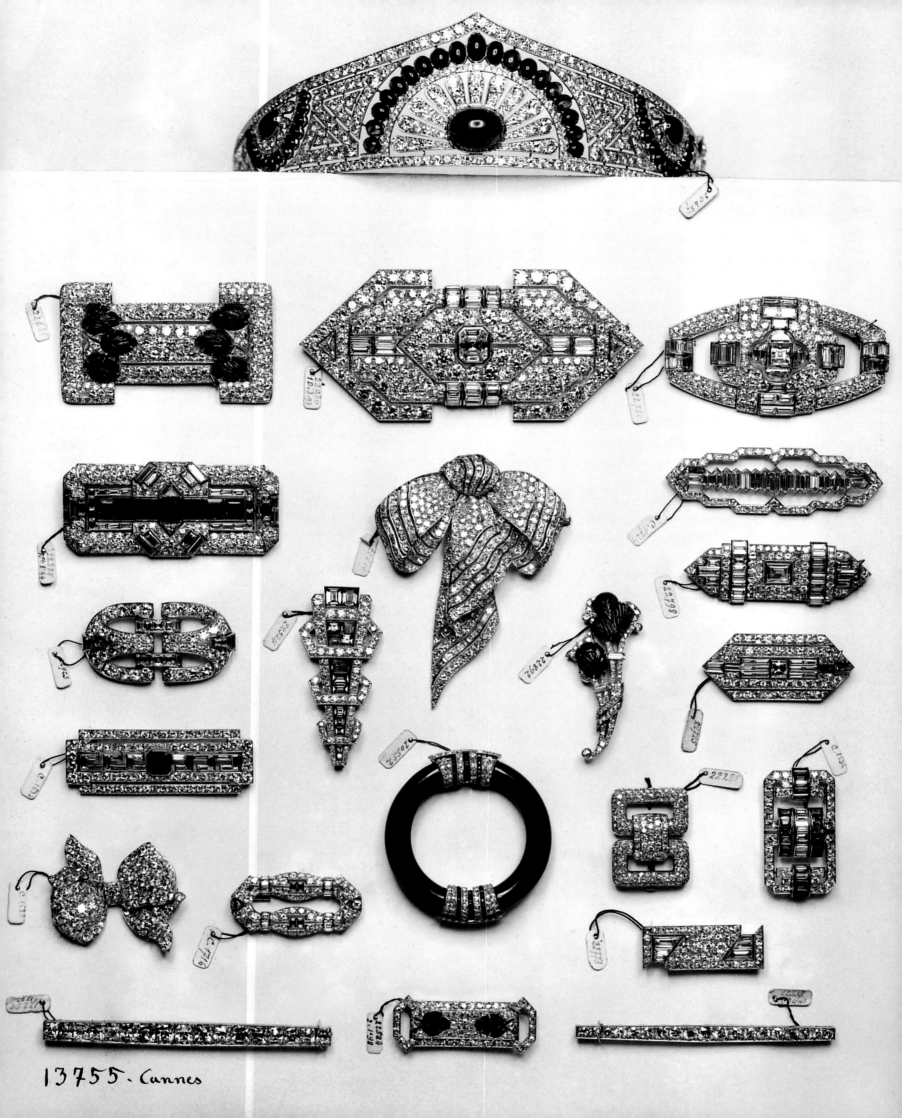

13755. Cannes

As jeweler to the cream of Paris society before the war, Chaumet could count on the trust of France's grand aristocratic families. The demands of social tradition and glamorous events ensured that orders flowed to the jeweler during the three seasons marking the high-society year. From February to June the Paris scene was filled with parties, balls, receptions, and evenings at the opera. In summer, Chaumet was present in the fashionable seaside resorts of Biarritz, Cannes, and Deauville[3]—photographs of stock sent to those different vacation destinations throughout the 1920s give an idea of the significance of the jewelry marketed there. Between 1917 and 1928 Chaumet also had stores in Vichy, "the queen of spa towns," whose hot waters drew an international clientele. In the fall, a return to family estates and the start of the hunting season provided excuses for placing new orders, like one made in 1927 by the Count of Greffuhle, who had a pin made for a hunting hat: it featured a hunting belt around a citrine from which sprang the pin feathers of a woodcock.[4]

Whereas, in general, the jewelry chests of these grand families were no longer being filled with extraordinary jewels and parures except for weddings or as marriage gifts—for which Chaumet remained the leading jeweler—orders flowed in from dynasties of industrialists and financiers. The cosmopolitan clientele of the interwar period, composed of millionaires from the United States and Latin America, as well as international diplomats, affirmed its social status by acquiring jewelry that clearly conveyed prosperity. The worlds of art and show business adopted similar practices: in 1930 Pablo Picasso gave his Russian wife, Olga Kokhlova, a monogram in diamonds of her initials. Olga had been a ballerina with Sergei Diaghilev's Ballets Russes when she met Picasso in February 1917 during performances of *Parade*. The already rich and famous Picasso married Olga in 1918 and gave her jewelry attesting to their rise to the cultural elite of the day.[5]

Immediately after World War I Chaumet relaunched the prospecting efforts that had helped the firm to grow during the Belle Époque. In 1921 and 1922 a unique event targeted the American market: a traveling show called The Salon of French Taste. Exhibitions were organized in New York, Philadelphia, and Chicago with the goal of familiarizing potential American clients with French decorative arts. Along with a few other Paris jewelers, Chaumet sent autochrome pictures—rather than real jewels—of designs that had made the company's reputation: pearl necklaces, bowknot brooches, head ornaments, earrings, and rings.[6] In 1924, a New York branch opened at 730 Fifth Avenue, extending these efforts.

Marcel Chaumet reinterpreted his father's vision of growth by using promotional methods suited to the times: advertising and exhibitions. In Paris the International Exposition of Decorative Arts in 1925 saw the consecration of the Art Deco style that Joseph Chaumet had pioneered in the sphere of jewelry as early as 1913–15. The Art Deco exposition was

3   Folder 148 (Deauville), folder 150 (Biarritz 1911–13), and
      folder 169 (Vichy 1917–28), Chaumet Archives.
4   Photograph no. 12053, dated January 21, 1927, Chaumet
      Archives.
5   Photograph no. 14792, dated April 2, 1930, Chaumet
      Archives.
6   Folder 354 (*Salon du Goût Français*), Chaumet Archives.

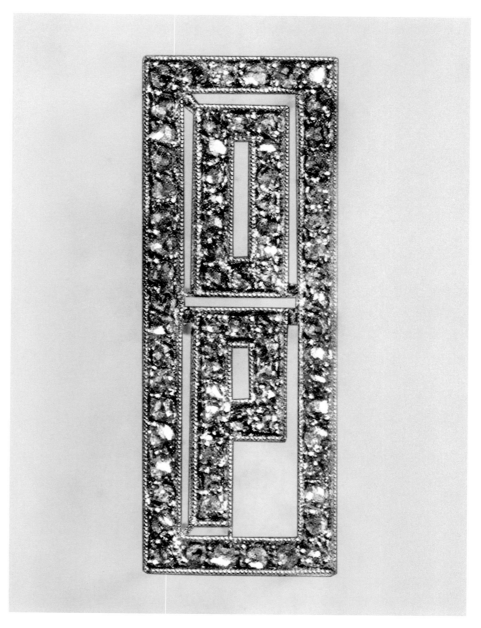

TOP

*Diamond monogram
with the initials of
Olga Picasso*, 1930.
Print from gelatin silver
bromide glass negative,
H. 9; W. 6.5 cm
Chaumet Paris Collection

BOTTOM

*Portraits of Pablo and
Olga Picasso*, 1919.

"Bunch of grapes" aigrette tiara, Joseph Chaumet (1852–1928), c. 1925. Gold, platinum, sapphires, rubies, diamonds, H. 4.5; W. 4.1; D. 1 cm Chaumet Paris Collection

followed in 1929 by a show of fine jewelry and precious metalwork at the Musée Galliera in Paris, in 1931 by the International Colonial Exposition (also in Paris), in 1935 by the Universal Exposition in Brussels, and in 1937 by the International Exposition of Arts and Techniques, once again hosted by Paris. It was time to celebrate a long heritage—in 1930 Marcel Chaumet marked the 150th anniversary of the firm by an exhibition and publication of the first historic study of the company, written by Gustave Babin and titled *Une Pléiade de Maîtres Joailliers* (A Host of Master Jewelers).

The whirlwind of the Roaring Twenties collapsed with the depression triggered by the Wall Street crash of 1929. Bankruptcies followed one another, debts deepened. Hard-hit American millionaires went back to the United States. Chaumet's turnover fell to seventeen million francs in 1932 after having hit a record eighty-four million francs in 1928.[7] But whereas other jewelers went under, Marcel Chaumet managed to weather the storm by taking radical measures. The New York branch was closed, the London store moved to less expensive premises, staff was cut at the Paris workshops, and the forty diamond-cutting benches in Auteuil were reduced to twenty-five. In such a grim climate, an order for three sets of matching jewelry in 1936 for the wedding of Princess Alice of Bourbon-Parma to the infante of Spain, Prince Alfonso of Bourbon-Two Sicilies, seemed like manna from heaven. These parures of pearls, sapphires, rubies, and diamonds were made from stones bequeathed by the prince's grandmother, Queen Maria Christina of Habsburg-Lorraine, who had received them from her uncle—Austrian emperor Franz-Joseph—at the time of her marriage to King Alfonso XII of Spain in 1879. The Spanish court, despite its exile after the proclamation of the Spanish republic in 1931, maintained its loyalty to the house of Chaumet. For that matter, after the death of Alfonso XIII in 1941, the King's collection of jewelry was sent for valuation to Chaumet's premises at 12, Place Vendôme in Paris.

THE CHALLENGE OF MODERNISM

After World War II ended, recovery was difficult. Although the workshop had not closed, output fell significantly. During those years of rebuilding, the "New Look" launched by designer Christian Dior revived the fashion industry. A new golden age of haute couture called for a new art of jewelry to match it. Given Chaumet's special role as jeweler to French nobility, the firm continued to embody a Parisian elegance characterized by sophistication and discretion. Yet change came in 1958 when Marcel Chaumet's two sons, Jacques and Pierre, were appointed co-directors of the firm. In 1961 a pioneering, inimitable jeweler named Pierre Sterlé joined the company, bringing new inspiration and a new creative thrust to it. In 1962, René Morin was hired. These two great designers, with their strong penchant for a free, whimsical—indeed bold—handling of natural motifs, combined with their thoroughly novel sense of line and movement, were a great asset to Chaumet in the 1960s and 1970s. Expansion was marked in 1968 by the purchase of Brussels jewelry company Wolfers and in 1970 by the acquisition of watchmaker Breguet.

7   Diana Scarisbrick, *Chaumet: Master Jewelers Since 1780* (Paris: Alain de Gourcuff, 1995), p. 223.

TOP
*Grand Prix diploma
awarded to Monsieur
Chaumet at the Inter-
national Exhibition of
Modern Decorative and
Industrial Arts*, Paris, 1925.
Chaumet Archives

CENTER
*Memorial diploma
awarded to Marcel
Chaumet at the Paris
Colonial Exhibition*, 1931.
Chaumet Archives

BOTTOM
*Grand Prix diploma
awarded to Monsieur
Chaumet at the Brussels
World's Fair*, 1935.
Chaumet Archives

FACING PAGE
*Pendant watch known
as the "Régence" watch*,
Joseph Chaumet
(1852–1928), 1924.
Platinum, frosted rock
crystal, diamonds, enamel,
H. 11; W. 3.4; D. 1 cm
Chaumet Paris Collection

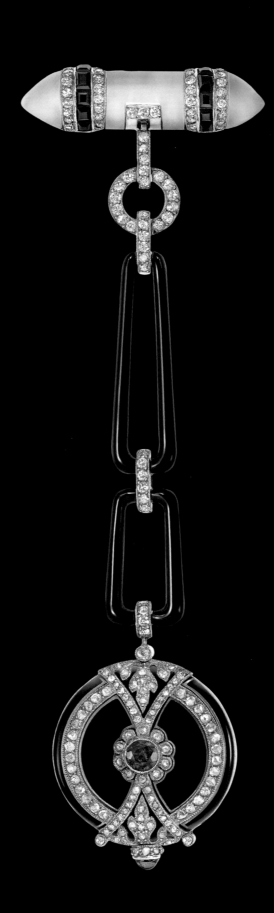

The international scope of orders and fashions led to a diversification of production. Responding to the needs of the day, jewelry of less costly materials was made, although without making any concessions in the quality and creativity embodied by Chaumet. This contemporary approach was epitomized by the 1970 launch of a boutique called L'Arcade. Its modern spirit targeted a broader clientele by offering attractive jewelry at competitive prices, all the while retaining the Chaumet label.

The revival of the 1960s was matched by institutional recognition. In 1962 Chaumet was included in an exhibition at the Musée du Louvre titled *Dix Siècles de Joaillerie Française* (Ten Centuries of French Jewelry). The Parisian firm was henceforth assured a place in the history of French taste and decorative arts. Its designs were found in the collections of the greatest museums. In 1976 this status earned Chaumet a commission from the Louvre to set the newly acquired Sancy diamond—just as Fossin had once set the same stone for the wife of Count Paul Demidov; the company also continued to work on some of the crown jewels on show in the Louvre's Apollo Gallery. In the same vein, Chaumet's founding of a heritage department to coincide with the company's bicentenary imparted greater scope to its long-held policy of passing on its tradition via the constitution of a collection of jewels and historic objects and the restoration of archived drawings and photographs. Ever since that date, Chaumet has not only organized its own events but also participated in over thirty international exhibitions devoted to the arts of the nineteenth and twentieth centuries.

    A new era in the history of Chaumet dawned after its declaration of bankruptcy in 1987 and subsequent acquisition by InvestCorp, an international investment corporation. The uninterrupted succession of four family dynasties—Nitot, Fossin, Morel, and Chaumet—came to an end as the twentieth century drew to a close. Branch stores closed: London (which had operated out of 178 New Bond Street since 1961), Geneva (opened in 1979), and New York (located at East 57th Street since 1984). First renamed Société Nouvelle Chaumet, and later Chaumet International, S.A., the company was bought by the LVMH group in 1999.

    Chaumet's rebirth was accompanied by a look back at its history. In 1995 came the first reference work to be based on archival material and historical documents, authored by Diana Scarisbrick and titled *Chaumet, Master Jewelers Since 1780*. The book was followed in 1998 by an exhibition at the Musée Carnavalet, *Chaumet Paris: Two Centuries of Fine Jewellery*, and by others held in the historic reception rooms of Chaumet's Place Vendôme premises, *Napoleon in Love* (in 2004) and *Le Grand Frisson: 500 Years of Jewels of Sentiment* (in 2008).

    Strengthened by its prestigious past, Chaumet found the inspiration to confront the transition to the third millennium. Keen to conquer new markets and new clients, notably the Near and Middle East (since the 1970s) and Asia (more recently), it now boasts a major network of stores throughout the world. They offer a range of emblematic jewels from tiaras to weddings rings, two of Chaumet's timeless signature items, as well as contemporary lines that have already become classics. The *Lien* line, launched by René Morin in 1980 and inspired by the favorite eighteenth-century motif of an intertwining ribbon "tie," has become the symbol of an emotional tie, a metaphor for love in all its forms. There can be no better conclusion than a reference to the company's first muse, Empress Joséphine. The line of jewelry that has borne her name since 2012 is inspired by the tiaras she so loved, which today yield timeless designs reminding us that Chaumet's unchanging identity has always been tied to excellence.

"Joséphine" ring, 2015.
Gold, diamonds
Chaumet Paris Collection

Chaumet's Pearls

Karine Huguenaud

Chaumet's expertise in pearls gained prominence in the early nineteenth century. In 1805, the tiara given to Pope Pius VII by Napoleon brought recognition to Nitot's talent as a jewelry maker, and demonstrated his ability to supply the 3,346 precious stones and 2,990 pearls that went into that unique creation. Nitot also considerably enriched the Crown pearls, originally for Empress Joséphine, who adored them and who owned several pieces, and later for Napoleon's second wife, Archduchess Marie-Louise of Austria. For their wedding in 1810, Nitot produced an ensemble of two necklaces, one comb, rows of pearls to wear in the hair, earrings, and bracelets, to which were added in 1811 a long necklace of 408 pearls and a tiara with 297 pearls. Because pearls are rare and it takes time to gather the required number, it wasn't until 1812 that a crown containing 1,233 pearls completed the ensemble.[1] The most prominent pearl in this piece stood out in the center of the tiara. On its sale by Nitot, it weighed 346,27 grains, that is, the size of a pigeon's egg, and was the largest known pearl in Europe at the time. When it was sold with the Crown Jewels in 1887, this pearl, named the *Régente*, or the Napoleon, was acquired by Fabergé. It was remounted in a pendant, and given by Prince Nicholas Yusupov to his daughter Zenaida, who gave it in turn to her son Felix in 1914 on his wedding to Irina of Russia.[2]

The firm's reputation for pearl jewelry endured after the First Empire. In 1851, the future Empress Eugénie purchased 169 pearls from Fossin for a six-strand necklace, and deposited 282 pearls with him for rethreading.[3] The pearl necklace became one of Chaumet's classics. A timeless, indispensable piece in every woman's jewelry collection, inherited from one generation to the next, remounted and rethreaded, enhanced and added to over the years, it was composed of one or several strands and generally graduated—with one larger, central pearl and pearls decreasing in size on either side. Joseph Chaumet saw it as "a sort of crowning, a consecration, a supreme refinement." A particularly elaborate version was the long, Indian-inspired Bayadère necklace. The term conjured up the tasseled chains worn by Hindu dancers (the word *bayadère* deriving from the Portuguese word *bailadeira*, dancer). Very fashionable in the interwar period, these long necklaces made up of multiple strings of tiny natural pearls and ending in tassel-like pendants wonderfully enhanced the *garçonne* (flapper) look. The *Salon des Perles* in the Hôtel Baudard de Sainte-James takes its name from the pearl stringers who worked on these masterpieces.

Joseph Chaumet, like the firm's founder, distinguished himself in the Belle Époque and the Roaring Twenties with his knowledge of stones and pearls, a specialty in which he excelled. On June 7, 1922, he gave a talk about his research on precious stones and cultivated pearls. Chaumet emphasized the danger of the Japanese artificial pearls that were coming onto the market, stressing the need to distinguish them from natural pearls in loyalty to the customer, as he had done in 1904 already with reconstructed or synthetic rubies. His interest in the subject even prompted him to study a business proposal in 1904 for a pearl fishery operation in Ceylan.[4] The Chaumet firm remained true to the principles of the master jeweler of the Belle Époque, using only natural pearls until the 1980s.

1   Bernard Morel, *Les Joyaux de la Couronne de France* (Paris: Albin Michel/Mercator), pp. 277 and 280. In 1812, the valuer's appraisal of the complete ensemble recorded a total of 3,232 pearls, valued at 1,223,429 francs. Today all that remains is the eagle at the top of the crown, the rest of the piece having been dismantled during the Restoration.

2   Hidden with the Yusupov jewelry collection in the family's Moscow palace during the Revolution of 1917, the Napoleon or *Régente* Pearl reappeared at Christie's New York in 1987. It was last sold at auction for 1.2 million euros at Christie's in Geneva in November 2005, making it the most costly pearl in the world.

3   Invoice ledger G (1851–52), p. 274, Chaumet Archives.

4   Folder 53 (Ceylan 1924), Chaumet Archives.

FACING PAGE

Design for an Indian set featuring pearls, emeralds, and diamonds, c. 1920. Graphite pencil, white chalk, ink wash painting, and white highlights, H. 53; W. 37 cm Chaumet Paris Collection

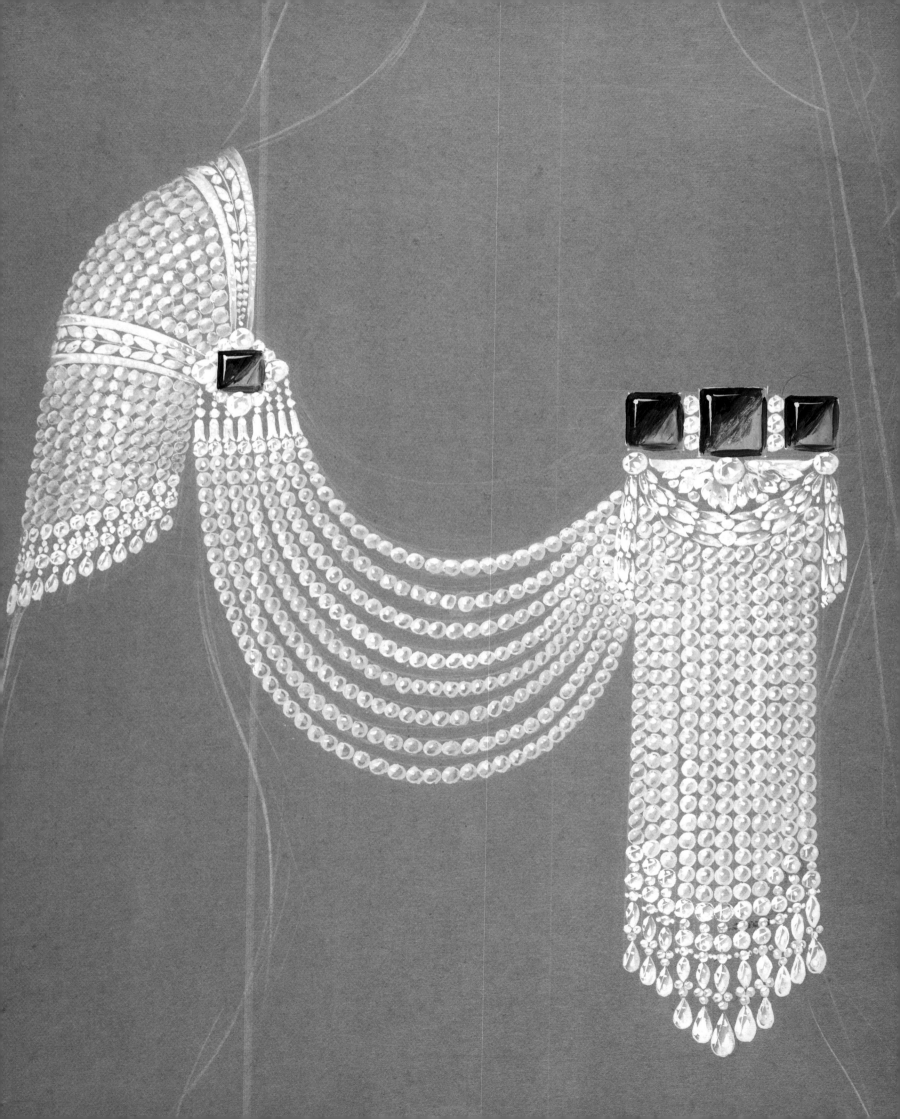

THE CHAUMET HERITAGE

Béatrice de Plinval

The "Lily" tiara from
La Nature de Chaumet
Collection (2016)
resting on invoice books
from Paris and London
(1914–25).

The Heritage Department was founded in 1980 by Jacques Chaumet, and has been headed for the last thirty-six years by Béatrice de Plinval. During this period, its main orientations have been defined, bringing about a policy of conservation, restoration, and exhibitions.

In the late 1970s, the Chaumet Archives were still kept in the storerooms where Joseph Chaumet had placed them in the early twentieth century. But the company had not yet taken the full measure of this unique heritage collection and its remarkable potential. Perhaps the time was not ripe. Over the following years, this widespread realization would determine the strategy of the great luxury houses.

FOUNDING OF THE DEPARTMENT

From 1978, in preparation for Chaumet's bicentennial in 1980, major renovation work began in the jewelry boutique and historic salons on the second floor of the Hôtel Baudard de Sainte-James. This was an opportunity to showcase a number of items from Chaumet's archive collections.

Jacques Chaumet, who wished to implement a conservation and restoration policy, entrusted me with this task.

The firm's guiding line would be the principles laid down by Marie-Étienne Nitot, founder of Chaumet in 1780. In choosing as successors not their descendants but talented jewelers whose mission was to maintain, enrich, and develop the house to the highest degree of competence, Nitot and his son made the continuation of excellence the driving force of Chaumet. To achieve this, it was essential to preserve its memory intact. This principle lies behind the rich diversity of documents and designs that make up the archival collections preserved and passed down from generation to generation. The time had now come to undertake the protection of this heritage, with determination and passion.

TROUBLED TIMES FOR THE ARCHIVES

When Jacques and Pierre Chaumet were forced to abandon their company in June 1986, we immediately undertook to protect the archives by putting the keys to the storerooms containing the drawings, accounting ledgers, and correspondence in a safe, to avoid them being dispersed. We also took care of the museum's jewelry and other objects.

A year later, in June 1987, lawyers representing the firm that had been shortlisted to take over the company were working on the conditions of the buyout. One of them, a Franco-American named Christian Romon, was also a *chartiste* (a graduate of the École National des Chartes), held a doctorate in the History of Art, and was a former pupil of Emmanuel Le Roy Ladurie. We saw this as a good omen, and hastened to invite him to visit our storerooms. A swift but accurate inventory of the collections enabled a report to be drawn up for the future owners and the judicial authorities on October 14, 1987. In this document, entitled "Report on preliminary review of the Chaumet private archives conducted October 7, 8, 1987," Christian Romon stressed the quality and quantity of the company's archives, which constituted an exceptional heritage collection of great historical and cultural value.

Having ensured that the Chaumet archive collection would appear in the deed of sale, it remained for us to find a way to safeguard the jewels and objects of greatest stylistic and historical importance, notably those conserved since the early nineteenth century. As these were not part of the buyout of the future Société Nouvelle Chaumet, they were to be dispersed at auction.

In 1988, we were able to negotiate the buyback of the museum's jewelry and objects for a reasonable sum with the judicial authorities' representative, who was aware of how important it was for Chaumet to conserve the finest works of its history. Thus the large Empire-period sketches, the portrait of Empress Marie-Louise, four tiaras, twenty-one pieces of jewelry, and other small items remarkable in their creative design and crafting would remain with Chaumet. We also managed to buy back some of the furniture from the reception rooms.

That same year an exhibition was being prepared at the Metropolitan Museum in New York titled *The Age of Napoleon: Costume from Revolution to Empire: 1789–1815*. Katell le Bourhis, the exhibition's organizer, asked us to loan our large Empire drawings and paintings, as well as the famous jewelry ensemble belonging to Empress Marie-Louise. The exhibition was a great success. And it was the first time Chaumet had exhibited all of its Empire collections abroad. It was an opportunity for visitors as well as the curators of the various lending museums to discover the value of our loans. A close relationship was forged with major institutions, marking the beginning, for Chaumet, of a significant institutional dialogue.

EXHIBITIONS AND PUBLICATIONS

In 1989, Hans Nadelhoffer, President of Christie's, Geneva, had just published a first work of historical reference for a luxury jewelry house—a publishing landmark in our sector. He often came to Paris and came to visit us several times. Together we put together a

Views of the storerooms where the historical records and the collection of preparatory plasters have been preserved since 1907. They have been gradually replaced by modern storerooms.

project for a book about Chaumet. His fascination and enthusiasm were palpable. We began discussions with publishers, but they came to nothing. Hans died of a terrible illness.

Our meeting with Diana Scarisbrick in 1989 proved to be a turning point. Her knowledge of Renaissance jewelry and gem carving had led her to study jewelry history, and the history of French jewelry in particular. She had already formed her opinion of Chaumet. At our first meeting at Place Vendôme, she said to us: "You know, I'm acquainted with all the luxury jewelry houses, but Chaumet has the finest history of Parisian jewelry making." To illustrate what she was saying, she quoted a New York-based collector renowned for his extraordinary taste and passion for jewelry, who had declared: "I would sell everything I own for the remarkable Chaumet drawings."

In 1991, we set to work with Diana and began to study, for the first time in the company's history, the archival collections in the storerooms, where everything had been meticulously put away through the generations and successive fashions since 1907, when Chaumet moved to its second address on Place Vendôme. The company's accounting ledgers and visitors' books were ferried between Paris and London in order to be studied. Every six weeks, a messenger loaded the books into the trunk of a car, crossed the Channel from Dieppe to Newhaven, arriving early in the morning at Diana's home at Chester Terrace, then returned by the night ferry with the books she had studied after the previous trip.

In 1995, the book *Chaumet, joaillier depuis 1780* was published by Alain de Gourcuff Editeur (English edition: *Chaumet: Master Jewelers Since 1780*). We asked Daniel Alcouffe, chief curator and director of the Department of Decorative Arts at the Louvre, to write the preface. In it, he observes:

> Although they may lament their disappearance, few historians of the eighteenth century can be surprised that the Germain or Riesener archives are not available to them. By contrast, we could be forgiven for supposing that historians engaged in studies of more recent periods would have the archives of the great nineteenth- and twentieth-century manufacturers at their disposal, whether or not the firms are still in existence. It is a sad truth, however, that whether through accident, indifference, or the regrettable lack of any body with the specific responsibility of preserving this type of documentation, the archives of the great manufacturing houses have all too often been lost, and sometimes not so long ago. Important firms who, like Chaumet … have endeavored to preserve their past and more particularly their archives, are therefore to be congratulated and encouraged.…
>
> Chaumet's links with the Département des objets d'art at the Louvre are long established, for among the clientele under the Second Empire are to be found Léon de Laborde, Horace de Viel-Castel, and Louis Clément de Ris, all of whom served as curators. In recent times, the firm has contributed on a number of occasions to the maintenance and presentation of the Crown diamonds exhibited in the Galerie d'Apollon. The Fossins were entrusted with the Sancy diamond for remounting when it was in the possession of the Demidov family; when it was bought by the Louvre in 1976 it was Chaumet who designed the setting in which it can still be viewed.

This book was essential in lending legitimacy to the organization of a large-scale retrospective exhibition. The year following its publication, Jean-Marc Léri, director of the Musée Carnavalet, proposed an exhibition of our historic collections in this museum devoted to the history of Paris. The show *Chaumet-Paris, Deux Siècles de Création* in 1998 gave impetus to a sustained policy of loans to major events worldwide, while offering Chaumet's Archives Department the capacity and the means to organize its own exhibitions: *Napoléon Amoureux, Bijoux de l'Empire des Aigles et du Cœur* in 2004, and *Le Grand Frisson, Bijoux de Sentiment de la Renaissance à Nos Jours* in 2008.

CHAUMET'S HERITAGE COLLECTIONS

Today, the archival heritage collections have a triple vocation: they are a source of inspiration for contemporary designers; they enable the authentication of antique jewelry pieces; and they constitute an indispensable source of reference for jewelry history and, more generally, for the history of the French decorative arts.

THE ANTIQUE JEWELRY COLLECTION

"Eagle fighting a snake" brooch, Joseph Chaumet (1852–1928), c. 1880. Gold, natural baroque pearl, diamonds, and rubies, H. 4.5; W. 6 cm Chaumet Paris Collection

Since 1980, Chaumet has developed a discerning acquisitions policy, one that will illustrate the changes in Parisian taste and preserve the memory of its creativity. From Neoclassicism to Romanticism, the Belle Époque, Art Deco, and, more recently, the 1970s, the Chaumet Collection features a particularly diverse range of styles and a quality of craftsmanship that remains exceptional to this day.

The 250 or so pieces making up this eclectic collection, most of prestigious provenance, echo successive fashions since the late eighteenth century. Their diversity, beauty, and richness bear witness to the uninterrupted transmission of excellence since the foundation of the jewelry house.

Today, Chaumet is making every effort to enhance and enrich its collections.

It is amusing to tell the stories behind each acquisition. Objects such as these have a destiny. They wait patiently for those who desire them. But for the meeting to take place, they must be recognized.

One day in the spring of 2000, a foreign dealer came to visit. He had come to ask us to authenticate three Chaumet clip brooches. Three sad, dirty, and broken objects were wrapped in old paper. As we set them out on a tray, one of them caught our eye. We recognized the hummingbird, a fine ruby and diamond brooch that could also be worn in an aigrette (headpiece), of which the drawing and original photograph dating from 1855 were still in our possession. It was in a pitiful state of disrepair. Hiding our excitement and unable to reveal our intentions, we asked our visitor if we could keep the three items in order to examine them, which he willingly accepted.

Three days went by before we could show the hummingbird to our president. We had to conceal our admiration and passion for this object because without his agreement, we would not be able to purchase it. But he shared our enthusiasm.

That day, a remarkable object entered our collections. It encapsulates the lightness, elegance, and poetry of the Chaumet style. We can not help thinking of the master jeweler who made it, who gave it that extra special touch.

Every object has a story. This is a simply beautiful one.

The Collection of Drawings

This is indisputably the foremost jewelry history collection of its kind in Europe and the United States. It forms an exceptional ensemble of 52,500 finished drawings, the oldest of which date back to the late eighteenth century. These working tools, used in the design of the pieces and to present them to customers for approval before a model is made in nickel silver, the final fitting stage before execution, are also works of art in their own right. Chaumet's designers deployed great technical and artistic skill in depicting the various stones and pearls, and in rendering their volumes, translucency, and shine. Their drawings were executed in graphite with touches of gouache on a wide range of white, gray, and black ocher paper, laid or vellum paper of variable weights, often on transparent paper.

The drawings were archived in albums put together by the designers before they retired from the company, either glued to the page or affixed with mounting corners. In 1995, we asked Dominique Vitart to take charge of this conservation and restoration work, which she continues to this day.

The Collection of Nickel Silver Maquettes

In the Belle Époque period, Joseph Chaumet had the brilliant idea of making three-dimensional models of the tiaras, and some of the larger necklaces and bodice brooches, in nickel silver, an alloy of copper, nickel, and zinc used by the apprentice jewelers. These mock-ups were the final, full-dimensional fitting stage of the design before the piece was executed.

ABOVE

*Studies of flowers:
pansy, daisy, poppy,
forget-me-not, and lilies
of the valley, c. 1890.*
Pen and black ink, brown
ink wash, white gouache
highlights, H. 14; W. 11.5 cm
Chaumet Paris Collection

FACING PAGE

*Engraved rock crystal bowl
with frame in gold and
gilded and enameled silver,*
Morel & Cie. design book,
1842–48.
Graphite pencil, gouache,
ink wash, gold highlights,
H. 34; W. 25 cm
Chaumet Paris Collection

Close to 600 tiaras form a masterly evocation of Chaumet's diverse creativity. They can still be admired in the *Salon des Diadèmes* (Tiara Room), where Joseph Chaumet had them displayed during the Belle Époque. They illustrate the many artistic themes of the firm, and remain a source of inspiration for special orders executed for customers who have noticed them.

The Photographic Collection

Having twice been obliged to move the drawings in order to protect them from the risk of flooding, and having used all our powers of persuasion in 1989 to urge the company's CEO to abandon the idea of dispersing them at auction, we were well aware that the photographic collection was at even greater risk. At the time no one was interested in the mountains of glass plates stored away in flat cardboard boxes covered with dust. They took up space in one of our large cellars that was coveted by other departments. There was a plan to have a big waste container delivered and have them destroyed. It was argued that the stock of jewelry cases could be stored there instead. At this point, we sought advice from Anne Cartier-Bresson, director of the City of Paris Photographic Restoration and Conservation Studio. On visiting the cellar, she could see how vulnerable this collection was. She recommended one of her pupils to us, Sabrina Esmeraldo, a graduate of the first photographic conservation and restoration course at the Institut National du Patrimoine (INP) in 1993.

In 1996, Sabrina set up her studio in the cellar with the aid of her assistant, Jorge Rivas-Rivas, and began the preservation of the collection of negatives from 1997 to 2003, and then, from 2003 on, that of the positive prints on paper. In 2013, she delivered a report synthesising twenty-three years of conservation work on this unique and exceptional collection. Over the years, with the recognition of photography as a major art form, many glass plates and prints have come to be considered real works of art.

The Archives Collection

While the archives dating from the First French Empire can now be consulted at the Archives Nationales in Paris, Chaumet still keeps all those assembled from the Bourbon Restoration period to the present. Invoice books and inventory books from Paris, London, and New York; visiting books; cash journals, books of stones, books of pearls, studio books; as well as all the customer files and the correspondence of Jules Fossin, Prosper Morel, Joseph Chaumet, and Marcel Chaumet totaling more than 20,000 letters, represent a truly valuable asset and resource. Our deep knowledge of these archives must today meet the requirements and demands of a great jewelry house in the twenty-first century. An ambitious project to computerize and digitize this exceptional collection has just been launched, for these heritage archives are essential to nurturing the appeal of the house.

The past reveals its codes, and the present redefines them, at a place and on a place where, since Nitot's day, our history was written. In his speech for the 250th anniversary of Place Vendôme in 1950, Paul Claudel said, "This is where France entertains, where France works, here she is true to herself, affirming her unity and her permanence through her long history."

FACING PAGE, TOP
Letter from Baron Ferdinand de Turckheim to Fossin, January 11, 1856. The Chaumet Archives holds records of all correspondence with the house's customers. The letters of Baron de Turckheim, a tax collector in Strasbourg, describe in great detail the orders he placed, here for a bracelet and a chatelaine, accompanying them with designs. Four signed pages, H. 21.5; W.13.5 cm Chaumet Paris Archives

FACING PAGE, BOTTOM
Annotated design sent to Fossin's Spanish agent, 1849. Graphite pencil, pen and black ink, ink wash, H. 11.5; W. 23.8 cm Chaumet Paris Archives

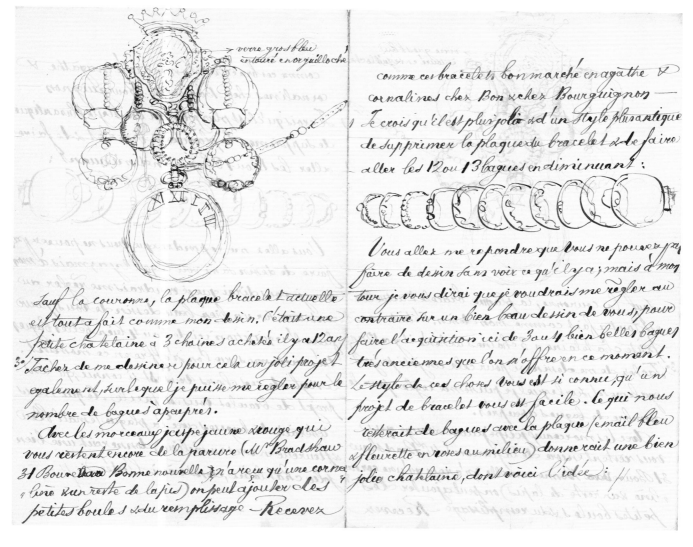

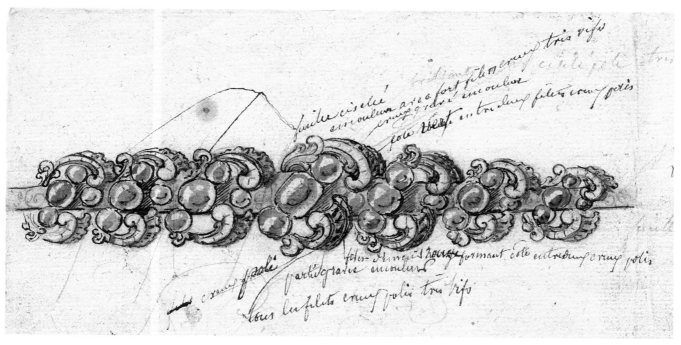

Chaumet and Photography

Sabrina Esmeraldo

At the end of the nineteenth century Joseph Chaumet set up a photographic studio in the company. His twin goals were to prepare for the Universal Exposition of 1900 and to produce photographic documentation for his scientific research into pearls and precious stones.

Thus over nearly a century, a series of photographers made visual records of objects produced by the house of Chaumet. Hundreds of thousands of photos were taken of pieces of jewelry and precious metalwork, of wax models, of designs, of settings, of jewels that were broken or were to be taken apart—anything that required a faithful visual record.

The oldest pictures reveal the photographer's efforts to enhance the arrangement of the jewels and the effectiveness of the photographic composition, to improve image quality through choice of negative and paper, and to organize the archive by numbering the shots. The first prints were all done on albumin paper or other printing-out papers with warm tones. Soon, however, photographers began using developing-out papers with more neutral tones. The backs of thousands of prints bear Kodak's Velox trademark, a paper that combined the advantage of contact printing (unenlarged, hence life-size dimensions) with swift development time.

We know the brands of the negatives employed because their original packaging served as archive boxes for the developed pictures. Very quickly a preference emerged for glass plate negatives made by Grieshaber, which Chaumet continued to use for fifty years.

The archive contains 33,000 glass plate negatives ranging from 6.5 x 9 cm (2½ x 3½ in.) to 30 x 40 cm (12 x 16 in.). Around 1910, company photographers tested flexible celluloid film, and roughly fifty shots survive in the collection, but this approach was soon abandoned.

Negatives on celluloid were finally introduced in the 1950s. A few experiments began in 1952 with medium-sized negatives, i.e., 13 x 18 cm (5 x 7 in.). In 1955 celluloid was extended to all five formats commonly used at Chaumet, ranging from 6.5 x 9 cm to 24 x 30 cm (9½ x 12 in.), while the largest format, 30 x 40 cm, was dropped. In 1964 photographers began using rolls of 120 film (60 mm), followed in 1968 by 135 film (35 mm). Color film made its appearance in the archive in 1974, as did black-and-white Polaroids with negatives. All told, there are over 34,000 celluloid negatives. Much of the archive from the 1970s and 1980s remains unexplored.

At first, prints were carefully glued in albums or onto large plates. They were also stuck on blue-cardboard file cards categorized according to type of jewel. Photos could also be cut up and used for various other purposes, visually illustrating invoices or ledgers. In the 1910s several prints were made of each negative, and stored in envelopes according to size. Systematically making a life-size negative and print of the objects was dropped in the 1970s, when the choice of format was determined, instead, by the requirements of the information to be conveyed.

The house of Chaumet's photographic archive thus provides an extensive view of the techniques and methods employed throughout the twentieth century. The quality of the items photographed also makes it exceptional. Indeed, Chaumet's entire output, from humblest cuff link to most extraordinary tiara, was exhaustively recorded. These photos have additional historic and documentary value in so far as they testify to the skill, inventiveness, and artistic value of jewelry by Chaumet, especially since many of the pieces were subsequently disassembled or lost.

The first glass plate:
Diamond necklace, 1890–95.
Gelatin silver bromide
glass negative, shot no. 1,
H. 24; W. 30 cm
Chaumet Paris Collection

N° 1

The Hôtel Baudard de Sainte-James

Romain Condamine

"Monsieur de Sainte-James was a tax collector, immensely rich.... He was a man of average height, fat and heavy, with a face strongly colored by that bloom one may acquire after the age of fifty if one is healthy and happy. Mr. de Sainte-James kept the most magnificent home, for he lived in one of the finest mansions on Place Vendôme, where he gave grand and good dinners that numbered thirty or forty people at least."[1] That is Élisabeth Vigée-Lebrun's recollection of the man who, appointed Treasurer General of the Navy in 1771—but known above all for his extravagant, folly-studded garden in Neuilly—undertook major redecoration work in his lavish townhouse on Place Vendôme, which since 1907 has been the headquarters of the house of Chaumet.

The *grand salon*, or main reception room on the piano nobile of this private mansion, or *hôtel particulier*, has retained its original appearance almost entirely. This is the very room that usually caught the attention of eighteenth-century chroniclers. Thus Luc-Vincent Thiéry, in a guide for travelers to Paris, recommended a visit to this "magnificent *salon* [which] is very richly decorated."[2] François Métra, meanwhile, noted that Sainte-James "spared no luxury in decorating his home" and added that "his *salon* alone cost 100,000 ecus."[3] An inventory of the treasurer's property, drawn up in 1787 by an appointed

expert, architect Jean-Baptiste Vincent Boullant, confirms those commentators' enthusiasm. The drawing room had a rich parquet floor and was lined by sixteen Corinthian columns, the space between the columns being filled with "vast expanses of mirror." To make the room appear even larger, mirrors were also placed on the inside of the shutters, set into gilded parquetry. From the cornice hung elegant garlands, also of gilded wood, "with tassels, intertwining ivy, wreathes of flowers, and cornucopias." Other garlands of "foliage, bead molding, and chains" were found on "magnificent wall chandeliers, which reflected in the mirrors."[4]

If this reception room was—and still is—so wonderful, that is because Baudard de Sainte-James sought out the finest artists of the day when he bought the mansion in 1777. He wanted it decorated with total harmony, down to the tiniest details of iconography. The design of the room and some of its furnishings is credited to François-Joseph Belanger, architect to Louis XVI's brother, the Count of Artois, while the wood paneling and gilded reliefs of naval trophies and marine flora and fauna are the work of brothers Jean-Siméon and Jules-Hughes Rousseau and a third decorative sculptor, Nicolas-François Lhullier. Finally, all the decorative painting was done by Jean-Jacques Lagrenée, a history painter and member of the Académie Royale.[5] The significance of this commission to Lagrenée's career can be seen

FACING PAGE

View of the historic grand salon of the Hôtel Baudard de Sainte-James.

PAGES 132–133

Charles Giraud, *View of the Historic Grand Salon of the Hôtel Baudard de Sainte-James, Then Owned by Mr. Basile Parent*, 1866.
Oil on wood
Private Collection

1   Louise-Élisabeth Vigée-Lebrun, *Souvenirs de Mme. Louise-Élisabeth Vigée-Lebrun* (Paris: H. Fournier, 1835), vol. 1, p. 275.

2   Luc-Vincent Thiéry, *Guide des amateurs et des étrangers voyageurs à Paris* (Paris: Hardouin & Gattey, 1787), vol. 1, p. 128.

3   François Métra, *Anecdotes secrètes du dix-huitième siècle* (Paris: Léopold Collin, 1808 [1787]), vol. 1, p. 390.

4   *Estimation des immeubles dépendants de la direction des biens du Sieur Baudard de St James*, unnumbered document dated October 11, 1787, Z1j 1171, Archives Nationales, Paris. Thanks to Emmanuel Sarmeo for sending us this source.

5   On the decorative works commissioned by Claude Baudard de Sainte-James for his Hôtel on Place Vendôme, see: Gabrielle Joudiou, "Les décors de l'Hôtel Baudard de Sainte-James," in Thierry Sarmant and Luce Gaume (eds.) *La Place Vendôme, Art, pouvoir et fortune* (Paris: Action Artistique de la Ville de Paris, 2002), p. 156; and Alexia Lebeurre, *Le décor intérieur des demeures à la mode dans la deuxième moitié du XVIIIe siècle (Paris et Île-de-France)*, dissertation supervised by Daniel Rabreau, Université de Paris I (Panthéon-Sorbonne), 2008. On the overdoors painted by Lagrenée, see Marc Sandoz, *Les Lagrenée, II.—Jean-Jacques Lagrenée, le jeune* (Paris: Éditions Les Quatre Chemins, 1988), pl. VIII and pp. 232–33.

FACING PAGE
View of the historic salons
of the Hôtel Baudard
de Sainte-James on the
Place Vendôme side.
Overdoor:
Jean-Jacques Lagenée,
*France Receiving the
Riches of the Sea*, 1751.
Oil on canvas

RIGHT
Eugène Delacroix
(1798–1863), *Portrait of
Frederic Chopin*, c. 1838
(cut and reworked
between 1863 and 1874).
Oil on canvas,
H. 46; W. 38 cm
Musée du Louvre, Paris

in the fact that he exhibited "sketches of the ceiling and the four overdoor panels in the reception room of Mr. de Sainte-James" in the Salon of 1781.[6] Those four medallions, which can still been seen over the doors today, depict *France Receiving the Riches of the Sea*, *Neptune and Amphitrite*, *Aeneas Abandoning Dido*, and *Abundance*.

Following the bankruptcy and death of Baudard de Sainte-James in 1787, the mansion passed through a number of hands until it became the Russian embassy in 1848.[7] From that date onward the *hôtel particulier* hosted its last glamorous occupants. Countess Delphine Potocka, a friend and patron of Frederick Chopin, housed the famous pianist there in a ground floor and mezzanine apartment in the left wing, overlooking the courtyard; sources inform us that the apartment had "an antechamber, dining room, drawing room, three bedrooms, dressing room, kitchen, pantry, [and] servants' room."[8] As indicated on a plaque on the front of the building, Chopin died there on October 17, 1849. This mansion was also where young Eugénie de Montijo, lodging there with her mother during a stay in Paris, met the president of the new republic, Prince Louis-Napoleon Bonaparte, who in 1852 would become emperor and would soon ask for Eugénie's hand in marriage.

The musical, romantic nineteenth century is still reflected in certain details of the mansion, notably the *grand salon*, as recorded in an 1866 painting by Charles Giraud. Worth noting in particular is the handsome ceiling painted in 1864 for the then owner, Mr. Parent, by Pierre-Victor Galland (who happened to be the nephew of Jean-Baptiste Fossin, the Nitots' successor).[9] The figure of Euterpe, muse of music, continues to preside over the combined heritage of all those artists who, since the age of Enlightenment, have been the pride of the house of Chaumet.

6 *Explication des peintures, sculptures & autres ouvrages de Messieurs de l'Académie Royale, qui sont exposés dans le Salon du Louvre* (Paris: Collombat & Hérissant, 1781), p. 13, no. 46.

7 On the various owners and tenants of the mansion, see: Fernand de Saint-Simon, *La Place Vendôme*, (Paris: Éditions Vendôme, 1982), pp. 379–95; Rochelle Ziskin and Thierry Claeys in Sarmant and Gaume, *La Place Vendôme...*, p. 291; and Philippe and Nicole Baudard de Fontaine, *Ces Messieurs Baudard de Sainte-James, trésoriers de la Marine* (Versailles: Mémoire & Documents, 2007), p. 87.

8 Undated document in private hands, *Hôtel Place Vendôme, 12 / États des locations*, fol. 1v.

9 Henry Havard, *L'œuvre de P.-V. Galland* (Paris: May et Motteroz, 1895), p. 58, and Jérémy Cerrano (ed.), *Pierre-Victor Galland, un Tiepolo français au XIXe siècle* (Paris: Somogy, 2006).

TIARAS AND THE ART OF JEWELS FOR THE HEAD

Diana Scarisbrick

Located in the Hôtel Baudard de Sainte-James, the *Salon des Diadèmes* has been showcasing Chaumet tiaras since 1907. Several hundreds of models in maillechort, an alloy of nickel, copper, and zinc, also called nickel silver, show the diversity of the House's designs.

Over the past two hundred years, Chaumet of 12, Place Vendôme has made more jewels for the head than any other Parisian jeweler. Furthermore, the Chaumet tiaras, bandeaux, aigrettes, combs, and pins have been recorded in ledgers, drawings, and photographs supplemented by almost 700 nickel silver replicas (*maquettes en maillechort*) of tiaras completed since 1900. Formerly displayed on the walls of the *Salon des Diadèmes* (Tiara Room), these replicas offered a range of design from which customers ordering new tiaras could choose the style most becoming to their particular looks. Evoking a world of historic names, great events, and outstanding personalities, a visit to the *Salon des Diadèmes* is still a unique experience.

I. NAPOLEONIC JEWELS FOR THE HEAD: 1802–1814

Like so much in its history, Chaumet's mastery of the art of making jewels for the head, and of the tiara in particular, begins with Napoleon. Before he came to power in 1802 the tiara was rarely seen at the courts of Europe because royal and noble women preferred to place less imposing aigrettes of jeweled flowers, leaves, and bowknots in their hair. However, faced with the challenge of establishing a new Imperial dynasty after the anarchy that followed the Revolution of 1789, Napoleon looked to jewelry, as he did all the arts, to assert the political authority he had won by his sword. Aware that, as the ancient Romans understood, there is no more powerful symbol of rank than a jewel that crowns the head, Napoleon revived the tiara for the Empress Joséphine, the Habsburg Archduchess Marie-Louise, whom he married in 1810, and the women of the Imperial family and court. Yet, although inspired by antiquity, these tiaras are quite different from those of the Greeks

ABOVE

"Ear of wheat" tiara,
François-Régnault Nitot
(1779–1853), c. 1810–11.
Gold, silver, diamonds,
H. 6.5; W. 15 cm
Chaumet Paris Collection

FACING PAGE

The "Ear of wheat" tiara
staged in the *grand salon*
of the Hôtel Baudard de
Sainte-James (detail of the
bronze statues decorating
the fireplace, caryatids
by Victor Paillard, mid-
nineteenth century).

Symbol of Ceres, Roman goddess of
prosperity, harvest, and fertility, the
ear of wheat was a preferred motif
in jewelry under the French Empire.
Empress Joséphine liked to wear ear
of wheat tiaras like the one pictured
here, consisting of nine stalks and set
with more than 66 carats of antique-cut
diamonds on a gold and silver mounting.
The movement and lightness of this
tiara of great formal modernity give the
illusion of a real bouquet of wheat blown
by the winds.

FACING PAGE

*Replica of the ruby and
diamond parure belonging
to Empress Marie-Louise:
coronet and tiara,* c. 1811.
Gold, silver, white sapphires,
zircons, and garnets
Chaumet Paris Collection

RIGHT

Gobelins Manufacture,
after Gérard,
*Marie-Louise, Empress of
the French,* 1814–15.
H. 78.5; W. 62.5 cm
Kunsthistorischen Museum,
Vienna

and Romans, which were made of gold and only occasionally enameled and set with colored stones. Instead, during the Napoleonic Empire, they were usually mounted with pearls and precious gems, particularly diamonds, so as to obtain an effect of brilliance.[1]

Designs, in accordance with the style devised for Napoleon by the architects Charles Percier and Pierre Fontaine were strictly classical: that is symmetrical in shape, with clear silhouettes and decorated with motifs derived from Greek and Roman art. One of the first, a tiara of ears of wheat, alluding to the goddess of prosperity, Ceres, was worn by the future Empress Joséphine at the first ceremony awarding the Legion of Honor.[2] Symbolic of victory, the laurel leaf tiara, which was on her head at the coronation of 1804, has been reproduced many times over the past two hundred years. In her turn, although lacking the graciousness of Joséphine, the Empress Marie-Louise had sufficient royal presence to sustain her role on all official occasions. Again, Nitot & Fils were commissioned to supply parures both for her private collection and for that of the state. Their greatest achievement was the historic parure of white diamonds comprising a tiara, comb, earrings, necklace, and belt, combining—as only the Nitots knew how—majesty with elegance. It was returned to the Crown Jewels Collection by the Empress Marie-Louise when she left France in 1815 and remodeled by the restored Bourbon monarchy.[3] The original splendor of Empire

1   Anne Dion-Tenenbaum, *Les parures dans le tableau de
     David,* in Sylvain Laveissière (ed.), *Le Sacre* (Paris: Musée
     du Louvre/RMN, 2004), pp. 30–32.

2   Countess of Rémusat, *Mémoire* (Paris: Calmann Lévy,
     1880), vol. I, p. 35.

3   Bernard Morel, *The French Crown Jewels* (Antwerp:
     Fonds Mercator, 1988), pp. 269–72.

jewelry is echoed by a garnet and white topaz replica of the great ruby and diamond parure delivered to the Empress Marie-Louise by Nitot in 1813. Copied by Chaumet from the original drawing, it is therefore a precious record of Nitot's intention. Another important example is the diamond and emerald parure that Napoleon gave the Empress for her private collection after the birth of their son, the King of Rome, in 1811, which was inherited by her Habsburg relations.[4]

Cameos and intaglios, greatly esteemed by the emperors of ancient Rome, were equally prized by Napoleon, who patronized the gem engravers of that city, Nicola Morelli (1771–1835), Giuseppe Girometti (1779–1851), and Luigi Pichler (1773–1854). Rather than keeping these items in collector's cabinets Napoleon had them set in jewelry, as did the Romans. His enthusiasm for these images depicting the divinities and heroes of mythology and ancient history was so great that in 1808 he authorized the removal of 82 cameos and intaglios from the state collection of the Cabinet des Médailles, which Nitot & Fils then mounted with quantities of pearls into a parure of tiara, matching necklace, belt, and bracelets for the Empress Joséphine. After their divorce, the same gems were remounted, again by the Nitots, into another parure for her successor, the Empress Marie-Louise.[5] The most deluxe designs were embellished with pearls and diamonds, wrought into classical motifs: lyre, Greek key, leaves of olive or laurel, acanthus and vine scrolls, palmettes and honeysuckles. This grandiose yet timeless style is represented by the tiara worn today by the Queen of Sweden, set with onyx cameos commissioned by Napoleon within pearl borders alternating with palmette and scroll between pieces. The gems were framed simply, in plain gold borders, perhaps outlined by a fillet of blue enamel. Because of the scarcity of hardstone cameos, tiaras might also be mounted with cheaper substitutes: coral and shell, both so much easier to carve. Essential as statements of rank, tiaras were also included in the relatively inexpensive sets of Berlin Iron, facetted steel, or black enamel and jet worn by the Empress with mourning dress.

Although the tiara was the most prestigious of Empire head jewels, it was only one of many designed to make women look their best. Typically, Empire was the bandeau of diamonds or pearls worn so low as almost to touch the eyebrows. Hair, whether dressed short in the simple *à la Titus* style, or smooth in front, plaited behind *à la Ninon*, or swept up into a chignon and framing the face, was kept in place by tortoiseshell or silver-gilt combs with tops mounted with Roman micromosaic plaques, with cameos, or diamond and colored stone classical urns and Cupid's quiver of arrows. Quantities of golden pins with pearl and diamond tops in the form of a lyre, the caduceus of Mercury, or an arrow, were placed in the hair beside the comb or fixed the lace veil to the back of the head. Such was the supremacy of Parisian fashion that even though France was at war with England these jewels, faithfully reported and illustrated in the *Lady's Magazine*, were quickly copied across the Channel, and by women in those continental countries occupied by French troops and ruled by a Napoleonic court.

"Cameo tiara of the Queen of Sweden" (Venus and Eros), detail, attributed to Nitot & Fils, c. 1810 (reproduced pp. 210–11). Gold, cameos in agate, and natural pearls Slottsmuseum, Stockholm, Royal Collections of Sweden

4   Diana Scarisbrick, "An Imperial Parure," *Apollo*, September 2004, pp. 80–83.

5   Ernest Babelon, *Catalogue des camées antiques et modernes de la Bibliothèque nationale*, Paris, E. Leroux, 2 volumes, 1897, pp. CLXIX-CLXXII.

II. ROMANTICISM: 1815–1848

As a result of the encouragement Napoleon had given to the art of jewelry and his success in using it as an expression of political power, the collapse of his regime did not mean hard times for the Parisian jewelers. On the contrary, the restoration of the Bourbon monarchy in France and the victory of the allied powers of Europe and Russia brought a desire to emulate the splendor of the Empire, for every ruler had learned from Napoleon the importance of asserting sovereignty by a show of courtly magnificence.[6]

It was in this atmosphere that Jean Baptiste Fossin and his son Jules, who succeeded Francois Regnault Nitot in 1815, won an international reputation for impressive jewels, represented by the diamond and spinel parure made for the Russian Princess Bagration (1783–1857), who lived in Paris from 1820. An even more important commission came from Prince Anatole Demidoff on his marriage to Princess Mathilde Bonaparte, niece of Napoleon, in 1841.[7] Some of these splendid jewels are depicted in her portraits: diamond crown with points tipped with pear-shaped pearls at the back of her head, and in the front, above the brow, a diamond acanthus leaf chain centered on the paved diamond Imperial eagle, symbolic of her Bonaparte blood.

Artists as well as jewelers, the Fossins also created jewels in an entirely new style. Turning away from the severe classicism of the Empire style, the Fossins revived the naturalistic theme characterising jewelry of the period before 1789. For their tiaras and bandeaux, they used leaves of ivy, volubilis, olive and chestnut, flowers of eglantine, hawthorn, acacia, jasmine and geranium, cactus, bulrushes and water lilies, as well as fruits such as grapes, cherries, and red currants with equal assurance. The flowers were set on trembler springs so that every movement showed them from a new and still beautiful point of view, and, for extra realism, Fossin introduced enamel, particularly green, for leaves. These garlands might be tied with ribbons, an eighteenth century motif also used on its own. Greatly impressed, *Les Modes* (1830) reported after a ball at the Austrian embassy that "never before had stones been mounted with such finesse, elegance, and taste. The heavy combs and severe tiaras had vanished while everywhere topazes, emeralds, rubies, and diamonds were ingeniously combined and set by Fossin's inimitable art to reproduce the many diverse forms of garlands, flowers, bouquets, and bowknots."

Some of the classical motifs—palmette, honeysuckle, Greek key, acanthus—so typical of the Empire, continued in fashion, as did the cameo tiara, sometimes set with hardstones, ancient or contemporary, but more often with the less expensive coral and shell. Evocative of Bacchus, the god of wine, festive amethyst or garnet grapes with diamond or green enamel vine leaves might be surmounted by a palmette, and supported by a band of Greek key. Three separate ornaments might be worn at the same time: a diamond bandeau round the head, a floral garland in the middle, and ears of corn in front of the comb at the back of the head. These expensive designs were adaptable; they might be split into a pair of brooches or different bouquets to pin to the bodice.

Diamonds were almost universally worn at court receptions since not only did they give brilliance to the appearance but could also, according to the *Lady's Magazine*, add to the charm of women no longer in their first youth. Moreover, tiaras, whether on their

"Amethysts" tiara, Jean-Baptiste Fossin (1786–1848), c. 1830. Gold, silver, diamonds, amethysts The Bedford Estates, Duke of Bedford Collection

6 Diana Scarisbrick, *Timeless Tiaras* (Paris: Assouline, 2002), pp. 208–12. 7 Chaumet Archives.

own or as part of a parure, were available in a great variety of other stones, precious and semi-precious. Masses of reasonably priced turquoises, golden and pink topazes, rich red garnets, chrysoprases, and aquamarines were set in light but showy stamped or filigreed and beaded gold mounts. These, being much less expensive, gave more scope for experiment than diamonds. Enamel was often introduced for extra color and gold was mixed with various alloys to come in shades of green, yellow, and pink. Red coral was also much appreciated, either faceted into beads, or with the natural branches standing up on the head. Possessing these alternatives to diamonds an elegant woman could avoid the embarrassment of being seen in the same tiara on two consecutive occasions.

Since this was the age of eclecticism, Fossin also found inspiration for hair ornaments in the world of the Renaissance and Middle Ages. There was the *ferronière* worn low across the brow, like a chain or necklace, centred on a pearl or colored stone drop perhaps hanging from the mouth of a chimera or framed in leafy branches enameled to match the color of the dress derived from the portrait of *La Belle Ferronière* by Leonardo da Vinci in the Louvre. Evocative of the age of chivalry were ducal *fleuron* crowns, worn high, surmounting a plait encircling the crown of the head, or much lower, as described by *Les Modes* (1838): "Coronets worn straight over the forehead are often seen.... They are placed today exactly as Raphael painted them on the brow of his angels." Another revival was named after the first love of Louis XIV, Marie Mancini, and whose ringlets framing the face had set a new fashion for the court of Versailles. The Fossin version of the Mancini's ornament for the head was composed of twin branches or bouquets falling down like showers against the cheeks and culminating in long fringes of diamonds or a contrasting colored stone such as opal.

The turban, toque, or beret covering the head was worn with numerous ornaments: bandeaux, chains of pearls, diamonds, and colored stones across the brow, and aigrettes and pins with jeweled tops standing out against the black or rich crimson velvet. However, for the opera and at balls the hair was increasingly shown off on its own, ornamented with flowers, feathers, and jeweled birds of paradise, one or more diamond arrows, golden snakes, fangs gripping a pearl drop, and aigrettes.

The Fossin design books contain many ideas—branches of leaves, flowers, bullrushes, ribbons, arabesques—for the decoration of the tops of tortoiseshell combs, some worn very high. However, this delightfully imaginative and creative period came to end with the Revolution of 1848, which drove Louis-Philippe, King of the French, into exile. The instability of the Republican government that followed led to a recession in the luxury trades that continued until the declaration of Napoleon III as Emperor of France in 1852.

III. COURT GRANDEUR: 1852–1900

During the second half of the nineteenth century industry flourished while investments in property and banking enriched the new European business class and the old aristocracy alike. Across the Atlantic the millionaires of North and South America grew wealthier every year. This prosperity, coinciding with decades of peace, low taxation, and no inflation provided the social background in which the women of the upper classes were permanently on show, and a husband's success could be measured by his wife's jewelry. In

"Leuchtenberg" tiara convertible into a brooch, attributed to Fossin, c. 1830–40. Gold, silver, emeralds, diamonds, H. 9; W. 14 cm Chaumet Paris Collection

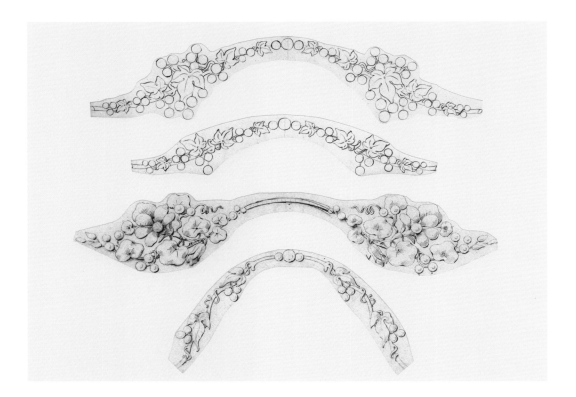

*Studies for naturalistic
head ornaments,
branches, foliage,
and flowers*, c. 1850.
Graphite pencil,
pen and brown ink,
H. 36.8; W. 52.8 cm
Chaumet Paris Collection

most European countries society was headed by a monarch who encouraged brilliance at court, and nowhere more so than in France during the Second Empire of Napoleon III.[8]

His marriage to Eugénie de Montijo in 1853 was followed by rounds of balls, dinners, and concerts held every year at the Tuileries in Paris and in the palaces of Versailles, St. Cloud, Compiègne, and Fontainebleau. Charles Worth ruled the world of fashion, creating sumptuous evening gowns that were worn with much jewelry. For the Empress, who set the standard, the crown jewels were remounted into parures that always included a tiara. More than this, the Emperor actively supported French participation in the International Expositions of 1855 (Paris), 1862 (London), and 1867 (Paris) where the jewelry stands, which always showed a selection of jewels for the head, attracted huge crowds and the French won most of the prizes. Jules Fossin remained active in the company until 1862, when Prosper Morel assumed control, followed by his son-in-law, Joseph Chaumet, in 1886.

As designs were static for some years after the Revolution of 1848, Fossin continued to supply crowns of jasmine flowers, branches, or coiffures of chestnut, ivy, and red currant leaves. However, by 1860 these naturalistic tiaras and bandeaux were contained in symmetrical frames of imposing proportions. The eighteenth-century motifs of trellis, bowknots, and ribbons were also introduced, perhaps as a consequence of the Empress Eugénie's passion for the time of Queen Marie-Antoinette. Classicism was given a stimulus after the purchase by Napoleon III of the celebrated Campana Collection of 1,200 items of Greek, Etruscan, and Roman jewelry for the Louvre in 1862.[9] This taste is represented by the triumphant laurel leaf tiaras ordered by the Duke of Doudeauville and by Princess Henckel von Donnersmark. Most popular of all were stars, perhaps because of their versatility, for they looked equally well whether in sets mounted on a tiara or worn separately as pins in the hair or as brooches on the dress.

8   Diana Scarisbrick, *Timeless Tiaras*, pp. 216–21.

9   Françoise Gaultier and Catherine Metzger, *Trésors
      antiques: bijoux de la collection Campana* (Paris: Musée
      du Louvre, 2004).

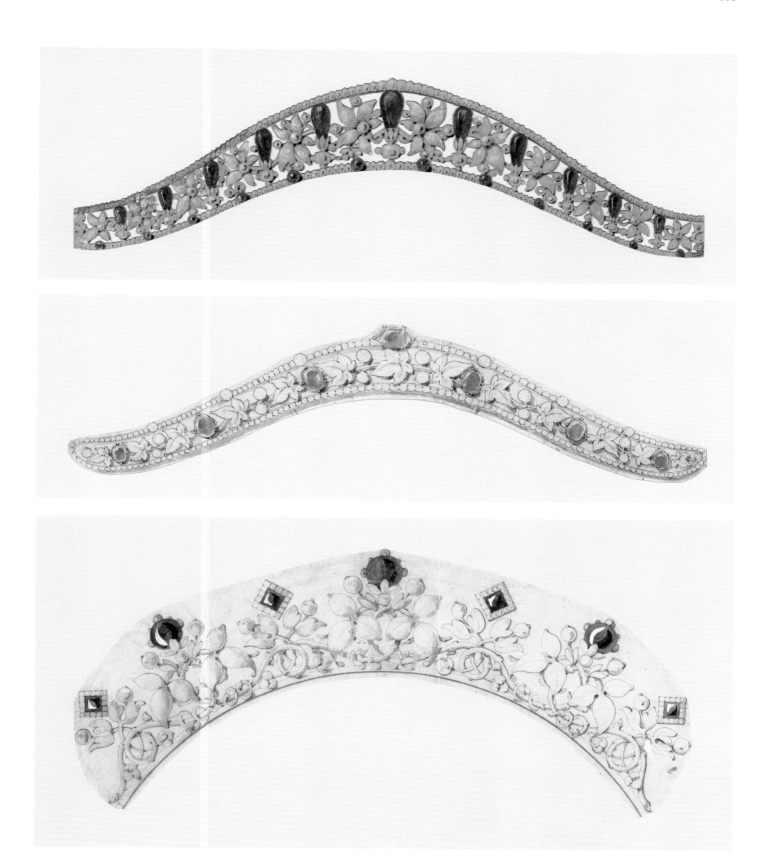

TOP

*Design for a
naturalistic tiara with pear
emeralds*, c. 1860.
Graphite pencil,
gouache, ink wash,
H. 12; W. 41 cm
Chaumet Paris Collection

CENTER

*Design for a
naturalistic tiara with
emeralds*, c. 1860.
Graphite pencil, pen
and black ink, ink wash
H. 10; W. 45 cm
Chaumet Paris Collection

BOTTOM

*Design for a
naturalistic tiara with
emeralds*, c. 1860.
Graphite pencil, ink wash,
and white gouache high-
lights, H. 14; W. 32.5 cm
Chaumet Paris Collection

As every woman aspired to look like the Empress, all who could afford to do so wore diamonds. This preference could be indulged more readily after the discovery of the mines of South Africa in 1867, which coincided with the introduction of electric light that suited diamonds' glitter and sparkle. Another change was political, for in 1870 the Second Empire fell, and after a difficult period of siege, famine, and anarchy, there was a return to order with the establishment of the Third Republic in France. The deep political divisions in French society were expressed by tiaras proclaiming loyalty to the exiled House of Orléans, such as the Duke of Doudeauville's paved diamond eagle carrying the Bourbon symbol, the fleur-de-lis. Another political statement, asserting her traditionally high rank, was made by the heraldic flowers atop the tiara of the Duchess of Luynes. Similarly, the impressive height of the *diadème ornements diamants et appliques poires de diamants* (diamond tiara with pear-shaped diamond points) made for the Duchess of Portland in 1897 was emblematic of her status at the court of Queen Victoria. Designed to look well from every angle, it suited her classically beautiful features and graceful silhouette to perfection.

Pearls, always a speciality of Chaumet since the Empire period, were particularly prized by Joseph Chaumet, who declared that for a woman they signified a kind of coronation, a consecration, the ultimate in refinement. For the women of the banking dynasties and the aristocracy he created splendid tiaras set with pearls of various tints—white, gray, and black—pear-shaped and round. (Like pearls, colored precious stones were now so much rarer than diamonds that the diamond and sapphire crown of the Polish Countess Lanckoronska (1894) drew all eyes toward her.)

However, this grandeur was not compatible with Republican principles and so at official receptions French and American women made do with aigrettes and combs instead of tiaras.[10] Chaumet's favorite themes were the stars, sun, the crescent moon, humming birds, feathers, ribbons tied into bowknots, flowers—marguerites, wild roses, gardenia, sunflowers, orchids—leafy sprays, bull rushes, ears of wheat, fine specimen pearls, briolettes (pear-shaped diamonds) falling down in a cascade like a small waterfall. They were designed to be placed in the hair with feathers, usually white, but sometimes matching the dress color, in front of the chignon. An American client, Mrs. Daisy White, married to a diplomat and who always dressed well with the right jewels, was pleased with the effect when dining with Queen Victoria at Balmoral in 1897: "I wore my black brocade Worth dress with tulle sleeves, a diamond and pearl chain, a diamond collar, with a row of pearls and an aigrette in my hair. Lady Lytton said I looked nice!"[11]

Combs were as important as ever, and *Queen Magazine* (1897) observed that "the prevailing mode of hair dressing requires the aid of combs of various shapes and sizes, broad side combs, small combs with long teeth, high back combs, besides forked pins. In all these blond tortoiseshell combs the preferred styles of ornamentation are the Louis XVI scroll and the Greek key pattern executed in diamonds and pearls."

PAGES 150–151
Henri Charles Antoine
Baron (1816–1885),
*Official Ceremony at the
Tuileries Palace during the
1867 World's Fair* (detail).
Watercolor and gouache
Musée national du Palais
de Compiègne

FACING PAGE
"Pansy flower" tiara,
attributed to Fossin,
c. 1850.
Gold, silver, and diamonds,
H. 7; W. 18 cm
Private Collection

10   Eugène Fontenay, *Les Bijoux anciens et modernes*
      (Paris: Société d'Encouragement pour la Propagation
      des Livres d'Art, 1887), p. 424.

11   Henry White Manuscript Collection, Margaret White
      Diary, 1897, Columbia University Rare Book and
      Manuscript Library.

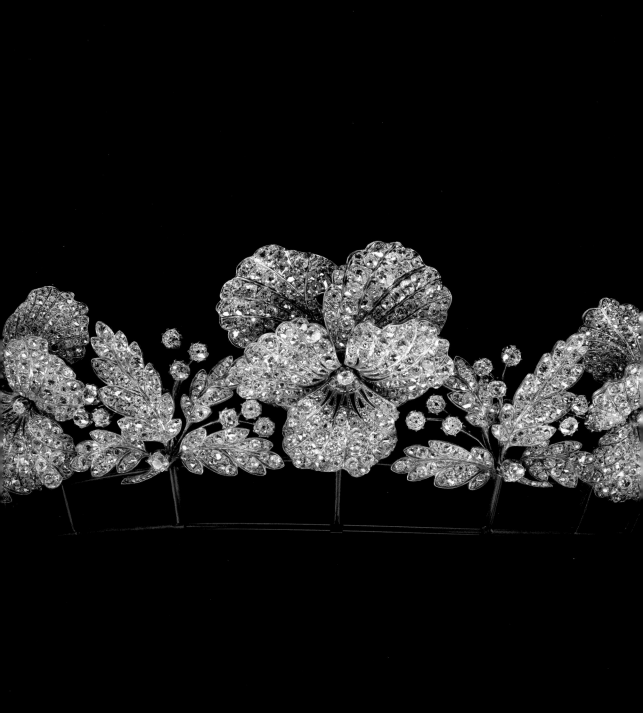

Miss A. Hughes photo

Walker & Boutall, ph. sc.

The Duchess of Portland
as Duchess of Savoy.

IV. TWENTIETH CENTURY I: 1900–1918

At the time of the International Exhibition held in Paris in 1900, the period of peace and prosperity known as the Belle Époque seemed to have reached its apogee. The luxury trades flourished and fashion, dominated by Worth, Redfern, Paquin, and Doucet was designed for the feminine, hourglass figure with small waist, full bosom, and leg of mutton sleeves. By day these outfits were crowned with huge hats, secured to the head by pins with jeweled tops exquisitely wrought as if each was an individual work of art. At night, ablaze with diamonds, the hair dressed high *à la Pompadour* and puffed out at the sides flattered the face and made a firm foundation for jewelry. Tortoiseshell combs with decorative galleries were essential, and the size and value of the other jewels worn was in ratio to the importance of the social event.

In all countries governed by a monarchy, tiaras were much in evidence. For German court receptions Chaumet supplied heraldic tiaras to Princess Henckel von Donnnersmarck and the Baron of Courlande. It was the same in Spain where the aristocracy followed the example of King Alfonso XIII, who ordered a turquoise and diamond tiara for his bride, Princess Victoria Eugenia of Battenburg (1906). That same year Princess Stephanie, daughter of Leopold II of Belgium, bought a fleur-de-lis tiara alluding to her royal Bourbon ancestry. In England, the coronation of Edward VII in 1902, court balls, state openings of Parliament, and gala performances at the opera brought out splendid dinner gowns worn with tiaras, and to meet the demand Joseph Chaumet opened a London branch in Bond Street. The greatest accolade came in 1914 when Russian Prince Felix Youssoupoff brought a large collection of family jewels to be remounted into parures for his bride, Irena, niece of Tsar Nicholas II. Among these superb commissions were a ruby and diamond tiara, a bandeau centered on a huge emerald, and an aigrette with the Polar Star diamond blazing like a great rising sun.[12]

12   Prince Youssoupoff, *Avant l'exil* (Paris: Plon, 1952), pp. 181–86.

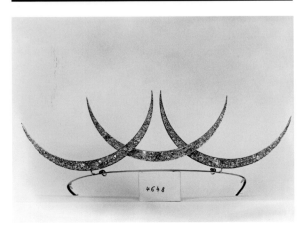

TOP

Study for a "Crescent moon and star" aigrette, c. 1900.
Graphite pencil, ink wash, and white gouache highlights, H. 11.9; W. 14.3 cm
Chaumet Paris Collection

CENTER, LEFT

Two "Crescent moon" aigrettes, c. 1900.
Print from gelatin silver bromide glass negative, H. 18; W. 24 cm
Chaumet Paris Collection

CENTER, RIGHT

"Crescent moon" in diamonds ordered by Prince Louis de Ligne, 1911.
Print from gelatin silver bromide glass negative, H. 24; W. 30 cm
Chaumet Paris Collection

BOTTOM, LEFT

Tiara with three crescent moons in diamonds ordered by the Count of Nadaillac, 1909.
Print from gelatin silver bromide glass negative, H. 18; W. 24 cm
Chaumet Paris Collection

BOTTOM, RIGHT

"Crescent moon" in diamonds for headdress ordered by Charles de Beistegui, 1911.
Print from gelatin silver bromide glass negative, H. 24; W. 30 cm
Chaumet Paris Collection

FACING PAGE

"Crescent moon" brooch convertible into an aigrette, Joseph Chaumet (1852–1928), c. 1890.
Gold, silver, diamonds, natural pearls, H. 4.2; W. 4 cm
Chaumet Paris Collection

FACING PAGE

Jeweled hatpin, Joseph
Chaumet (1852–1928).
Chaumet Paris Collection

1912, Platinum, rock crystal,
aquamarine, and diamonds,
H. 22.5; D. 3.5 cm

1913, Platinum, agate, diamonds, cabochon sapphire,
H. 24.5; D. 5.5 cm

1914, Platinum, rock crystal,
diamonds, sapphire,
H. 21.5; D. 4 cm

ABOVE, LEFT

Jeweled ball-head hatpins,
Joseph Chaumet
(1852–1928), c. 1915.
Platinum, onyx, rose-cut
diamonds, H. 22; D. 2 cm
and H. 14; D. 3 cm
Chaumet Paris Collection

ABOVE, RIGHT

Jacques-Émile Blanche
(1861–1942), *Portrait of
Actress Gilda Darthy,
a Chaumet Customer*,
c. 1905–10.
Oil on canvas,
H. 116; W. 89.5 cm
Musée des Beaux-Arts,
Rouen

With the emergence of the Art Nouveau movement around 1900, the jewelry world was divided into two camps, but Joseph Chaumet chose not to adopt the style associated with René Lalique. Although some of his naturalistic designs, particularly that of a bat with openwork wings perched on top of the head, come close to Art Nouveau, his chief source of inspiration was the art of eighteenth-century France, which his customers also regarded as the high point of elegance and refinement.

He adopted motifs not so much from the jewelry of that time but from architecture, with silver and porcelain, inspired by the wrought iron decorating buildings and from the trimmings on upholstery and curtains. Wild roses, jasmine, daisies, pinks, lilies of the valley, and anemones were arranged in wreaths, or set asymmetrically in sprigs, in baskets and bunches, sometimes on trembler springs so the diamonds shook with every movement of the head. There are fern leaves combined with the versatile ivy with or without berries. The theme of water, as used by the rococo silversmith, is expressed by the shell, by seaweed and the bullrush, this last used so often that it could almost stand as a signature for Chaumet. Ideally suited for the glitter and sparkle of diamonds at well-lit formal evening events was the *chute d'eau* (waterfall), a motif also reinterpreted many times by Joseph Chaumet. Other favorites were the trellis, or *mesh en résille* pattern, ribbons, bowknots, festoons, tassels, and fringes. The classical olive and laurel branches, palmettes, ears of corn, running scrolls of vine, and acanthus received a new lease of life. However, the most popular and versatile motif from the art of Greece and Rome was the meander or key pattern: angular or rounded in single or double lines, intricately interlaced, sometimes softened by ribbons or trails of foliage. The linking of these different elements by swags and festoons led to the name "garland" style to distinguish the tiaras from this period from those that came before and after. An innovation, which remained

The TATLER

Vol. XXVII. No. 349. { REGISTERED AT THE GENERAL } POST OFFICE AS A NEWSPAPER London, March 4, 1908. Sixpence.

Lafayette

PRINCESS STEPHANIE, THE WIFE OF ELEMER, COUNT LONYAY

i   a

in favor until the mid 1930s was the wing tiara, which derived from the winged helmets of the Valkyries in Richard Wagner's famous opera, *The Ring*. Another success was the Mary Stuart tiara, with the circlet forming a V over the brow, derived from the veil and cap she wore as a young widowed Queen of France in 1560.

Chaumet also created *diadèmes russes* derived from the picturesque national headdress or *kokochnik*, which being flattering to the looks had an appeal beyond the large Russian clientele. The halo shape might be paved with diamonds, or filled in with acanthus scrolls, arabesques, or an overall pattern of five petaled flowers. While the majority date from the period 1900–1914, Chaumet went on making them, one of the last being for the Russian-born Lady Zia Wernher in 1934. Another favorite with Russian customers such as the Princesses Youssoupoff and Ouvaroff was the dramatic and sumptuous *diadème soleil* (sunray tiara) with as many as three layers of diamond sunbeams radiating from a large central stone.

This was the high point in the history of the tiara and many women reserved their best stones for it. These rich red rubies, sapphires, dark green emeralds, brilliant

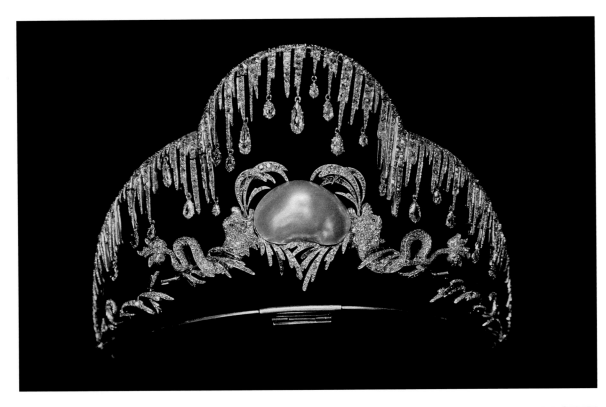

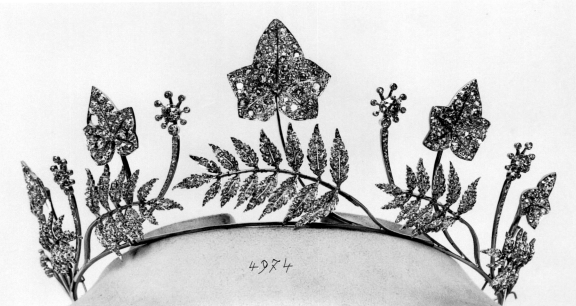

TOP

"Waterfall and dolphin"
tiara, c. 1900.
Print from gelatin silver
bromide glass negative,
H. 13; W. 18 cm
Chaumet Paris Collection

CENTER

"Fern and ivy" diamond
tiara ordered by the
Viscountess of Flers, 1910.
Print from gelatin silver
bromide glass negative,
H. 18; W. 24 cm
Chaumet Paris Collection

BOTTOM, LEFT

Diamond "Flower"
tiara ordered by
Princess of Pless, 1908.
Print from gelatin silver
bromide glass negative,
H. 18; W. 24 cm
Chaumet Paris Collection

BOTTOM, RIGHT

Diamond "Flower"
tiara ordered by
Count Léo d'Ursel, 1912.
Print from gelatin silver
bromide glass negative,
H. 18; W. 24 cm
Chaumet Paris Collection

diamonds, and iridescent pear-shaped pearls are usually displayed rather simply, standing up in points or appliqués linked by twisted ribbons, hanging from bowknots, and swinging within arcading. Nothing seems to have inspired Chaumet more than a collection of pear-shaped diamonds that he mounted on leafy stems for the marriage of the future Duchess of Gramont in 1904. When simplification became the rule around 1910, he introduced the motifs of the overlapping disc (*écus comptés*), the geometric interlaced circle, and the lozenge.

Although still inspired by the art of the reigns of Louis XV and Louis XVI, the tiaras he offered now were much lighter than those of the previous period, thanks to the finesse of platinum settings that were so thin as to be almost invisible, thus giving full value to the brilliance of the large stones and the sparkle of the smaller. The bright white surface of this metal, so strong that it could be used to delicate effect in small quantities, was broken up by the millegrain technique into beads that reflected the light coming from the diamonds in countless points, so that not only the stones but the metal itself seemed ablaze with fire. A further refinement was the use of colored stones cut to measure the settings. These new techniques made such a difference that quantities of old family tiaras were brought into Chaumet for remodeling in the "modern style," especially for marriages.

But the world was changing. Around 1910 threats of revolution shook the political stability of many countries. New taxes led to a decline in formal entertaining for which grand parures were de rigueur and people now began to hold small dances, dinners in restaurants, and card parties at home. Moreover, under the influence of Paul Poiret women's dress changed, evoking a chapter from *One Thousand and One Nights* instead of the classical elegance of the Petit Trianon of Queen Marie-Antoinette. The smart women who adopted his avant-garde fashions wore straight, loose-fitting tunics patterned in shapes and colors inspired by the costumes designed for Madame Ida Rubinstein in *Scheherazade* and the other pageantries of Diaghilev's *Russian Ballet*.[13] Since the tall, majestic tiaras-fenders were not compatible with this silhouette, the aigrette worn with osprey feathers acquired a new lease of life, as did the jeweled fillet or bandeau encircling the head. Since the narrow dimensions of the bandeau, single or double, did not leave much room for decoration the motifs were restricted to Greek key, festoons, honey suckle, and trails of leaves. One of Chaumet's greatest successes was the platinum, onyx, and diamond bandeau created in 1913 for the American portrait painter Romaine Brooks, who, much influenced by Aubrey Beardsley, dressed and lived in a house entirely decorated in black and white without a single note of color. This dramatic contrast anticipates the Art Deco style that emerged after World War I.

V. Twentieth Century II: 1918–1939

The period between the end of World War I and the declaration of World War II in 1939 covers the years of frenetic extravagance between 1918 and the New York stock market crash of October 24, 1929, followed by a gradual return to stability in the 1930s. During these years, jewelry was created in a new style to coincide with the changed

---

13 Paul Poiret, *En habillant l'époque* (Paris: Grasset, 1974), pp. 64–77.

conditions of women's lives marked by the cutting of hair into short bobs and the simplified dresses created by Chanel, Paquin, and Lucien Lelong for slender boyish figures with neither hips nor busts.

Chaumet had to adapt to this new world. Although the lucrative Russian clientele had disappeared with the Bolshevik Revolution, the demand for luxury continued from both "old and new money" elsewhere. There were also numerous diplomatic wives whose elitist existence was governed by protocol and formality and who now included the Japanese attending the Peace Conference at Versailles, and who had adopted Western dress and jewelry. There was some falling off in orders from those with "old money" but the majestic garland style tiara was far from being out of fashion, although it was not seen so often. Since this rather conservative clientele did not always wish to abandon their favorite styles, these were modernized too, the traditional motifs being enclosed within a triangular frame rising to an apex above the brow.[14]

At the same time, Chaumet proposed a more up-to-date alternative in the strictly non-traditional style that crystalized at the Exposition des Arts Décoratifs held in Paris in 1925. Known as Art Deco, after the title of the groundbreaking exhibition, it is characterized by a simplification of line, the dominance of geometric shapes (circles, squares, rectangles), strong contrasts of color, and of opaqueness and transparency, of cabochon and faceted, *calibré*-cut stones. The platinum mounts were reduced to mere skeletons, diamonds were cut to moon and oblong, as well as square and round, shapes. For Lady Wimborne, a leader of fashion in London, Chaumet created one of the first Art Deco parures, including a ruby and diamond tiara, which she wore low on the brow *à la Joséphine*, with long earrings.[15]

However, although the most important, the tiara is only part of the long story of jewelry for the head. In response to the ever changing demands of fashion there has also been a succession of less imposing but nonetheless charming and graceful ornaments. It shared a place with the less ceremonial bandeau that, in encircling the head in a narrow flexible glittering band, admirably supplemented the low style of coiffure, loosely waved and parted in the middle, and drew attention to the line of the profile. Decorative motifs such as the overlapping discs (*écus comptés*) and trails of leaves used for tiaras were scaled down to suit the smaller proportions of the bandeau, and long lines of diamonds were twisted together into a braid or plait or formed into geometric motifs.

14   Diana Scarisbrick, *Timeless Tiaras* (Paris: Assouline, 2002), pp. 232–35.

15   Osbert Sitwell, *Laughter in the Next Room* (London: MacMillan, 1949), p. 228.

ABOVE AND FACING PAGE
"Scrollwork" tiara belonging to the Marquise de Talhouet, Joseph Chaumet (1852–1928), 1908.
Gold, silver, diamonds, H. 6; W. 16 cm
Two prints from gelatin silver bromide glass negatives, H. 18; W. 24 cm
Chaumet Paris Collection

FACING PAGE

"Marie Stuart" aigrette,
Joseph Chaumet
(1852–1928), c. 1910.
Gold, silver, natural
pearls, and diamonds,
H. 10 cm (without the
feathers); W. 13 cm
Chaumet Paris Collection

RIGHT

*Design for the "Marie
Stuart" aigrette,*
Joseph Chaumet
(1852–1928), c. 1910.
Graphite pencil, gouache,
H. 8; W. 18.5 cm
Chaumet Paris Collection

After this decade of great luxury came to an end with the stock market crash of October 24, 1929, Chaumet struggled to survive the economic depression which followed. In these difficult times Marcel Chaumet, who had succeeded his father in 1929, was supported by those Parisian customers who were still determined to shine at the opera and other formal events. The desire to keep abreast of fashion led to the destruction of many glorious creations of the previous generation, positively encouraged by Chaumet, who in 1930 offered to "remodel a jewel, however flattering it had been, however splendid it still was, and bring it up to date." In response, Spanish royal family stones were reset into modern parures for the marriages of Princess Beatriz, Don Jaime, and Don Juan in Rome (1935), and of Prince Alfonso de Borbón in Vienna (1936). These Chaumet tiaras of the 1930s were in tune with the soft curls of the longer hairstyles and the slender, yet more feminine silhouettes of the stately evening gowns of Molyneux, Patou, Schiaparelli, and Vionnet in Paris, and of Norman Hartnell in London. No longer worn low on the brow, they now stood high, encircling the head like a halo. The platinum mounts were thinner than ever, and the diamonds and colored stones, *calibré* cut to ever more precise geometric shapes, were mounted in strong, emphatic designs. Much used in the 1930s was the palm branch motif, set with diamonds to each side of an important central stone, a type made for the Grand Duchess of Luxembourg and for the wife of the Governor General of Canada, the French born Countess of Bessborough.[16]

At the same time there were others who bought jeweled brooches to fasten veils and to shimmer in their well-dressed hair. *Vogue,* for instance, described the two diamond clips holding a white camellia over the ear of the dark haired Princess Jean de Faucigny Lucinge, and how a "smart Parisienne placed a very narrow bandeau of diamonds high above her brow." These jewels for the head were designed to play several roles: the bandeau could divide into bracelets, or be clasped round the neck, and the clip or brooch was equally versatile.

16 Diana Scarisbrick, *Tiara* (Boston: Museum of Fine Arts,
San Francisco/Chronicle Books, 2000), pp. 148–49.

6649

The London branch at 22 Bruton Street benefited from the celebrations that marked the Silver Jubilee of George V in 1935, and the coronation of George VI in 1937. Lady Howard de Walden ordered a new tiara from Chaumet for her coronation ball at Seaford House in London, where Sir Henry "Chips" Channon was impressed by "the gorgeous cavalcade of our best tiaras." Unfortunately, although the economic situation improved considerably toward the middle of the 1930s, the outbreak of World War II in 1939 brought another crisis and it was not until after the peace of 1945 that Chaumet returned to "business as usual."

VI. FROM MID-TWENTIETH CENTURY TO THE PRESENT: 1945–2017

After World War II, although tiaras were regularly seen in New York at the Metropolitan Opera, it was some time before they reappeared in Europe. England lead the way, and they were brought out for the ball held at Buckingham Palace in celebration of the marriage of the future Queen Elizabeth II to Prince Philip of Greece in 1947, and again in 1950 when President Auriol of France came on a state visit to England. Impressed by the brilliance of the tiaras, the diplomat Jacques Dumaine observed that "Queen Victoria's world has returned as if by magic." [17]

The high point of English postwar splendor was the display that accompanied the coronation of Queen Elizabeth II in 1953: the sight of the women guests massed together blazing with diamonds at the service in Westminster Abbey made an unforgettable impression. Elsewhere in Europe, there were other brilliant scenes. In Rome, according to *Vogue* (1951), at the coming out ball of Princess Maria Camilla Pallavicini, "all attending it would remember the extraordinary beauty of the jewels—tiaras, necklaces, and bracelets—

17   Jacques Dumaine, *Quai d'Orsay 1945–1951* (Paris: Julliard, 1956), pp. 468 and 476.

ABOVE
Kokoshnik-shaped Russian tiara in diamonds and pearls ordered by M. de Beistegui, 1914. Print from gelatin silver bromide glass negative, H. 18; W. 24 cm Chaumet Paris Collection

FACING PAGE
Three designs for bandeaux, c. 1920. Graphite pencil, black ink, white gouache, H. 30;2; W. 22.9 cm Chaumet Paris Collection

LEFT
*Chaumet Place
Vendôme n°12*, 1920.
Preparatory study
for an advertisement:
tiaras and bandeaux
worn *à la Joséphine*.
Charcoal, gouache, and
India ink on tracing paper,
H. 77; W. 55.5 cm
Chaumet Paris Collection

FACING PAGE
*"Oak leaf" bandeau
tiara ordered by
Baron Henri Hottinguer,*
Joseph Chaumet
(1852–1928), 1913.
Platinum, diamonds,
H. 4; W. 33 cm
Private Collection

PAGE 172
*Sapphire and diamond
set given as a wedding
present to Princess Alice of
Bourbon-Parma,* 1936.
Print from gelatin silver
bromide glass negative,
H. 30; W. 40 cm
Chaumet Paris Collection

PAGE 173
*Tiara from the
"Bourbon-Parma" parure,*
Marcel Chaumet
(1886–1964), 1936.
Platinum, rubies, diamonds,
H. 4; W. 23 cm
Private Collection

adorning the ladies present." It was the same in France, at balls held at Versailles, at the Hôtel Lambert, at the Château de Groussay, the Hôtel de Mery, and elsewhere where stars of stage and screen, as well as the wives of the captains of industry, wore Chaumet tiaras, bandeaux, and aigrettes with their Dior and Balenciaga gowns. To partner the Dior and Balenciaga gowns, the Chaumet tiara of this time was designed as a halo of diamonds radiating light over the hair and the features.

The great change in social attitudes that occurred during the 1960s sent not only the great couture houses into retreat, but also the jewelers, who took some time to adjust to the new situation. There was still a demand for aigrettes of platinum set with both round and baguette diamonds in increasingly abstract designs, and Chaumet continued to make tiaras for the occasional wedding. Then, from the 1980s an opportunity to create many more was given by the late King of Morocco. Attached as he was to symbols of royalty, King Hassan ordered them not just for his daughters, but for his infant granddaughters so as to look their best at court and family celebrations.

Over the past twenty years, there have been other signs that the tide is turning toward a revival of the fashion for jewels for the hair—although not from Buckingham Palace, where they seem to have been given up except for state visits. Instead, it is private individuals who have rebelled against the drab uniformity of dressing down to a point where almost no distinction is made between clothes for work and pleasure, between day

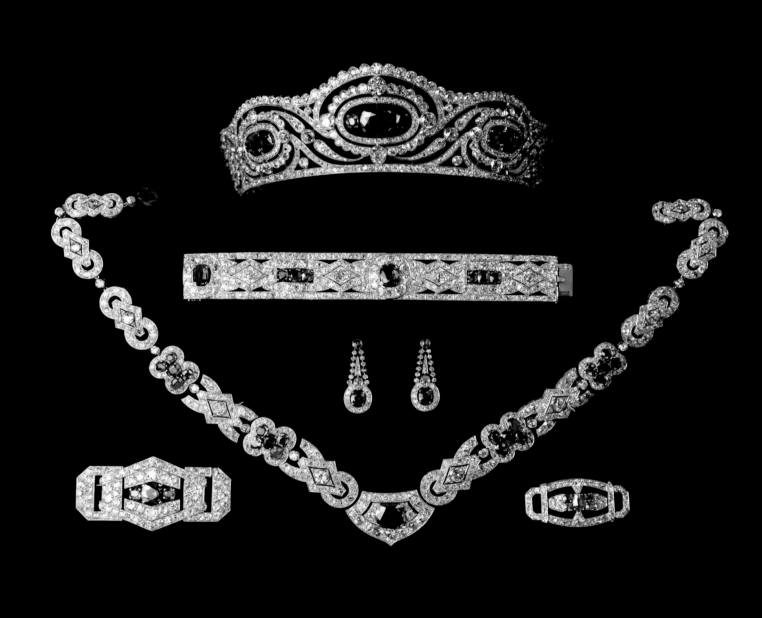

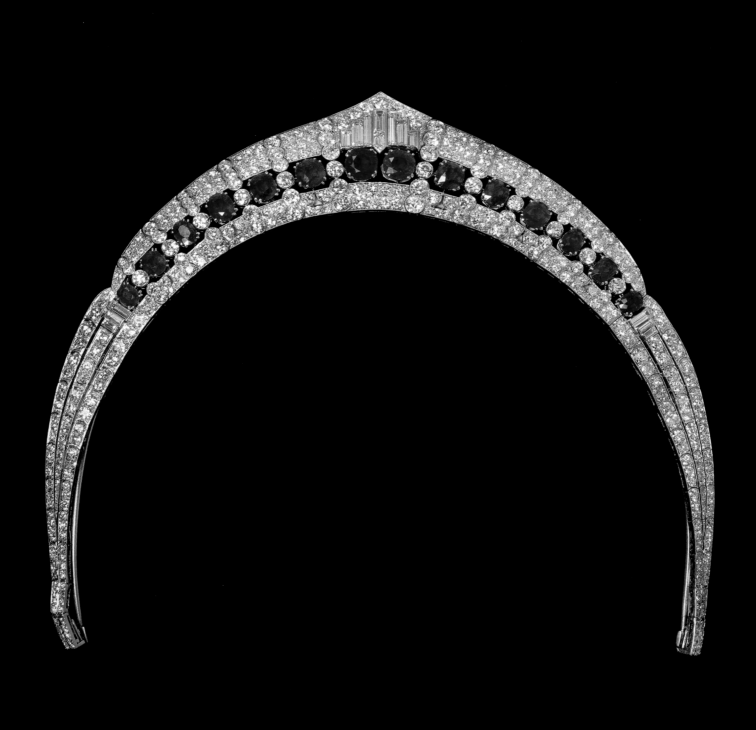

In her memoirs, *Times to Remember* (Garden City, N.Y.:
Doubleday, 1974), Rose Kennedy wrote: "As a matron
I would wear a tiara in my hair. I didn't own one. It had
simply never occurred to me before coming to England
that I would ever need one. My new and sympathetic
friend Lady Bessborough lent me hers and it proved
to be exactly right, most flattering and magnificent.
(It fitted very well and had many brilliant diamonds
including a gorgeous marquise diamond in the front.
With a few temporary adjustments and arrangements,
it was perfect. I was so grateful to her for the thought.
I remember my children—Bobby and Teddy as well as
the girls—were extremely impressed.)"

and evening. Such clients have ordered complete parures of tiara, earrings, and necklaces in simplified but attractive designs of bowknots, tassels, flowers, principally set with versatile all white diamonds and pearls, and less often with colored diamonds. The success of these jewels and the huge popular appeal of *Tiara* exhibitions in Boston (2000), London (2002), and Tokyo (2007) further encouraged Chaumet to design ornaments for the head so as to accentuate the individuality and charm of twenty-first-century women. With the appointment of Stella Tennant in 2003 as the face of Chaumet, her combination of aristocratic birth with the casual freedom of the "rock chick" look proved that tiaras of both traditional and contemporary designs could be worn to great effect with the slender silhouettes and modern hair styles, both long and short, sleek or tousled. Worn across the head so as to light up the hair, the flat openwork bandeau, flexible and as supple as a ribbon, has proved a particular success, drawing attention to the wearer without overwhelming her. These tiaras combining tradition, modernity, and wearability are inspired by the riches of the Chaumet Archives. Most recently, Chaumet has created the Joséphine design alluding to the very first tiaras created by the firm for the wife of Napoleon, whose patronage established Chaumet as Europe's leading jeweler. However, while inspired by the taste and elegance of the Empress Joséphine, in contrast to the tall and heavy ornaments made two hundred years ago, Chaumet's versions of today encircle the head with the maximum of brilliance and the minimum of weight. These magical jewels transform every woman into a princess, standing out from the crowd, as has been the role of the tiara throughout history.

ABOVE, LEFT
Anne Gunning Parker, later Lady Nutting, wearing a Chaumet tiara set with round and baguette-cut diamonds, Henry Clarke (1918–1996), 1953.

FACING PAGE
"12 Vendôme" tiara, 2015. Platinum, white gold, and diamonds, H. 6; W. 15.8 cm Chaumet Paris Collection

"Fuchsias" Tiara, Known as the "Bourbon-Parma" Tiara

Philippe Thiébaut

The prestigious wedding of Prince Sixtus of Bourbon-Parma and Hedwige de la Rochefoucauld Doudeauville, celebrated in Paris on Wednesday, November 12, 1919, was duly chronicled in the columns of *Le Figaro*, principal record of society life from the Belle Époque to World War II:

> Despite its immense size, Saint François Xavier Church could barely accommodate the exceptionally elegant company of guests that had gathered to attend the wedding of H.R.H. Prince Sixtus of Bourbon-Parma, artillery captain in the Belgian army, Grand Cross of the Order of Leopold, holder of the French and Belgian Croix de Guerre, and Miss Hedwige de La Rochefoucauld, daughter of the Duke of Doudeauville, Chevalier of the Legion of Honor, holder of the Croix de Guerre, and of the Duchess of Doudeauville. Naturally, this splendid wedding ceremony was followed by the most glamorous of receptions. The Doudeauville mansion—rightly considered one of the finest in Paris— had been brightly illuminated for the occasion, to bring out the extreme elegance of the Duchess's lady guests, as well as the splendor of the jewels in the wedding basket and the superb gifts on display in the great rectangular salon on the upper floor.
>
> —*Le Figaro*, December 4, 1919

Taking pride of place in this wedding basket was a diamond tiara with fuchsia motifs by Chaumet, today in the Chaumet Heritage Archive Collections. Small fuchsia flowers in suspension were a common theme in Chaumet's naturalistic creations. The stamens, represented by briolette drop diamonds mounted as pendants, feature a technical characteristic that became a style: pear-shaped diamonds mounted in a trompe l'oeil. The diamonds set together in a discreet pear-shaped mount created the illusion of a single stone.

The archives trace the dialogue between the jeweler and the family.

EXTRACTS FROM THE VISITORS' BOOKS, FEBRUARY–NOVEMBER 1919:

FRIDAY, FEBRUARY 7, 1919:
Duchess of Doudeauville: "Withdrew from her deposit one diamond choker which she is leaving for tiara project."
Duke of Doudeauville: "Came to view Tiaras mock-up, asked us to make mock-ups and wax layouts for the tiara with a view to using a diamond choker from the Duchess's deposit, dismantle this choker for the layout on wax, will come back Monday morning."

MONDAY, FEBRUARY 10, 1919:
Duchess of Doudeauville: "Presented her with a tiara mock-up with a layout on wax using the diamonds from the choker belonging to the customer. Accepted the model, asked us to draw up an estimate of the price of mounting this tiara with supply of necessary diamonds."

SATURDAY, SEPTEMBER 20, 1919:
Duchess of Doudeauville: "Request by Princess Albert Radziwill that we begin execution of the diamond tiara in preparation and that has been laid out on wax since the beginning of the year."

WEDNESDAY, SEPTEMBER 24, 1919:
Duchess of Doudeauville: "For the diamond tiara project with stones—only wishes to spend 10,000 francs and a part-exchange of stones; we are to prepare a new drawing taking this into account. Will come back tomorrow morning."

THURSDAY, SEPTEMBER 25, 1919:
Duchess of Doudeauville: "Firm order for a diamond fuchsias tiara using her stones, with removable lower band, agreed price 10,000 francs in cash and three diamonds in part-exchange. Delivery November 6."

TUESDAY, NOVEMBER 4, 1919:
Duchess of Doudeauville: "Order of bust to present row and string of pearls at the jewelry exhibition. Deliver tiara Monday evening and bring showcase Tuesday morning."

The Crèvecœur "Wheat Ear" Tiara

Diana Scarisbrick

There cannot be many tiaras that have remained in the family of the original owner for more than two hundred years, but this is the case of the Crèvecœur wheat ears.

Their story began in 1779 with the appointment to the French Legation in Philadelphia of the handsome, young, and clever diplomat from Strasbourg, Louis Guillaume Otto (1754–1817). In the 12 years he spent in America, he became friends with the leading figures of the new republic and rose to the position of Chargé d'Affaires. His first marriage to the daughter of the famous Livingston family of New York ended with her death in childbirth.

In 1790 he married again to América Francès Saint-Jean de Crèvecœur (1770–1823), known as Fanny, daughter of Michel-Guillaume de Crèvecœur (1735–1813), a nobleman who went from Normandy to Canada as an army officer in 1754, and later settled in Pennsylvania and New York. A man of wide scientific interests covering medicine, topography, botany, farming, and steamships, M. de Crèvecœur became famous in Europe after the publication of his *Letters from an American Farmer* in 1782. A shrewd observer, he was impressed by the self-reliant, independent American character, expressed his admiration for Quaker humanitarianism and his dislike of slavery, and provided an optimistic view of the emerging society: "without ancient prejudices and manners, where individuals of all nations are melted into a new race of men." The young couple arrived in Europe in 1792 and eventually Louis Guillaume Otto resumed his diplomatic career. Recognizing his talents, Napoleon sent him to London to negotiate the terms of the Peace of Amiens, then to the court of the Elector of Bavaria, and, most importantly, in 1810 to Vienna to settle the marriage contract with the Archduchess Marie-Louise. In recognition of his services, Napoleon created

him Count de Mosloy and, according to family tradition, gave Countess Fanny the diamond "Wheat Ear" tiara, alluding to her father's interest in agriculture. In her turn, their daughter, Sophie, as the wife of Count Pelet de Lozère, successively Minister of Education and of Finance during the reign of Louis-Philippe, would have worn it to receptions at the Tuileries. After her death in 1874, the tiara passed to her cousin, Robert Saint-John de Crèvecœur, and then to his descendant, François-Jean Saint-John de Crèvecœur, who had it remodeled on his marriage to Martine de Hottinguer in 1910.

As the attribute of Ceres, the goddess of the harvest and of prosperity, the wheat ear motif was adopted by the women of the Imperial court; an example, set with diamonds, was worn by the Countess of Valette who carried the ceremonial train of the Empress Joséphine, and is depicted in the painting by J.L. David of the coronation of 1804. It remained in fashion throughout the nineteenth century, worn in different ways, standing high on the crown of the head, or low on the brow as a garland, hanging down beside each cheek, combined with other motifs such as cameos, bull rushes, and lilies of the valley. At the time of the marriage of François-Jean de Crèvecœur, it was brought up to date by Chaumet using elements from the earlier tiara. This new, light design, which was composed of six wheat ears resting on curvilinear stems, with those at the centre meeting at an apex, could also be worn on the bodice as a stomacher. Exemplifying the finesse of Chaumet's craftsmanship, this Belle Époque interpretation of a classical theme has been worn on special occasions by generations of Crèvecœur wives and daughters through the twentieth century into the present, evoking the links between their ancestor and the emergent American republic.

"Wheat Ear" tiara known as the "Crèvecœur," 1910. Gold and diamonds Private Collection

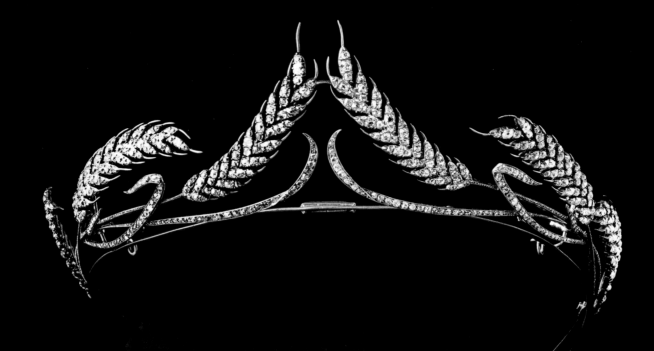

PART TWO

FROM ONE EMPEROR TO THE NEXT: JEWELER TO MONARCHS

IMPERIAL
COMMISSIONS

Anne Dion

The first piece to which we can associate the name of Nitot is the sword made at the request of First Consul Napoleon Bonaparte in October 1801, which was adorned with the *Régent* diamond.[1] Bonaparte wanted a sword for ceremonial occasions, and in fact he wore this one during celebrations for the second anniversary of his accession to power.

The *Moniteur universel* justified, with some embarrassment, this abandonment of republican simplicity for the display of monarchical pomp. "Although the lavishness and finery of diamonds are in fact suited only to women, the grandeur, beauty, and rarity of the *Régent* diamond makes it an exception."[2] The sword was also worn during Napoleon's coronation in Notre Dame Cathedral, thereby transforming it into a symbol of imperial power. Although there is no surviving documentation on the commission, it is most likely that the order went to goldsmith Jean-Baptiste-Claude Odiot, whose maker's mark is found on the sword. When François-Régnault Nitot, Marie-Étienne's son, was instructed to remove the gems for inclusion in a new sword in 1812, he carefully preserved the original. In 1852 François-Régnault unsuccessfully proposed that this sword, kept in a sarcophagus-like reliquary crowned by a gilt-bronze eagle, be used for Napoleon's tomb.[3] What role, then, had Marie-Étienne played in the original commission of 1801? Most probably he mounted the crown jewels, with which he was very familiar, having been involved in valuing and preserving them during the French Revolution. His expertise as a connoisseur of gems was also recognized during the Consulate period because in October 1801 he was asked, along with the jeweler Foncier, for his opinion on the twelve finest stones in the state's collection of gems.[4]

1   Jean-Pierre Samoyault and Colombe Samoyault-Verlet, *Château de Fontainebleau, Musée Napoléon Ier* (Paris: RMN, 1986), pp. 17–19.

2   *Moniteur universel*, 21 Brumaire X (November 2, 1801).

3   The sword passed from François-Régnault to his son, General Nitot (1812–1899), then to his grandson,

Lieutenant-Colonel Nitot, who in 1905 gave it to Prince Napoleon in Brussels.

4   Ernest Theodore Hamy, "L'émeraude du pape Jules II au Museum d'histoire naturelle (1798–1805)," *Bulletin du Museum d'histoire naturelle*, 1896, p. 50.

Couronne de Charlemagne.

Marie-Étienne may have been similarly consulted for the so-called "Charlemagne crown." The commission for the new imperial regalia (laurel wreath, scepter, hand of justice, globe) and the restoration of the so-called "Charlemagne regalia" went to goldsmith Martin-Guillaume Biennais (1764–1843). Some ancien régime regalia had survived the Revolution—Charles V's scepter, sword, and spurs—but not the hand of justice or the crown. Yet a memorandum claims that Biennais dismantled the crown and its cameos, refurbished the stones, made new settings, and reassembled the whole thing. This forged document, probably the idea of Vivant Denon, who was charged with overseeing the ostensible restoration, was probably designed to suggest a revived link with the Carolingian empire. Although Nitot's name is not mentioned, the family's preservation of a watercolor drawing of the crown pleads on behalf of his participation.[5] The reference works asserting that he made the crown, however, only date from the mid nineteenth century.[6] If Nitot did any work on the crown, it probably entailed—as on the sword—setting the cameos.

Cameo crown, known as "Charlemagne's crown," Marie-Étienne Nitot (1750–1809), 1804. Ink, watercolor, and gouache highlights on paper, H. 49.3; W. 35.6 cm Chaumet Paris Collection

THE POPE'S TIARA: A TURNING POINT IN MARIE-ÉTIENNE NITOT'S CAREER

The remainder of the coronation finery was supplied by jeweler Bernard-Armand Marguerite (circa 1768–1843), who succeeded his father-in-law, Edme-Marie Foncier, and who remained Joséphine's favorite supplier (as Foncier had been). Marguerite supplied all the empress's jewelry, the emperor's Grand Cross of the Legion of Honor, the new hat braid studded with twenty-six diamonds, and two rings for the empress and emperor, adorned respectively with a ruby and an emerald. On the other hand, Napoleon turned to goldsmith Henri Auguste (1759–1816), who had also been commissioned by the City of Paris to make a large silver-gilt dinner service, to make the gifts the new emperor gave the pope, namely a tiara and set of altar ornaments.

Although the tiara, now in the Vatican Collection, has lost its splendor due to repeated removal of gems and the elimination of the bas-reliefs, a drawing shows how it originally looked.[7] The tiara was composed of a series of three gold crowns, one above another, against a base of white velvet. Each crown included a band edged with rows of pearls and contained a hexagonal bas-relief depicting, respectively, the re-establishment of religion in France (1801), the Concordat (1802), and the coronation (1804); scrollwork supported vine leaves and fleurons. At the top of the tiara was a ribbed emerald that Napoleon had confiscated from the Vatican treasury in accordance with the Treaty of Tolentino in 1797— here it was being elegantly restored to its owner. We do not known whether this gesture met with the approval of Nitot, who in 1801 had listed the emerald as one of the twelve finest stones in the Museum d'Histoire Naturelle and had advocated its preservation.[8]

5 Neither the date nor history is known for the Chaumet firm's set of watercolors, but they are homogeneous in style and might be contemporary with the objects they depict, in which case they cannot be prior to 1812, when the emperor's sword was executed. The objective seems to have been to commemorate the most important works. The drawing of the crown differs from the actual object by one cameo.

6 Honoré d'Albert Luynes, *Exposition universelle de 1851. Travaux de la commission française sur l'industrie des nations,* Paris, Imprimerie impériale, 1854, p. 203; Henri Vever, *La bijouterie française au XIXe siècle (1800–1900)* (Paris: H. Floury, 1906–8) vol. 3, pp. 32, 34, 39.

7 *Chaumet* exhibition 1998, no. 14, p. 27; *Pie VII face à Napoléon* exhibition 2015, nos. 52–53, pp. 124–25.

8 Hamy, "L'émeraude du pape Jules II...," p. 50.

LEFT

Details of the three bas-
reliefs: *the Reestablishment
of Worship* (1801),
the Concordat (1802), and
the Coronation (1804)

FACING PAGE

*Design of the papal
triregnum of Pius VII*,
Marie-Étienne Nitot
(1750–1809), 1805.
Watercolor on paper, India
ink, and gouache highlights,
H. 48.5; W. 35 cm
Chaumet Paris Collection

TIARE DONNÉE PAR S. M. I. ET R. NAPOLEON I.
À SS. PIE VII.

François Gérard
(1770–1837), *Emperor
Napoleon I in His
Coronation Robes*, 1806.
Oil on canvas,
H. 223.3; W. 147.2 cm
Musée Fesch, Ajaccio

Design of this tiara was claimed by architect François Debret (1777–1850): "Around the time of his coronation, Napoleon commissioned his goldsmith, Mr. Auguste, to make a tiara enriched with the finest stones, plus altar ornaments in silver-gilt, as a present for Pope Pius VII, who had come to Paris to crown him. Being at the time in contact with the goldsmith, I composed various objects for him, supplying the designs." [9]

Although the imperial household gave the order to Auguste, several elements attest to Nitot's participation. Auguste had requested an advance for the purchase of the gemstones,[10] but poor management of his business led him before justices of the peace on several occasions, thus documenting his debts to Nitot. In August 1805 Auguste paid Nitot 91,752 francs,[11] while a decision by a Paris court on October 18, 1805 stated that he still owed 6,000 livres.[12] When Marie-Étienne Nitot died in 1809, an outstanding debt of 10,000 francs remained, and in order to meet it Auguste had to sign over an equivalent amount from the sum owed him by the imperial household for the gifts given to Pope Pius VII.[13]

It was a Nitot—certainly François-Régnault, then aged twenty-six—who would take the tiara to Rome. On May 22, Auguste handed the tiara over to Nitot, to be "taken to the Grand Chamberlain in Milan in a carriage belonging to Mr. Auguste and arranged with all the care required for traveling posthaste while protecting the precious object and keeping it safe." The jeweler was escorted by a non-commissioned officer in the guides commanded by Napoleon's brother-in-law, Joachim Murat.[14] Nitot made a stop in Milan, where Napoleon was being crowned king of Italy, a favorable opportunity that ultimately made the Nitots' fortune. The presentation of the tiara in Milan was recounted by the *Journal des débats*, which noted that the tiara "was made in Paris by Mr. H. Auguste for the jewelry work and by Mr. Étienne Nitot for the setting of the gems." [15] Mademoiselle Avrillion, Joséphine's lady's maid, who noted Nitot's "elegant and neat attire" upon his arrival, introduced him to the empress; according to Avrillion's account, the shrewd merchant Nitot "did not show up empty-handed; he was carrying jewels of the finest quality, in order to present them for Their Majesties' selection." [16] The selected items were handed over to Mademoiselle Avrillion, who had to carry them on every gift-giving occasion, privately regretting that she herself never benefited from even a modest ring.[17] On his way back from Rome, Nitot stopped over in Genoa—where the court was staying subsequent to the French Empire's annexation of the Genoese republic—in order to present "some highly precious things" once again.

This voyage proved crucial, because it drew Joséphine's attention to the Nitots. The empress, whose favored jeweler had first been Foncier, followed by Marguerite, bestowed the title of "Official Jeweler" upon the Nitots. This favor gave new impetus to the career of father and son, insuring their renown. Both were very proud of the title, for that matter, never failing to mention it.

9   Leniaud, Jean-Michel, *Saint-Denis de 1760 à nos jours* (Paris: Gallimard-Juliard, 1996), p. 60.

10   Auguste spent over 150,000 francs on gems, diamonds, and pearls on 28 Ventôse XIII (March 19, 1805) and obtained an advance for that amount on April 1, 1805. Archives Nationales, Paris, O² 32. See Gastinel-Coural 2005.

11   21 Thermidor XIII (August 9, 1805). Archives Nationales, Paris, Min. centr. XIV/560.

12   Archives Nationales, Paris, O² 32.

13   Ibid., contract drawn up before Maître Potron, October 1810.

14   Ibid., Archives Nationales, Paris, O² 150.

15   *Journal des débats*, 3 Messidor XIII (June 22, 1805).

16   Marie-Jeanne-Pierrette Avrillion, *Mémoires de Mademoiselle Avrillion, première femme de chambre de l'impératrice, sur la vie privée de Joséphine, sa famille et sa cour*, edited by Maurice Dernelle (Paris: Mercure de France, 1969), p. 111.

17   Ibid., p. 158.

NITOT AND SON, SUPPLIERS TO THE NEW GERMAN KINGDOMS

His travels enabled François-Régnault to seize new opportunities. Napoleonic diplomacy wove a web of connections—political, military, and matrimonial—with the southern German states of Baden, Bavaria, and Württemberg. Nitot would soon profit from these connections. In January 1806 the French court sojourned in Munich for the marriage of Eugène de Beauharnais to Augusta Amelia of Bavaria, the daughter of the Elector Maximilian, whom Napoleon had elevated to the rank of king. François-Régnault went along. It was furthermore through Nitot, who asked about the names to be engraved on the wedding ring, that Joséphine learned that Napoleon had decided to adopt her son Eugène as his own.[18] The emperor, recounted Avrillion, commissioned Nitot to make for the bride a diamond parure (matching set of jewelry) costing 300,000 francs, as well as several other parures, probably at Joséphine's urging. The whole order came to the tidy sum of 821,969 francs.[19]

The new king of Bavaria, Maximilian I, planned a coronation ceremony (which was ultimately canceled). On May 3, 1806, Maximilian announced that he had asked for designs for two crowns, a scepter, a globe, and a sword from Paris,[20] while charging his own court jeweler, Borgnis from Frankfurt, with execution of the designs. Borgnis hastily began assembling the gems required by the plans, taking stones from the Bavarian state treasury and from the Palatinate globe, and making purchases in Paris. The pearls, notably the ones for the queen's crown, were purchased from the court banker Seeligmann, who in fact held a monstrance received as compensation for the loss of the left bank of the Rhine. The most valuable gem, a large 35.5-carat blue diamond owned by the Wittelsbach family, would be added to the king's crown after it arrived in Munich. The regalia was delivered in March 1807. Borgnis's detailed accounts neglected to mention the name of the artists in Paris to whom he turned. A letter from the Nitots to Napoleon nevertheless reveals their role—in January 1807, in fact, they pressed the emperor to pay a balance of 250,000 francs because they found themselves in difficult straits at a time when they "were charged with supplying the crowns and regalia of Bavaria as well as various fairly substantial items to Prince Jérôme Napoleon."[21]

Among the surviving regalia, the scepter, sword, and a case for seals bear the mark of goldsmith Biennais. The embroidered purple velvet baldric was supplied by the embroiderer Picot.[22] Although an original mark no longer exists on the queen's crown, altered in 1867, the king's crown and globe bear the mark of Jean-Baptiste Leblond. When Leblond had his punch made around 1803–4, he was working from premises at 3, Rue des Fossés-Saint-Germain-l'Auxerrois, but by 1809 he was a subtenant of the Nitots and owed them significant sums. The trade directory for 1810 lists Leblond as residing at 1, Rue Saint-Nicaise, the side entrance to the Nitots' building. It would therefore appear that Leblond was working for our jewelers, and that the presence of his mark on the Bavarian regalia confirms their attribution to the Nitot firm.

Crown of Maximilian I, King of Bavaria, Martin-Guillaume Biennais and Jean-Baptiste Leblond, goldsmiths, Nitot & Fils, jewelers, 1806–7. Gold, pearls, diamonds, emeralds, sapphires, and rubies, H. 23.3; D. 26.5 cm Residenz Schatzkammer, Munich

18 Avrillion, *Mémoires de Mademoiselle Avrillion...*, pp. 138–39.

19 Nitot's petition to the Emperor, February 15, 1806. Archives Nationales, Paris, O² 537.

20 Sabine Heym, Prachtvolle *Kroninsignien für Bayern—aber keine Krönung*, catalog of the exhibition *Bayerns Krone 1806*. 200 Jahre Königreich Bayern, 2006, p. 37.

21 Nitot, letter to Emperor Napoleon, January 16, 1807. Archives Nationales, Paris, O² 30.

22 Delivered on October 22, 1806 for 240 francs. Picot ledger, folio 172, Brocard Collection, Department of Prints & Drawings, Musée du Louvre.

The king's crown is a closed (or arched) one. The lower band, edged with rows of pearls, is dotted with alternating diamonds and colored gems; above it is a ring of diamonds and pearls, from which rise, in alternation, diamond rosettes and gold vine leaves set with a large emerald, constituting the bases of the arches that converge to hold the crowning ball topped by cross. The Bavarian queen's crown, prior to its alteration, is known from an 1827 portrait of Queen Theresa by Joseph Stieler. It was a small, closed crown also capped by a ball and cross; above a band dotted with gems and edged with pearls and a row of scrollwork there rose large pear-shaped pearls and pearl-studded palmettes. Finally, the globe displays a similar pattern of bands edged with pearls and alternating colored stones that are round, square, or diamond-shaped. The design for this crown being comparable to Auguste's tiara,[23] perhaps the design of the Bavarian royal insignia should be ascribed to Debret.

In 1807, a German newspaper reported that the Paris jeweler Nitot, who had made the Bavarian crowns, was also working on the crown for Württemberg.[24] In fact, Frederick I of Württemberg was elevated to the rank of royalty at the same time as the king of Bavaria. He was proclaimed king on January 1, 1806. During a ceremony of homage to the new monarch in his new château on January 6, 1807, the new crown and scepter were presented for the first time.[25] The crown (now in the Württemberg Landesmuseum, Stuttgart), subsequently altered by Wilhelm I, displays similarities with the Bavarian crown that make its attribution to Nitot likely. It has the same gold band edged with rows of pearls from which rise vine leaves at the base of eight arches supporting a ball and cross, all set with diamonds and emeralds.

In July 1807, Catharina, Frederick I's daughter, had already received a diamond parure delivered by Nitot when she married Napoleon's youngest brother, Jérôme, in the Tuileries Palace in Paris.[26] Once installed on the throne of Westphalia, King Jérôme and his queen accorded the Nitots a warrant of official supplier. From the Nitots Jérôme primarily commissioned decorations for the royal order that he instituted on December 25, 1809.[27] Nitot did not always deliver swiftly enough, however: on February 10, 1810, Jérôme's master of the wardrobe, Marinville, complained that he had received only fifteen knight's crosses, one insignia, and four plaques without crosses, which did not meet the number of anticipated awards, and he furthermore ordered four necklaces, two of which—one gold, the other diamond—had to be ready for Jérôme's upcoming arrival in Paris for Napoleon's marriage to Marie-Louise.[28] Nitot was usually asked to furnish items that were pavé-set with diamonds, whereas Biennais supplied the enameled gold insignia. In May 1810 Nitot received an order to use diamonds worth 32,000 francs that the king had given him to make two large crosses and five commander's crosses and their bow, the rest going to small crosses.[29] Nitot subcontracted the embroiderer Picot to do the embroidered plaques, or at

FACING PAGE

Jean-Baptiste Regnault (1754–1829), *Portrait of Empress Joséphine, Wife of Napoleon I, Wearing a Diamond and Emerald Jewelry Set*, c. 1809. Oil on canvas, H. 59.4; W. 46.8 cm Fondation Dosne-Thiers, Paris

PAGE 196

Necklace and earrings of the Grand Duchess Stephanie of Baden, Nitot & Fils, 1806 (modified in 1820). Gold, silver, emeralds, and diamonds. Necklace H. 20.5; W. 20 cm. Earrings H. 5.7; W. 2.4 cm Victoria and Albert Museum, London

PAGE 197

Intaglio set, Nitot & Fils, c. 1809. Gold, silver, nicolo agate, and natural pearls. Necklace 13 cm. Brooch H 3; W. 5.5 cm. Earrings H. 4.5; W. 2 cm Chaumet Paris Collection

23   Ottomeyer 1979 attributes the crown to Percier, and consequently the tiara as well; we have seen that the design of the latter was by Debret.

24   *Dresdner Anzeigen*, 1807, p. 219.

25   *Königreich Württemburg* exhibition, 2006.

26   See Archives Nationales, Paris, O² 29 or 400 AP 84; letter from Duroc to Daru, August 6, 1807 (O² 6 piece 98).

27   A case made by Nitot for the order is preserved at the Stadtmuseum in Kassel (inv. no. 286). See *König Lustik* exhibition 2008, no. 168.

28   Letter from Marinville to Nitot dated February 10, 1810. Masson Collection, Bibliothèque Thiers, Fondation Dosne-Thiers, Paris, Ms 41, ledger of Marinville correspondence 1809–12, pp. 33–34. My thanks to Guillaume Nicoud for supplying this information.

29   Ibid., May 8, 1810, p. 38.

least the stripes when the center of the decoration was bejeweled.[30] On rarer occasions Nitot supplied a snuffbox or other box with monogram or portrait,[31] or books of chased gold to house miniatures by Jean-Baptiste-Jacques Augustin.[32] He also furnished a watch, like the one whose design is still archived in the Chaumet firm. The posthumous estate inventory of Marie-Étienne Nitot also lists, as part of the merchandise on the premises, snuffboxes bearing the monogram of Catharina of Württemberg, queen of Westphalia. Although significant sums were owed to Nitot in 1810, by 1811 mention was made only of paying the balance on existing debts—Nitot vanished from Marinville's correspondence in 1812. It can therefore be supposed that delays in delivery became tiresome and that the Westphalian court no longer patronized him.

From Joséphine's Patronage to the Crown's

As official jewelers to Empress Joséphine, the Nitots appear in her personal accounts as early as the fall of 1805.[33] Although the content of these orders unfortunately escape us, the sums are impressive. A list of expenses for 1806 mentions 86,846 francs for Nitot.[34] A summary of unsettled debts as of January 1, 1810—we must suppose that part of them, at least, were paid—shows that Joséphine owed Nitot nearly 100,000 francs for the year 1807, 23,000 francs for 1808, and over 208,000 francs for 1809.[35] When Nitot died, Joséphine still owed him 73,722 francs.[36] The Nitots knew how to meet Joséphine's every wish. On being criticized for not following the required procedures when supplying the imperial household, they pointed out that they habitually displayed "the promptest obedience" toward the empress.[37]

In March 1807 appraisals were made of a hydrangea-themed garland and a matching set of diamond jewelry comprising a tiara, comb, double-strand necklace, pair of three-strand bracelets, and earrings "reminiscent of the taste for old pendant clusters but more to modern taste." The diamonds won praise for their quality, their water, and above all their perfect match,[38] underscoring one of Nitot's main strengths, namely the ability to select and match stones. Openwork settings, a Nitot specialty, enhanced their sparkle. And "modern taste" revealed an ability to keep up with the times.

A Nitot bill for jewelry delivered in July 1809 provides a sample of the variety of items ordered by the empress: a pearl belt, an asteriated opal ring, a fine turquoise-and-brilliant parure featuring oval and pendant turquoises, a pair of pearl cluster earrings

PAGES 198–199
"Oak leaves" set with cornelian intaglios, Nitot & Fils, Antoine-Pierre Chanat's stamp, c. 1809. Gold, enamel, cornelian. Necklace L. 46.3 cm. Comb H. 11.3; W. 11.1 cm. Earrings H. 4.7; W. 1,7 cm Private Collection

FACING PAGE
Jean-Baptiste Isabey (1767–1855), *Portrait of Empress Joséphine in Front of Her Mirror,* 1808. Watercolor, ink wash, lead pencil, and pen, H. 25.5; W. 17.6 cm Musée du Louvre, Paris

30   Entries for November 23, December 20 and 27, 1809, and January 2 and March 3, 1810. Third Picot ledger, Brocard Collection, Department of Prints & Drawings, Musée du Louvre.

31   Entry for June 1, 1810, Marinville correspondence ledger 1809–10, pp. 39–40. Masson Collection, Bibliothèque Thiers, Fondation Dosne-Thiers, Paris.

32   Ibid., order for two books, August 13, 1809.

33   In July 1806 Joséphine's intendent, J.-C. Ballouhey, paid Nitot the sum of 10,000 francs invoiced on 29 Vendémaire XIV (October 21, 1805) and another 6,000 francs invoiced 25 Brumaire XIV (November 16, 1805). Bibliothèque Municipale de Gray, MS 17, ledger of H.M. the Empress's accounts.

34   Masson Collection, Bibliothèque Thiers, Fondation Dosne-Thiers, Paris, MS 31.

35   Ibid., MS 30, summary list of payments made by Mr. Duménil. Of the 331,028 francs claimed, 260,000 francs were finally paid, figures confirmed by the act of liquidation of Marie-Étienne Nitot's estate.

36   Serge Grandjean, *Inventaire après décès de l'Impératrice Joséphine à Malmaison* (Paris: RMN, 1964), note 160, p. 61.

37   Letter dated March 26, 1807. Archives Nationales, Paris, O² 153.

38   Affidavit of appraisal, March 4, 1807. Archives Nationales, Paris, O² 30.

MALACHITES ENTOURÉE

with six pear-shaped pearls, and tassels of gold or blue enamel to adorn purses.[39] Nitot also undertook to set coral cameos already belonging to Joséphine on a parure of chased gold and pearls (comprising bandeau, comb, necklace, and earrings), perhaps not unlike a bracelet and pins owned by Queen Hortense (now in the Musée national des châteaux de Malmaison et Bois-Préau). Joséphine was known to love cameos and carved stones, notably buying coral from Scotto and cameos from Capperone.

At the start of the reign, the jeweler Marguerite had supplied Joséphine with a ruby-and-diamond parure that was later given to Nitot for reworking. In January 1808 the new set was ready: the origin, weight, and number of rubies was rigorously verified in the presence of Marguerite.[40] The matching set now included a tiara, necklace, belt, comb, and pair of earrings. In 1809 this parure was once again altered, or at least enhanced, since in addition to these items the appraisal mentioned cluster earrings plus a spray to which a garland could be adapted.[41]

The relationship of trust between Nitot and the empress was clouded by just one incident. When, during Joséphine's divorce, her jewelry had to be sorted to distinguish her personal gems from those of the crown, a dispute arose over briolette diamonds removed from one of the crown tiaras by Nitot. But an investigation established the truth of the matter, leaving the Nitots' honest reputation intact.[42]

Nitot & Fils steadily ousted Marguerite as supplier to the crown. In 1806, a commission was split between them: Marguerite supplied fifty snuffboxes, Nitot forty-two boxes and twelve rings.[43] The prices charged by Marguerite served as guidelines for the Nitots' early deliveries when they were appraised, but this comparison turned to the Nitots' advantage because their diamonds were judged to be much finer in quality.[44]

While staying in Mainz in late 1806 and early 1807, during Napoleon's campaigns in Saxony and Poland, Joséphine placed orders with Nitot for over 83,000 francs' worth of snuffboxes, watches, and costume jewelry to be liberally distributed to local authorities and servants.[45] This type of jewelry, given away as presents,[46] became an important part of the Nitots' business with the crown. The matching sets of jewelry might vary in value, from Brazilian topazes, Brazilian rubies, amethysts, pearls, opals, and chrysoprases, always combined with brilliants, or else a simple necklace and pair of earrings. Imperial munificence often translated into the gift of a snuffbox, which could vary in kind and value. Marie-Étienne's posthumous estate inventory notably mentions a gold box decorated with an enamel portrait of Madame de Maintenon, and others in tortoiseshell with portraits of the likes of Madame de Montespan, Cardinal Richelieu, and "the great Turenne painted in enamel by Petitot," valued

39   Bill for 99,313.08 francs dated July 1, 1809. Masson
     Collection, Bibliothèque Thiers, Fondation Dosne-Thiers,
     Paris, MS 30/233.

40   Ibid., MS 30/202, January 22, 1808.

41   Affidavit of appraisal dated January 19, 1810; the figure
     of 109,937.80 francs included only newly supplied rubies
     and labor. Archives Nationales, Paris, O² 30. At the
     time of Joséphine's death, the spray and garland were
     unaccounted for. The brooch known as the "Beauharnais
     spray" is sometimes assumed to come from the set, but

     the brooch contains only ten rubies whereas the original
     cluster and garland together ontained 130.

42   Montesquiou investigation and report, August 1810.
     Archives Nationales, Paris, AF IV 1711 B, pp. 131–33.

43   Archives Nationales, Paris, O² 30.

44   Ibid. O² 30, appraisal dated March 8, 1807.

45   Ibid., O² 30 and O² 770.

46   Maze-Sencier Alphonse, *Les Fournisseurs de Napoléon Ier
     et des deux impératrices* (Paris: Henri Jaurens, 1893).

at 3,000 francs. More standard were snuffboxes with a monogram or a portrait of Napoleon or, more rarely, of Empress Marie-Louise and even, in 1813, Marie-Louise as regent. A diamond monogram might be topped by a crown, or even ringed with larger or smaller diamonds. Price could vary from 2,000 to 17,000 or even 20,000 francs.[47] The portraits were often done by Jean-Baptiste Isabey, consistently paid 600 francs, or else by Robert Lefèvre, Guérin, Saint, or even the more obscure Gilliard. Such portraits could also adorn diamond-studded medallions of often greater value.

Napoleon's marriage to Marie-Louise was an occasion for magnificent gifts— the emperor's sisters Caroline, Elisa, and Pauline, along with Eugène's wife Augusta Amelia, were each given a medallion valued at nearly 50,000 francs.[48] Napoleon generously distributed rings, often monogrammed, gold repeater watches, lapel watches, and so on. The beneficiaries of this largesse often passed them on fairly quickly. Count Charles Clary, chamberlain to the Austrian emperor, admiringly described his gift for his wife: "On the lid one sees [Napoleon's] portrait, marvelously painted by Saint, very flattering but a good likeness. Inside the cover there is an eagle and a border of [swirls] and bees in blue enamel, that are the prettiest things in the world."[49] The count initially considered selling just the twenty-six diamonds framing the miniature portrait, but then with a somewhat guilty conscience decided to sell the whole thing minus the portrait—"Nitot, who made it, will give me 13,200 francs."[50]

NAPOLEON'S MARRIAGE TO MARIE-LOUISE: LAVISH ORDERS FOR NITOT

When Marie-Étienne Nitot died in September 1809, the stock of merchandise was valued at 1,333,275.19 francs. When the estate was liquidated the following April, it was stated: "The trading firm having done considerable business since the death, due to the marriage of H.M. the Emperor and King to H.I.H. the Archduchess Marie-Louise of Austria, there remains only merchandise to the value of 215,000 francs." So 1,118,275.19 francs of gems and jewelry were sold!

Nitot was the exclusive supplier of extraordinary parures destined for Marie-Louise in 1810. Back in Vienna, Marshal Louis-Alexandre Berthier had already given Marie-Louise a miniature portrait of Napoleon by Isabey, set by Nitot with twelve large diamonds.[51] The emperor gave Marie-Louise two large matching sets of jewelry—one of emeralds and diamonds, the other of opals and diamonds—composed of a tiara, a mesh necklace with bezel settings, a pair of earrings, and a comb. The Louvre now holds the necklace and earrings from the emerald and diamond parure.[52] The necklace was composed

---

47 One snuffbox was delivered on February 10, 1810, for 29,546 francs, while another delivered on April 7, 1810, was worth 17,338 francs. Archives Nationales, Paris, O² 29 A.

48 Ibid., O² 29 A, affadavit of appraisal of twenty-one medallions, July 2, 1810.

49 Charles de Clary-et-Aldringen, *Trois mois à Paris lors du mariage de l'empereur Napoléon Ier et de l'archiduchesse Marie-Louise* (Paris: Librairie Plon, 1914), pp. 246–47. The description is accompanied by a sketch.

50 Ibid., p. 325.

51 The medallion evaluated on February 20 was subsequently enlarged at Napoleon's request, and reassessed on June 8; two diamonds had been added and its value increased from 155,000 to 175,000 francs. Archives Nationales, Paris, O² 30, 32, 34, and 41.

52 Appraisal dated June 8, 1810. Archives Nationales, Paris, O² 30. See Dion-Tenenbaum 2004 and Morel 1988, pp. 282–88.

of palmettes of brilliants alternating with large emeralds (some round, some diamond-shaped) rimmed with brilliants, from which hung splendid pear-shaped emeralds. Two very fine pear-shaped emeralds were used for the earrings. The tiara, whose center featured a large, diamond-shaped emerald, is now at the Smithsonian Institution in Washington, but its emeralds have been replaced by turquoises.

In addition to these gifts, which belonged to Marie-Louise personally, for the benefit of the crown jewels Nitot produced two dazzling parures—one of diamonds, the other of pearls—as well as others of lesser value but greater whimsy. Since the pearls were difficult to acquire all at once, delivery of the set was done in stages: in the month of April 1810 Marie-Louise had already received a three-stand necklace, another single-strand necklace of large pearls, a comb, bracelets, earrings, and strings of pearls for the hair;[53]

ABOVE, LEFT
Double-row pearl necklace,
early nineteenth century.
Gold or silver, diamonds
Private Collection

ABOVE, RIGHT
A pair of earrings
belonging to
Empress Joséphine,
early nineteenth century.
Diamonds, pearls,
H. 4.5; W. 1.5 cm
Musée du Louvre, Paris

FACING PAGE
Frederik Westin
(1782–1862), *Joséphine*
of Leuchtenberg Wearing
the Tiara and Necklace
Inherited from Her
Grandmother, 1836.
Oil on canvas
Rosendal Palace,
Stockholm,
Maltesholm slott,
Kristianstad

Empress Joséphine was passionate about pearls and owned several pearl jewelry sets crafted by the Emperor's official jeweler, Nitot. Unfortunately, as is often the case with jewels, most of them have been given away, lost, or remounted since; very few have remained in their original state. This is why this exquisite pair of earrings featuring two large pear-shaped pearls, weighing respectively 134 and 127 grains, topped by diamond-set caps, seems even more valuable. The necklace featuring a double row of pearls and seven detachable pear-shaped pearls topped with diamond-set caps is exceptional both for its beauty and provenance. It once belonged to Princess Augusta of Bavaria, wife of Eugène de Beauharnais, son of Empress Joséphine. It was then passed down to the latter's granddaughter, also named Joséphine, who became Queen of Sweden in 1844 after her marriage to the heir to the throne, Prince Oscar of Sweden, the future Oscar I. The cameo tiara worn in this portrait still belongs to the Royal Collections of Sweden.

53   April 7, 1810, valued at 178,408 francs. Archives
Nationales, Paris, O² 32.

SACRE DE SA MAJESTÉ L'EMPEREUR NAPOLÉON I.er

a tiara arrived in November 1811 once a large, flawless, egg-shaped pearl weighing 337 grains had been acquired; a closed crown topped by an imperial eagle was only delivered in July 1812. The eagle would be preserved by the jeweler Bapst after the crown was taken apart during the Restoration.[54] The diamond parure, of a lavishness unparalleled in the nineteenth century,[55] is known from a portrait of the empress painted by Robert Lefèvre in 1812. The tall tiara was organized around a large central palmette with, at its base, a large oval diamond "with slight aquamarine water, weighing 25 carats," purchased from Nitot; at its top was a crown diamond known as the *fleur-de-pêcher*; the portrait offers a glimpse of the comb behind the tiara. The belt was composed exclusively of rose-cut diamonds, with a central palmette echoing the one on the tiara. The girandoles, or cluster earrings, each featured three pendants of extraordinary pear-shaped diamonds. The parure also included a necklace[56] and a pair of bracelets with very rare "portrait" diamonds (that is to say, flat stones beneath which a portrait could be placed). The crown of brilliants was adorned with an enameled gold garland of laurel leaves in the middle of the bandeau, and was topped by an eagle of brilliant-cut and rose-cut diamonds.

Although more modest, a parure of mosaic work reflected the taste for antiquity (now in the Louvre).[57] The comb, necklace, pair of bracelets, and earrings were adorned with ten tiny glass mosaics—probably done by Roman craftsmen—depicting ancient ruins (notably the tomb of Caecilia Metella, the Forum, and Tivoli). The highly elegant setting is composed of vine leaves and bunches of grapes in delicately chased gold.

The marriage also swelled the collection of crown jewels with a few items for the emperor's use, notably a large cross of the Order of the Legion of Honor, and an epaulette braid.[58] The braid was adorned in the middle with the Hortensia diamond, which had been added to the crown jewels under Louis XIV. The insignia of the various orders established by Napoleon and his brothers during the Empire period were among the jewels consistently supplied by the Nitot firm, as already noted for Jérôme's Westphalian order. But Marie-Étienne Nitot's posthumous estate inventory also mentioned stars for the Legion of Honor, crosses for the Order of La Réunion (Holland) and the Order of the *Couronne de Fer* (Iron Crown) in brilliants.

ORDERS FOR THE CROWN JEWELS AFTER 1809

In 1812, Napoleon instructed that the diamonds on the first consul's sword be removed and used on a new sword, along with stones from a ruby crown.[59] There was a clear evolution from the consular sword, with its still-timid pomp (despite the *Régent*

PAGES 208–9

Cameo tiara, attributed to Nitot & Fils, c. 1810. Gold, agate cameos, and natural pearls Slottsmuseum, Kungl. Husgeradskammaren, Royal Collections of Sweden

FACING PAGE

Empress Marie-Louise's emerald parure, François-Régnault Nitot (1779–1853), 1810. Gold, diamonds, emeralds Musée du Louvre, Paris

54 November 28, 1811, pearl tiara valued at 221,547 francs, and July 22, 1812, crown valued at 110,279.35 francs. Archives Nationales, Paris, O² 32.

55 Ibid., O² 32. Most of the set was appraised on April 1, 1810, and valued at 1,645,446.55 francs; while the crown was appraised on April 10, and the rosettes and bezel-set stones on August 18.

56 Regnault's portrait shows the necklace delivered in 1811.

57 Anne Dion-Tenenbaum, "Une parure en or et mosaïque de Marie-Louise donnée par les Amis du Louvre," *Revue du Louvre et des musées de France* 5 (December 2001), pp. 16–17.

58 Affadavit of appraisal dated May 8, 1810. Archives Nationales, Paris, O² 32.

59 Ibid., as discussed later, this ruby crown, delivered in 1810, was soon taken apart and replaced by a new one on November 21, 1811.

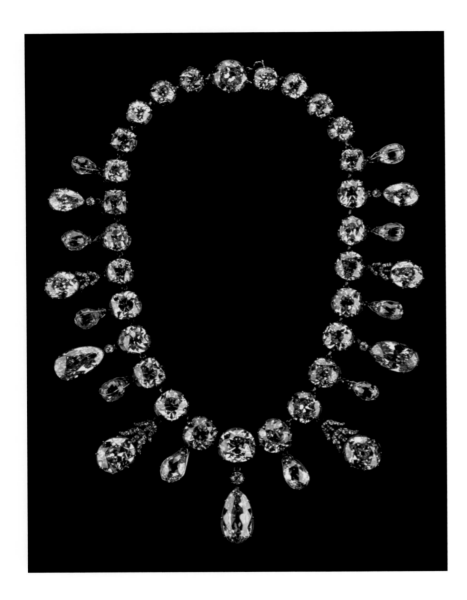

LEFT

*Empress Marie-Louise's
diamond necklace,*
François-Régnault Nitot
(1779–1853), 1811.
Gold, silver, and diamonds
National Museum
of Natural History,
Smithsonian Institution,
Washington D.C.

FACING PAGE

Robert Lefèvre
(1755–1830), *Portrait of
Empress Marie-Louise
Wearing the Great
Diamond Parure,* 1812.
Oil on canvas,
H. 222; W. 153 cm
Chaumet Paris Collection

diamond), to the new sword that blazed with imperial symbolism. "The hilt is decorated with diamonds of prodigious size, among them being the one known as the *Régent*, which forms the knob of the pommel. Diamonds of various shapes have been arranged with perfect taste to compose designs that represent the imperial eagle, winged thunderbolts, and bees. The scabbard is similarly enriched with gems, presenting ornamentation of the same kind, set against a base of crimson velvet. The belt, of gold-embroidered white velvet, is also covered with rose-cut diamonds of the greatest beauty, forming various designs."[60]

As soon as he was old enough to wear official dress, the King of Rome wore, like his father the emperor, a plaque of brilliants of the Order of the Legion of Honor and an epaulette of brilliants.[61]

60   *Journal de l'Empire*, January 16, 1813. See also Nitot's
       bill dated November 16, 1812, for 82,010.94 francs
       (Archives Nationales, Paris, O² 32) and Picot's delivery

to Nitot of the embroidered white baldric on October 18,
1812 (Brocard Collection, Louvre).
61   January 6, 1814. Archives Nationales, Paris, O² 30.

The crown treasury was nevertheless expanded largely for Marie-Louise's use. In October 1810 Nitot delivered a turquoise-and-diamond jewelry set, then another parure of Oriental rubies and diamonds in January 1811.[62] The latter is known from a gouache in the Chaumet Collection. Composed of a tiara, a crown, a necklace, a comb, a pair of earrings, a pair of bracelets, and a belt, it featured rosettes with a ruby at their center, linked by fine chains of diamonds. During the year 1811 other additions to the crown jewels included a parure of sapphires and diamonds, then another of amethysts and diamonds. The empress's gown and hair were thereby embellished by 150 ears of wheat of eight different sizes, all in openwork settings lined with gold.[63] An ear-of-wheat tiara in the Chaumet Collection evokes those jewels, combining naturalism with mythological allusions to Ceres.

In May 1808 Napoleon had eighty-two cameos withdrawn from the medal cabinet in the Bibliothèque Impériale. In 1812 twenty-four were set in gold with pearls for Marie-Louise to form an ancient-style parure composed of a bandeau, necklace, comb, pair of bracelets, earrings, belt plaque, and medallion.[64]

MARIE-LOUISE'S PATRONAGE

In addition to the jewels belonging to the crown, Marie-Louise had her own constantly growing collection of finery. To mark the birth of the King of Rome, she received a parure based on Brazilian rubies (pink topazes), two garlands of openwork hydrangea on stems and springs,[65] and a magnificent diamond necklace boasting nine large pendant brilliants and ten big briolette-cut diamonds. This necklace, now in the Smithsonian Institution, can be seen on the above-mentioned portrait of Marie-Louise by Regnault. A little cluster of hydrangeas, given in 1816 by Hortense (then Countess of Saint-Leu) to the Benedictine monastery of Einsiedeln, evokes the exquisitely tasteful naturalism of these jewels. Finally, Marie-Louise had diamonds that she brought from Vienna reset in a more fashionable parure, notably including a "flexible, gold-backed openwork" tiara.[66]

Marie-Louise also became a very faithful client of Nitot from her own purse, as demonstrated by an expense ledger kept by her intendant, Jean-Claude Ballouhey.[67] Although Joséphine had launched the Nitot firm by making it one of her suppliers, she nevertheless turned to other jewelers including not only Foncier and Marguerite, but also Friese, Devillers, and Pitaux; Marie-Louise, however, patronized Nitot exclusively. In July 1810 she bought a small parure of pearls, then in March 1812 a set in turquoise, brilliants, and pearls, plus bands and bracelets to compliment of parure of Brazilian rubies.[68] Like

Day parure adorned with mosaic work belonging to Empress Marie-Louise, François-Régnault Nitot (1779–1853), 1810. Gold and mosaic work framed with blue glass paste. Necklace L. 45 cm. Bracelets L. 18.5 cm. Comb H. 11 cm. Earrings H. 4.3 cm Musée du Louvre, Paris

62   October 10, 1810, turquoise-and-diamond parure assessed at 179,119.30 francs and January 16, 1811, ruby parure worth 406,352.33 francs. Archives Nationales, Paris, O² 29 A and 32.

63   Delivered on August 10, 1811, billed at 305,283.12 francs. Archives Nationales, Paris, O² 32.

64   Ibid., O² 32. July 12, 1812, jewelry set billed at 49,382.65 francs.

65   These garlands of hydrangea were given an additional seventeen leaves and fifty flowers on April 4, 1813. Affadavit of appraisal dated June 9, 1813.

66   Necklace delivered June 8 and appraised on July 6 at 376,275 francs; the others on March 8. Archives Nationales, Paris, O² 30.

67   Ledger titled *Écrin de Marie-Louise*, Masson Collection, Bibliothèque Thiers, Fondation Dosne-Thiers, Paris, Ms 37; and *Journal des recettes et dépense faites poiur le service de S.M. i'Impératrice et Reine*, Bibliothèque Municipale de Gray, Ms 18–20.

68   July 20, 1810, 11,000 francs; March 31, 1812, 51,955.22 francs. Bibliothèque Municipale de Gray.

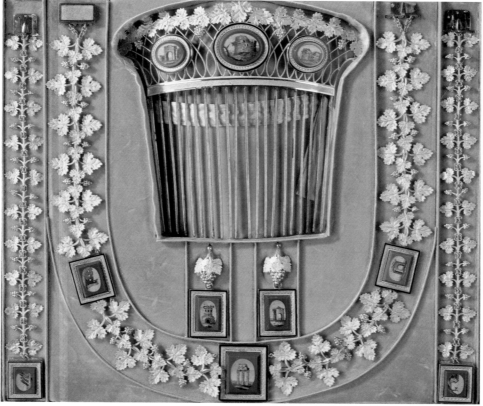

Glaive
de S.M.L'Empereur et Roi

M.E. Nitot et fils.

Napoleon, she regularly bought snuffboxes, watches, and rings to distribute as gifts, such as a lapel watch of enameled gold ringed with pearls, given in 1813 to Fanny Soufflot, the young King of Rome's companion. Her taste inclined naturally toward sentimental jewelry. For example, in September 1810 she spent 2,238 francs on three acrostic bracelets of semiprecious stones "forming the names of Their Majesties and the dates of their births written in small rose-cut diamonds." The third of these bracelets commemorated the date they first met in Compiègne, March 27, 1810, and the day of their wedding in Paris, April 2, 1810. In February 1811 she had a pearl bracelet set with a portrait of her brother, the archduke. After the King of Rome was born, she ordered a small almanac case of enameled gold and pearls, with an allegory of the birth of the heir, as well as several bracelets with the infant's portrait, combined with colored stones sometimes spelling the name of Napoleon, sometimes her own, with locks of hair. Marie-Louise had full confidence in Nitot's taste. After Napoleon abdicated on April 27, 1814, she asked Ballouhey to have some souvenir jewels made, such as a bracelet with the portrait of her lady-in-waiting, the Duchess of Montebello, and she also instructed him to have the miniature portrait of herself by Isabey set in a bracelet of "colored stones, or small chains or small pearls. I rely on Nitot's good taste for this."[69]

Although the neoclassical taste dominated Nitot's deliveries to the crown, the jeweler also innovated in designs whose style prefigure the Romantic period. Such is the case with a surprising gold "Gothic girdle" delivered on July 19, 1813.[70] The plaque on the girdle features an ancient cameo donated by Pauline Bonaparte, surrounded by "six crescent-shaped onyxes, plus two round ones forming the buttons, and six little oval onyxes." From this cameo falls a very long, increasing flared pendant, composed of gold latticework containing stars, bees, and palmettes, and ending in tassels. Only a few years later the Duchess of Berry would become very fond of such belts inspired by the Middle Ages.

69 Letters from Empress Marie-Louise to Mr. Ballouhey. Masson Collection, Bibliothèque Thiers, Fondation Dosne-Thiers, Paris, Ms 30.

70 Ledger titled *Écrin de Marie-Louise*, Masson Collection, Bibliothèque Thiers, Fondation Dosne-Thiers, Paris, Ms 37; and appraisal dated July 25, 1813, of 10,540.07 francs, Archives Nationales, Paris, O² 30. See also *Chaumet* exhibition 1998, p. 34.

The Consul's Sword, Called "Coronation Sword"

Karine Huguenaud

A cornerstone of Marie-Étienne Nitot's spectacular success was the sword made for First Consul Napoleon Bonaparte, as decreed by Bonaparte himself on 18 Vendémiaire X (October 10, 1801). He ordered that the ceremonial sword should glitter with all the fire of the French crown jewels, notably the fabulous *Régent* diamond.[1] Discovered in the Indian mine of Golconda, this legendary 140-carat diamond was named after Philippe d'Orléans, regent of France, who bought it in 1717 for the sum of two million livres.[2] It graced the coronation crown used by Louis XVI and Louis XVI, and was the single most precious gem owned by the French monarchy. Stolen during the Revolution, it was later found but then pawned during the Directory period; and it was a treasure that Bonaparte constantly tried to recover after he came to power in 1799.

Based on an inventory of the crown jewels drawn up in 1791, the estimated value of the stones set on the sword amounted to 360,950 gold francs, to which should be added the estimated value of six million francs for the *Régent* alone.[3] So when wearing the consul's sword, Napoleon was flaunting the reconstituted treasury of the French nation. This ceremonial weapon certainly symbolized the first consul's power in a dazzling way, yet it also clearly testified to France's renewed prosperity and healthy coffers following the torment of revolution.

Bonaparte's decision to wear the crown jewels for the first time since the fall of the ancien régime clearly made a political statement. Setting himself up as the new master of France in the tradition of kings with their divine right, Bonaparte invested the consul's sword with a symbolic dimension designed to project a legitimacy he still lacked, and which he would further assert by founding the nation's fourth dynasty. It was moreover this insignia of government that Emperor Napoleon chose to carry when he was crowned in Notre Dame Cathedral on December 2, 1804, rather than an ancient-style sword, as the famous painting of the event by Jacques-Louis David would have us believe.[4] It was also this sword that Napoleon wore in the official portrait by Gérard featuring all the regalia—imperial cloak, crown, scepter, hand of justice, globe, and grand neckchain of the Order of the Legion of Honor.

Three grand names are linked to the making of this key item of Parisian jewelry and precious metalwork. Odiot is credited with the overall design and goldsmithery, Boutet with the damascened blade, and Nitot with setting the roughly forty-two diamonds weighing a total of 254 carats, exact details of which are known thanks to a report filed when they were removed and weighed on June 18, 1812.[5] On that date, Napoleon ordered Nitot & Fils to work on a new sword to hold the crown jewels: it was to be a traditional sword with baldric, more warlike in appearance than the elegant Louis XVI-style consular épée whose symbolic impact, undermined by the invention of imperial regalia for the coronation, no longer met the needs of a consul who had become Caesar. François-Regnault Nitot removed the diamonds from the first sword to make the new one, but he managed to obtain from the government the supreme honor of being allowed to buy the original épée, stripped of its gems, which he replaced by perfect facsimiles of glass and rock crystal.[6]

Kept as a precious relic in the Nitot family until the early twentieth century, in 1905 the consul's sword was given by Edgar Nitot (great grandson of Marie-Étienne Nitot and grandson of François-Regnault Nitot) to Prince Victor Napoleon, the official representative of the imperial family, then living in exile in Brussels. It entered the French national collection in 1979, and is today held by the Musée Napoléon Ier in the Château de Fontainebleau.

1 "The Minister of the Interior shall have made for the First Consul of the Republic a sword the hilt of which will be set with the *Régent* diamond and other diamonds judged necessary…taken from those diamonds currently in the public treasury." Memo of decree dated 18 Vendémiaire X, sent to the ministers of public education and the treasury on 19 Vendémiaire. Archives Nationales, Paris.

2 The diamond weighed 426 carats when discovered, then was cut to 140.640 carats. The cutting produced secondary stones that were sold to Peter the Great, Tsar of Russia. Bernard Morel, *Les Joyaux de la Couronne de France* (Paris: Albin Michel/Mercator, 1988), pp. 186–88.

3 Ibid., p. 250.

4 See Karine Huguenaud, "L'épée consulaire dite Epée du Sacre," *Bulletin de la Société des amis du musée de la Légion d'honneur et des ordres de Chevalerie* 17 (2014), pp. 5–14.

5 Napoleon Archives, 400 AP 4, Archives Nationales, Paris.

6 Ibid.

FACING PAGE

Consular sword, also known as Napoleon I's "Coronation Sword," Nicolas-Noël Boutet (1761–1833), Marie-Étienne Nitot (1750–1809), Jean-Baptiste-Claude Odiot (1753–1850), 1802.

Gold, sanguine jasper, gemstones, tortoiseshell, steel, leather, L. 96; W. 12; D. 8 cm Musée national du château de Fontainebleau

Marie-Louise's Gothic Girdle

Karine Huguenaud

Napoleon's marriage to Marie-Louise of Hapsburg-Lorraine, daughter of the Austrian emperor, represented a high point for Nitot & Fils. In 1810 the firm made stunning jewelry included in the wedding gifts to the bride, designed not only to seduce the future wife but also to underscore the new regime's glamour with regard to one of the oldest monarchies in Europe. Right up to Napoleon's downfall, Nitot & Fils delivered items destined for the new empress's personal use, as well as for the crown jewels. One of the most novel creations, made in 1813, was an elaborate belt of finely chased gold studded with pearls, featuring a plaque with an ancient cameo ringed by six crescent-shaped sards and six oval sards, set with pearls. Dubbed the "Gothic girdle," this lavish, refined accessory was perfectly suited to female dress during the Napoleonic period. Empire gowns, typical of the neoclassical fashion that influenced the arts and dress from the late eighteenth century onward, were made of light, gauzy fabrics that fell in a pure, simple line to the feet, and had short puff sleeves flanking a bodice that ended just below the bust, creating a very high waist. This particular cut favored the use of a belt either to mark the high waist or to adorn the long skirt. This inspired a new style of belt called "Gothic" because it was inspired by the long girdles worn by women in the Middle Ages, which fell from the waist to the lower edge of the gown. Marie-Louise's Gothic girdle thus featured a long, vertical, openwork pendant that widened as it fell; its forty panels were connected by hinges and two thin strips on the edges, designed to lend it flexibility and thus allow it to follow the silhouette perfectly.

The emergence of the Gothic style indicated fascination with nascent Romanticism. Marie-Louise was a skillful artist herself and did several watercolors in 1812 and 1813 showing her penchant for Gothic architecture and fashion. Its introduction into the art of jewelry prefigured the revival tastes of the 1820s and 1830s, revealing Nitot's visionary genius. In a bold synthesis of styles, Nitot managed to incorporate—with a rigorous, harmonious symmetry—neoclassical motifs and Napoleonic emblems (palmettes, bees, stars, laurel wreaths) along with lobed tracery of medieval inspiration.

This masterpiece was orchestrated around the ancient cameo that links the long pendant to the two horizontal belts. It was a present from Princess Pauline Borghese to her new sister-in-law, Marie-Louise. Archeological objects were fashionable gifts at the time, and this rare example from the Hellenistic period shows Apollo playing the cithara after having slain the Python, which lies at his feet. The female figure on the left has given rise to several hypotheses: she might be Apollo's mother, Leto, who was persecuted by the Python, or perhaps the prophetess at Delphi (called Pithia), whose protector was the Python. Or maybe she is Euterpe, the muse of music, who appears on a cast version of this same cameo.[1] Pauline, who was Napoleon's favorite sister, came

---

1   A glass cast in the Paoletti Collection (Gabinetto Gemme, Museo di Roma) describes the subject as "Apollo vincitore del serpente Pitone, et la Pitia." See Lucia Pirzio Biroli Stefannelli, *La collezione Paoletti: stampi in vetro per impronte di intagli e cammei* (Rome: Gangemi, 2007), p. 43, no. 180. Another cast, made by engraver Tommaso Cades for the German Institute of Rome in 1829, is listed in the Classical Art Research Center and The Beazley Archive at Oxford. It shows a variant of the female figure holding an *aulos* (a single-reeded flute that was played in pairs during the classical period), who is thus identified as Euterpe (400005857, Cades, 4.I.E.58).

**PAGE 223, LEFT, AND
FACING PAGE**
*Gothic-style belt belonging
to Empress Marie-Louise*,
Nitot & Fils, 1813.
Gold, natural pearls, and
onyxes, L. 83 cm
Chaumet Paris Collection

into possession of one of the finest collections of ancient cameos in the world following her marriage to Prince Camillo Borghese. Perhaps this cameo was once part of it. Marie-Louise remained highly attached to this unique accessory and kept it until the end of her life, bequeathing it to her dear friend Lady Burghersh, née Wellesley-Pole (hence niece of the Duke of Wellington), later Countess of Westmorland.[2] The empress's girdle, along with its original case of red morocco leather gilt-stamped with the imperial arms and bearing the extremely rare mark, *M. E. Nitot & Fils à Paris No. 1*, entered the Chaumet Collection in 2014.

2   Codicil 89 of Marie-Louise's will left the Gothic girdle, which had remained her private property, to Lady Burghersh, Countess of Westmorland (testament dated May 22, 1844, Archivio dello Stato, Parma), who passed it on to her second daughter, Lady Rose Weigall. Sold at Christie's on February 22, 1894, it was acquired by Mr. Arbuthnot Guthrie, and later by Colonel Sir Neville Chamberlain, who sold it at Christie's on May 28, 1935 (lot 126). It resurfaced at the sale of the Calvin Bullock Collection on May 8, 1985 (once again at Christie's in London, lot 24), where it was acquired by Mohamed Mahdi Altajir before entering the Chaumet Collection in 2014.

ROMANTIC JEWELRY

Isabelle Lucas

"We live in an age of universal investigation, and of exploration of the sources of all movements."[1] In 1827 Alfred de Vigny thus expressed the drive for experimentation and discovery that motivated an entire generation to extend its pursuits into unprecedented realms. In the thirty-three years spanning the Bourbon restoration (1814–30) and the July Monarchy (1830–48), this powerful urge sparked a revival not just of the economy and the structure of French society but also a profound transformation of art in all its dimensions.

Indeed, the Romantic movement developed a new artistic idiom through its probing of the very depths of being. Goldsmiths and jewelers met the technical challenge of the fashionable new aesthetic by inventing new manufacturing techniques and resurrecting neglected or forgotten skills and methods. The exploration of possibilities offered by an extended range of materials was matched by the adoption of original themes and shapes. Jewelry, mirroring the Romantic sensibility for vibrant feelings and colors, embraced the movement's multifarious nature and embodied its evolving profusiveness. Although this context was conducive to unbridled creativity, it is possible to pinpoint a few of the main themes of the art of the day: historic revivalism, Orientalism, the celebration of nature, and the expression of feelings. Whereas this last constituted a major creative inspiration—since jewelry was associated with the expression of sentiment—the others reflected a desire to echo the new artistic trend on a private, personal level.

1   Alfred de Vigny, "Truth in Art," *Cinq Mars*, trans. anonymous (New York: Current Literarture Publishing Company, 1910), p. IX.

REVIVAL STYLES

"The age of a second Renaissance has dawned in Europe," rejoiced Adrien de Lavalette in 1842. "And the honor of this felicitous outcome should be attributed to historic scholarship. By studying the artistic wealth of the past, we have acquired almighty admiration for the masterpieces that each century has bequeathed us…. Nowadays, each century pays us tribute and offers us inspiration. Fashion … allows us to delve into the artistic riches of every period and every land."[2] The rise of this inherently fluctuating influence over an evolving society ultimately multiplied the number of trends deemed fashionable. Delphine de Girardin even mocked the way her fellow ladies dressed, "borrowing one idea from every country, from every religion, from every persuasion, and from every age." She cited, pell-mell, "hats in the style of Mary Stuart, or Henri IV, Mancini- or Fontange-style coiffures, Spanish hairnets and Egyptian turbans."[3] Dress fashion drew its faithful partner, jewelry, into this headlong race for novelty.

The primacy accorded to history, whose task—according to the Romantic attitude—was to revive the most everyday features of bygone eras, induced artists to abandon the classical ideal for the colorful poses that study of age-old archives revealed to them. An interest in the Middle Ages, which the Restoration had painted as being pleasantly picturesque, was soon accompanied by exploration of periods with features as distinct as the Renaissance and the reign of Louis XV. The July Monarchy spawned a kaleidoscopic vision of artistic styles representative of pre-nineteenth-century historical periods, from which designers tried to forge a contemporary version. Drawings and documents in the Fossin archives shed light on how jewelry was adapted to this new iconography and to unprecedented formal features.

An idealized Middle Ages (initially thought to end only with the Baroque period) was elevated into a favorite motif, bringing a storybook feel and an old Gothic aesthetic to the subjects of kings Louis XVIII (reigned 1814–24) and Charles X (1824–30). It entranced celebrities of the day such as the Duchess of Berry, who would dress up for costume balls as a medieval queen or as Mary Stuart. Then there was the young convent-school girl imagined by Gustave Flaubert in the form of Emma Bovary, who "would have wished to live in some old manor like those chatelaines with long figures who, under the trefoils of their ogive arches passed their days … watching the approach from a distant landscape of a cavalier with white plume on a galloping black horse."[4] The meticulous if whimsical reconstructions of "troubadour-style" paintings and stage sets served as inspiration for parties, interior decoration, and finery for the social elite, won over by the historical tales of Goëthe and Walter Scott. In the absence of reliable sources, jewelers used their

Alexandre-Jean Dubois-
Drahonnet (1791–1834),
*Portrait of the Duchess
of Berry*, 1828.
Oil on canvas,
H. 224; W. 171.5 cm
Musée des Arts Décoratifs,
Paris, on deposit from the
Musée de Picardie, Amiens

2   Adrien de Lavalette, "L'art du dix-neuvième siècle," *La Sylphide* (1842), p. 360.

3   Delphine de Girardin, *Le vicomte de Launay: Lettre parisiennes* (Paris: Michel Lévy Frères, 1857), vol. 2, p. 46.

4   Gustave Flaubert, *Madame Bovary*, trans. William Walton (Philadelphia: George Barrie & Sons, 1896), pp. 61–62.

imagination, as Fossin did in 1822 when designing a "Gothic" necklace for the Duchess of Berry, who unhesitatingly demonstrated her penchant for medieval-style jewelry by richly adorning herself with it for a full-length portrait exhibited at the Salon of 1827. Like other society ladies, she was a keen advocate of the extension of this style to all items of finery by importing figures from fashionable novels of chivalry and ornamentation often derived from late-Gothic architecture.

The influence of the literary revival of medieval tastes did not wane when King Louis-Philippe succeeded Charles X. In 1835, Esmeralda costumes still prevailed at artists' balls: "It is claimed that women who wear it re-read *The Hunchback of Notre Dame* in order to identify fully with the heroine," reported the *Gazette des salons*.[5] In the 1940s, Fossin's clients were still enjoying jewelry crowned with arches, such as "Gothic-gallery bracelets" adorned with pearls or formed by a "large chain of openwork arches." Then there were relief versions of Romantic book illustrations showing a knight in prayer or accompanied by his damsel, such as a bracelet decorated with a kneeling knight, listed in Fossin's 1842 inventory, and "small figures of cavalier and lady" etched onto the plaque of one purchased by the Marquise of Miraflores in 1839. Halberd-shaped brooches and pins in the form of a chased gold glove holding a gem (which varied depending on the client's wishes) recall the supremacy accorded to the military class in those harsh, brawling centuries. Meanwhile, the Middle Ages as ardent defender of the Christian faith was reflected by a host of angels who, draped in long gowns, populated jewelry. Grouped in pairs, these angels might flank a fragment of Gothic architecture or hold a shield surmounted by a crown, as seen in one particularly appreciated design for a seal ring; or else they protected a portrait mounted on a bracelet. In 1842 the Marquis of Vogüé bought a pin with a silver-gilt figure of the archangel Michael in a Gothic setting of chased gold; Prince Mikhail Galitzin and General Gaspard Gourgaud, however, preferred one that showed the archangel slaying the dragon, carved in gold-damascened steel.

Most of the many pieces of jewelry listed under the sibylline label of "Gothic style" resist precise description, however. The Marquis of Tillet was one of those people who had a very marked taste for it. In 1840 he ordered a large parure (or matching ensemble) of chased, engraved gold, with highly refined ornamentation of black and white enamel, studded with emeralds, pearls, and brilliants; the set included a tiara, a bandeau, a necklace with pendant, a *sévigné* (bow brooch worn between the breasts), and two shoulder pins. To this Tillet added a round crystal flacon with engraved gold Gothic ornamentation, carried on the arm with a large chain. This design must have been fashionable because during that same period Fossin sold very similar models to Baroness James de Rothschild and to the wife of banker Achille Seillière.

As scholarship progressed, however, the Renaissance era assumed greater autonomy and unrivaled glamour. Following the 1829 success of his historical play, *Henri III et sa cour* (Henry III and His Court), Alexandre Dumas claimed that his actors "have resuscitated men

FACING PAGE, TOP
Three chivalric scenes in the neo-Gothic style for bracelet plaques, c. 1840. Graphite pencil, pen and black ink, gouache wash, H. 7; W. 12.2 cm
Chaumet Paris Collection

FACING PAGE, CENTER
Design for a medieval-style corsage ornament, c. 1840. Graphite pencil, pen and black ink, H. 9.8; W. 5.4 cm
Chaumet Paris Collection

Design for a medieval-style belt buckle, c. 1840. Graphite pencil, pen and black ink, H. 4; W. 6.2 cm
Chaumet Paris Collection

FACING PAGE, BOTTOM
Design for a medieval-style belt buckle, 1830–40. Graphite pencil, pen and black ink, H. 9; W. 11 cm
Chaumet Paris Collection

Design for a medieval-style brooch, 1830–40. Graphite pencil, pen and black ink, H. 9.8; W. 11 cm
Chaumet Paris Collection

and rebuilt an era."[6] At the dawn of the 1830s the Renaissance made a notable entrance into the decorative arts thanks to the designs of Claude-Aimé Chenavard, whose anthologies of ornamentation were veritable encyclopedias of patterns. The rich inventiveness of Renaissance jewelry was a godsend to Fossin and other jewelers, who produced many designs of elaborately worked chain, worn as a sautoir or around the forehead like the woman in the Leonardo da Vinci portrait known as *La Belle Ferronnière*. The Countess of Grimberg and the Countess of Toreno both ordered several *Ferronnière* bandeaus as late as 1838, but once the decade-long fad was over they would convert them into other items of jewelry.

Old-master paintings, anthologies of ornament, and antique objects made it possible to steep oneself in the spirit of an age admired for its refinement and ingenuity. In 1836 *La Mode* reported on an elegant collection of wedding gifts "with diamonds mounted by Fossin in the 'François I' style," as well as a parure of gold and malachite inspired by a chain alleged to have belonged to Pope Alexander VI.[7] Paolo Veronese's portraits of women prompted Fossin in 1842 to set a *sévigné* with large pearls for the Countess of Valanglart. Madame Boigues brought the jeweler two enamel reproductions of Raphael's *Madonna of the Chair*, which she had bought in Rome and wanted to have set on brooches, rimmed by a frame featuring a chased cherub's head. The Florentine goldsmith and sculptor Benvenuto Cellini—praised to the skies for the proud, rebellious figure suggested by his autobiography, his picaresque adventures, his glamorous clients, and his magisterial œuvre, all so appealing to the Romantic spirit—was then ascribed many fine pieces of precious metalwork made during the Renaissance. Thus Anatole Demidov, an enthusiastic art love and collector, asked Fossin in 1844 to make a bracelet that copied one of Cellini's purported designs. Demidov repeated the commission the following year for a "bracelet topped with a fleur-de-lis of chased gold, white enamel and ruby, based on a drawing of a bracelet by Benvenuto Cellini."[8]

Most clients who bought "Renaissance style" jewelry, however, contented themselves with some characteristic ornament. Thus Madame Thiers chose a chatelaine enlivened with a little grotesque figure of chased, engraved, and enameled gold in the form of a caryatid, while in 1840 Countess Duchatel bought a bracelet centered on two emerald- and pearl-studded tritons flanked by a series of small shells punctuated by a pearl. There were countless jewels in the form of strapwork, a swirling, decorative motif that framed the paintings in the François I gallery at the Château de Fontainebleau—in fact, that symmetrical motif became emblematic of Renaissance revival art. Putti, fauns, chimeras, mermen and mermaids, like angels and dragons, whether carved in relief or in the round, enjoyed the same decorative duality they had had during the Renaissance. An enameled gold pin commissioned in 1842 by Baron de Knyff featured a skull and crossbones—whether inspired by an aristocratic whim, a Romantic attraction to death, some scholarly allusion, or spiritual

Designs for chatelaines,
c. 1840.
Graphite pencil, pen and
black ink, gouache, ink
wash, H. 37; W. 53 cm
Chaumet Paris Collection

6   Alexandre Dumas, *Henri III et sa cour: drame historique
     en 5 actes et en prose* (Paris: Vezard, 1933 [3rd ed.]), p. IX.
7   *La Mode* (4th quarter, 1836), p. 246.
8   Invoice ledger D, fol. 32–33, Chaumet Archives.

concerns, this memento mori that underscored the vanity of worldly concerns, which was a frequent theme of seventeenth-century jewelry. Meanwhile, pins that bore images of Charles IX or Henri III in chased and enameled silver or gold expressed the Romantics' fascination for the last monarchs of the Valois dynasty, as well as for the lavish elegance seen in portraits of them.

At the same time, a revival of the pleasant lifestyle under Louis XV, which acquired new appeal, called for special furnishings, "Watteau-style" fans, "Pompadour" sachets of scent and private little costume suppers. Jewelry displaying the charm of rococo art was suddenly coveted, whether surviving intact or in the form of fragments. Many clients had brooches made from eighteenth-century enamels of putti framed by chased sentimental motifs symbolizing that sensual period, as exemplified by a "group of putti in grisaille on lilac ground" set in ribbons and swirls of engraved gold for the Countess of Beaumont, and by a "little cupid after Van Loo" transformed into a medallion topped by a ribbon bow of blue enamel for Prince Theodore Galitzin. Similar settings graced countless portraits of ancestors. One old painted enamel, set in a framework of ribbons with a small quiver, was the main feature of a chatelaine that Fossin made in the Louis XV style for a Mr. Ternaux. An apparently antique chatelaine that Fossin sold to Anatole Demidov in 1842 proved that this jewel accessory's return to fashion added value to authentic vestiges of eighteenth-century decorative inventiveness, which were highly sought after.

Although the abundance of orders favored a variety of designs, one motif that best seemed to convey the essence of the "Pompadour" style was a bouquet of diamond florets set on a base of blue enamel or glass. Placed in a rococo-inspired surround of swirling lines, this decorative motif was chosen by Marquise de La Gorce for the fastener and the little plaques set between the chain links of her chatelaine, as well as by Duchess Strozzi in 1843 for an imposing corsage ornament formed of three plaques joined by chains enhanced by tassels of brilliants. The desire to see a little bouquet of rose-cut diamonds glitter on the finger, set off by a blue or purple base and placed upon a marquise-shaped ring—characteristic of the ancien régime—was so popular that jewelers Philippi and Dutreih, who made it their specialty, supplied numerous examples to Fossin. Jules Fossin's mother-in-law, Madame Delalande, chose to enlarge this design to the size of a bracelet whose central bouquet was placed upon a little bow of rose-cut diamonds on a blue enamel base. The rich setting of a large desk seal ordered by the Duke of Nemours represented a refined variant on this highly valued motif, endowing it with a scattering of little bouquets of chased gold and painted enamel that contrasted with the pale blue enamel base.

A taste for jewelry inspired by classical antiquity still survived, if overshadowed by the unprecedented diversification of historical sources that stimulated creativity. That taste, already fueled by study of the humanities, was reinforced by trips to Italy. The souvenirs brought back home—usually cameos or tiny mosaics—furnished the raw material for finery that was always genteel, such as an "antique-style" bracelet of chased gold that Fossin set in 1840 with two monsters, a Medusa-head cameo and a cluster of coral talismans evoking the Neapolitan superstition of *jettatura* (evil eye); that same year Fossin also made a large, "Pompeii-style" parure of pearls and cameos comprising a bandeau, a *sévigné*, a chain, and two shoulder pins.

Necklace from the "Bunch of grapes" set, Fossin & Fils, c. 1825. Gold and turquoises, H. 18; W. 18 cm Chaumet Paris Collection

ORIENTALIST JEWELRY

The era's drive for knowledge and exploration also led to the discovery of exotic landscapes, climes, and peoples. The quest for the roots of European culture, combined with a desire to encounter other civilizations, drew artists and scholars to the Orient. Following Bonaparte's Egyptian campaign and the scholarly studies it prompted, an educated French readership enthusiastically welcomed the 1811 publication of the first Romantic travel account, Chateaubriand's *Itinéraire de Paris à Jérusalem (Itinerary from Paris to Jerusalem)*, recording the author's journey through Greece, Turkey, Palestine, and Egypt. During the Restoration, a young Léon de Laborde, whose family and friends were clients of Fossin, crisscrossed the Near East with his father, then traveled to Egypt and Petra. These same lands were also being explored by diplomats and scholars. For example, the future botanist Gustave Thuret, an attaché at the French embassy in Constantinople, returned from Syria and Egypt with talismans that he asked Fossin to set in Algerian-style silver rings (based on models he supplied) and brooches surrounded by a large chased gold and green enameled ring inscribed *Damas* [Damascus] *1842* on the back. The vogue for talismans, which dated back to the eighteenth century, remained strong. Fossin continued to set amulet stones inscribed with good luck charms in Arabic, which people clearly continued to value in so far as Princess of Lieven had her heart-shaped turquoise talismanic medallion repaired in 1844.

The French conquest of Algeria from 1830 onward familiarized society with the landscapes and mores of the Islamic Orient. Many artists, including Eugène Delacroix and Horace Vernet, returned with lively, colorful visions of North Africa. French women began wearing burnouses and fabrics given to them by relatives fighting on the other side of the Mediterranean. In 1840, the Duchess of Orléans was seen leaving the Théâtre des Italiens wearing "a white burnous from Africa, of wide, coarse fabric," similar to one among her wedding gifts in 1837.[9] At that time arose the fashion for Algerian-style parures with spherical elements, the demand being so great that Fossin produced countless variants on this theme. The simplest were of entirely gold, but most included pearls and gold balls either engraved

LEFT

Tiara from the "Bunch of grapes" set, Fossin & Fils, c. 1825. Gold and turquoises, H. 5; W. 19 cm
Chaumet Paris Collection

FACING PAGE

Project for an Oriental-style set, c. 1840. Graphite pencil, pen and black ink, gouache, ink wash, H. 22.5; W. 20.6 cm
Chaumet Paris Collection

9   *La Sylphide* (January 1840), p. 27.

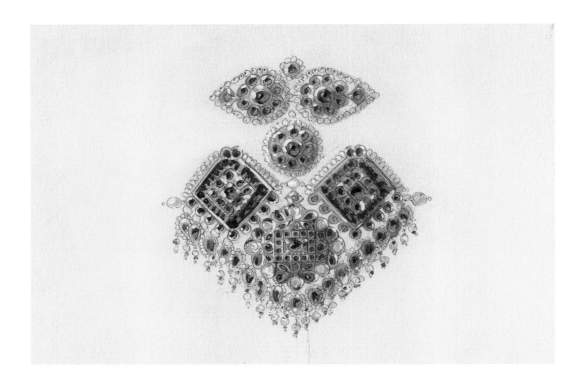

or enameled, on which were etched a network of gold lines; other balls were composed of coral, lapis, onyx, and other brightly colored stones such as garnets and turquoises. This motif became dominant—Fossin set a large Scotch pearl in a pin in Algerian fashion, with a network of engraved gold threads. A new entry joined the list of his annual inventory, namely "burnous pins," in which a little chain united two distinct models decorated with balls of pierced or ribbed gold, or of semiprecious stones (malachite, lapis, cornelian) perhaps underscored by a network of gold threads or even rose-cut diamonds.

The Oriental influence could also be seen in gold or enameled lucky charms featuring odalisques, scimitar-shaped brooches pavé-set with diamonds, and other items. One remarkable, if little developed, series involved items of gold-damascened steel or iron, whose execution required the skills of specialists, namely the damascener Roucou and the chaser Vechte. Two clients in particular commissioned rare, highly elaborate designs. In 1844 Countess Le Hon ordered an iron cane knob inlaid with Arab lettering in gold; the previous year she had already asked several artisans to participate in making a gold-damascened steel bracelet adorned with a "large plaque of steel with damascene and repoussé work, surrounded by brilliants, featuring a bas-relief of the battle of the Amazons" (a theme associated with the Orient through the presumed Asian origin of the female warriors). Meanwhile, a bracelet ordered by Madame de Lalande in 1844 displayed assertive decoration and virtuoso execution, being a large spring bangle of steel covered with gold ornaments chased in relief; its ends terminated in monster heads of chased steel of supposedly Oriental inspiration, with eyes and nostrils incrusted with gold, and a collar of rose-cut diamonds.

Further afield, India embodied the perfect Orient in the minds of exotically inclined Romantic artists, for it was full of sensuality and mystery. A few Fossin jewels allude to that legendary country, such as a so-called Moghul bracelet, a turquoise ring set in a gold "Indian body" with two monster heads, and parures enriched with colorful stones. The term *bayadere* (dancing girl) was applied to necklaces evoking Hindu dancers, whom Théophile Gautier immortalized in an enthusiastic account when they performed in Paris in 1838. The

vision they sparked in his imagination even before seeing them was probably typical of the way many of his contemporaries perceived women from the Orient. "There was something distant, splendid, magical, and charming that one vaguely imagined as a whirlwind of sun, where gems and dark eyes sparkle in turn."[10] It was perhaps to reinforce her already distinct charm that in 1841 Countess Le Hon purchased an Indian parure, including a necklace of six large, round plaques set with emeralds, rubies, opals and rose-cut diamonds, attached by several strands of large pearls, closed by a clasp of chased and repoussé silver-gilt.

Scarcely less magnificent but highly prized was jewelry featuring exotic animals such as tigers, leopards, panthers, and elephants. They would be arranged symmetrically on spring bangle bracelets and brooches, whereas pins would either hold a caparisoned elephant and its mahout or else separate those two figures into a pair. Anthony de Rothschild boldly ordered a bracelet with an enameled gold elephant head at each end, painted in various colors and set with rose-cut diamonds; Queen Maria Amelia selected another bracelet that met in "two fantastic leopard heads." The better to express the imagined lavishness of the Orient, these jewels orchestrated the colors of enamel and stones in highly sophisticated compositions. Although the lion adorned all kinds of jewelry (its head often set with rubies and turquoises), it was not truly representative of Romantic exoticism, being part of the classical repertoire. On the other hand, the dangers of Oriental shores were wonderfully evoked by a crocodile lurking in a clump of grass and reeds of gold-damascened iron, which adorned a riding crop owned by French botanist Gustave Thuret. The numerous designs featuring animals were related to the naturalist trend that emerged and developed within the Romantic movement.

BELOW AND FACING PAGE
Bracelet in the shape of a bird defending its nest, Henri Duponchel (1794–1868) and Jean-Valentin Morel (1794–1860), c. 1845. Molten chiseled gold, natural pearls, H. 2.8; W 18.2; D. 2.8 cm Musée du Louvre, Paris

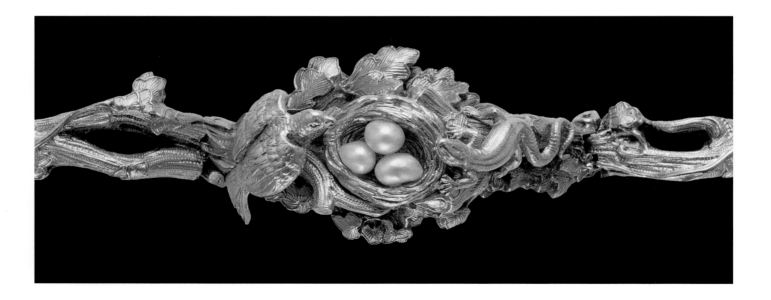

10　Théophile Gautier, "Les devadasis dites bayadères," *La Presse* (August 20, 1838).

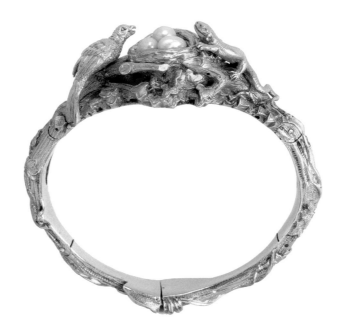

NATURALISM

A feeling for nature—a key element of Romanticism, which imbued it with soulful expressions—accompanied the exploration of the physical world. Furthermore, since the late eighteenth century the attention brought to bear on nature had profoundly affected the domestic environment, to the great benefit of botany and horticulture. Interest in the animal kingdom also grew apace, triggering spectacular changes in animal art. People liked to plaster "their walls with the faces of their dogs, their horses, their cows, their bulls, and their rams." [11] Jewelry joined the parade. Fossin sold many bracelets, brooches, and pins with animal subjects, just as he composed parures—even including tiaras—on this theme. In 1841 Delphine de Girardin declared them to be the jewels in vogue, drolly offering a long list of species comparable to the picturesque fauna found at Fossin, which began to rival symbolic animals (which had previously been the only acceptable kind). [12]

In keeping with the Romantic penchant for raw nature, wildlife predominated, ranging from birds to reptiles and from mammals to insects. A desire for realism placed the animals in their setting: a lizard would laze on a reed, while flies would settle on vine leaves. Most animals were made of chased gold with enameling to enhance the naturalist illusion. Some would be of semiprecious stones, like a glimmering little owl of labradorite or a bird of petrified palm that Jules Fossin kept for himself. Approaching the category of luxury jewelry, insects such as a gold-and-diamond butterfly studded with emeralds and rubies might grace a brooch (a motif that would enjoy a great future). High society's favorite pastime of hunting also provided the impetus for a rich gallery of heads—fox, wolf, boar, horse—and of hares, pheasants, partridges, and wild ducks, all evoking the tiny sculptures of similar inspiration brilliantly carved by hunting enthusiast Hubert Obry. One highly appealing bangle bracelet featured two heads of greyhounds.

11   Girardin, *Le vicomte de Launay*, vol. 3. p. 157.   12   *Le Furet des salons* (November 17, 1839).

Serpents

Isabelle Lucas

During the Romantic era, by far the most popular animal was the snake, making Boileau's seventeenth-century verses ring true: *Il n'est point de serpent ni de monstre odieux / Qui par l'art imité ne puisse plaire aux yeux*[1] (There is scarcely a monster or horrid snake / that will not please the eye if artfully made.) The term "fascination" seems appropriate given the impressive number of sales and the variety of designs. Men as well as women fell under the serpent's charm.

The often green enameling, the occasionally chased and engraved scales, and the sparkling, gem-studded eyes and head indicated a desire to combine a faithful reproduction of the animal with a wish to dazzle the eye with lavishness and undulating lines. The range of variations was infinite, from a modest pin with a small enameled gold snake holding a pearl to a bracelet composed of a "long snake winding two and a half times around the arm," enameled in green and set with brilliants from head to tail, with ruby eyes. A snake's suppleness notably allowed for a multitude of compositions. Fashion magazines, which noted the growing infatuation with serpents right from the Restoration, commented on the persistence of this preference even while incidentally displaying a certain irritation. "I resent fashion's exaggerated use of snakes and lizards in the finery it invents," stated *La Mode* in 1839 when describing a gown adorned with lizards, which suggested the repugnant image of a "woman delivered to the beasts."[2] At the Salon of 1847 sculptor Auguste Clésinger in fact demonstrated the danger of that connection by showing his *Woman Bitten by a Serpent*, the latter being wrapped around her arm like a bracelet. As Théophile Gautier stressed, "[Clésinger's] *Woman Bitten by a Serpent* ... caused a stir. Many groups crowded around the gracious death throes of this quivering marble, this modern Cleopatra prey to some mysterious aspic, her bare arm ringed by a bracelet by Fossin or Froment Meurice."[3]

Yet the snake's popularity has never waned, whether ascribed decorative or symbolic value. Testifying to the vitality of the naturalistic trend, its obsessive presence was rivaled only by floral and foliate themes.

1   Nicolas Boileau, *L'Art poétique* (Paris: Denys Thierry, 1674).
2   *La Mode* (June 15, 1839), p. 329.
3   Théophile Gautier, "Salon de 1848," *La Presse*, April 23, 1848.

ABOVE
Woman bitten by a snake (detail), Auguste Clésinger (1814–1883), 1847. Marble Musée d'Orsay, Paris

FACING PAGE
Study for the "Snake" bracelet ordered by Countess Le Hon, 1847. Graphite pencil, pen and black ink, watercolor wash, H. 15,2; W. 8.9 cm Chaumet Paris Collection

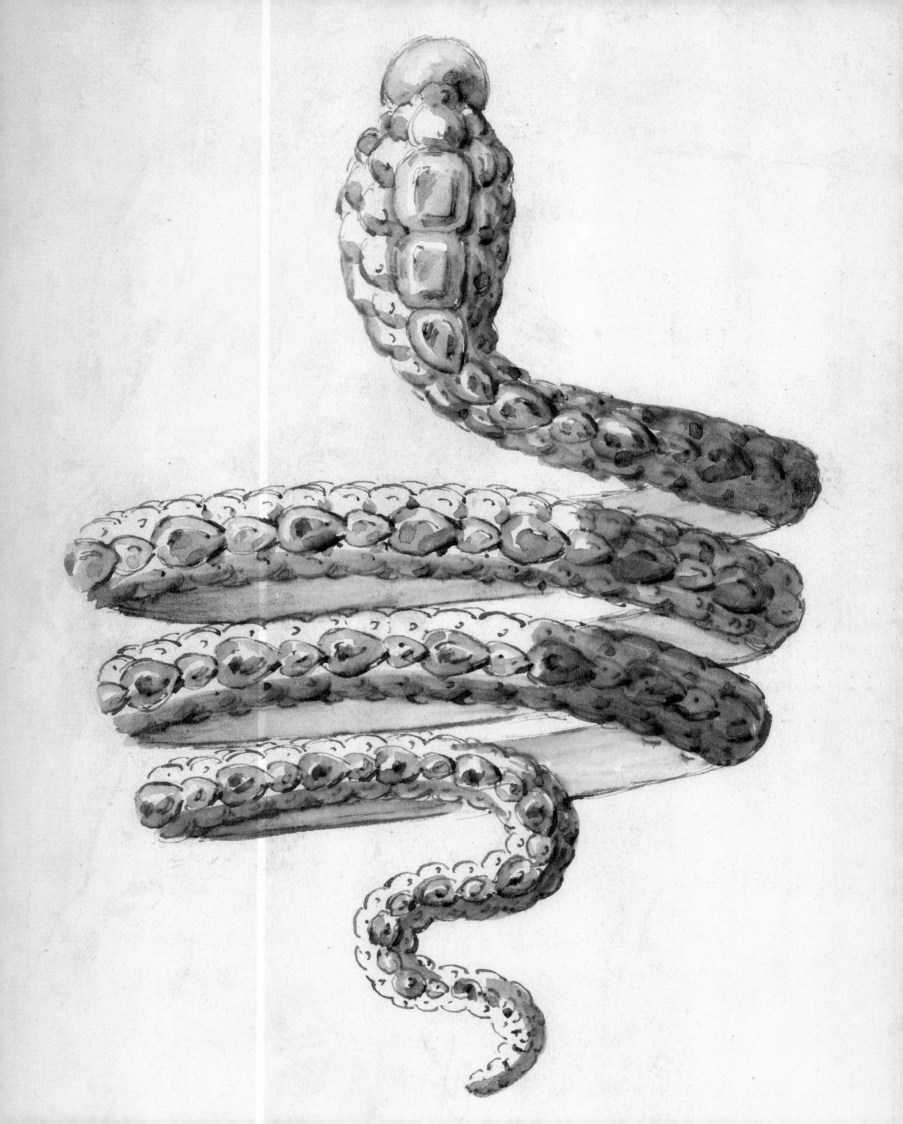

A few lines by Théodore de Banville illustrate the extent to which, in 1850, naturalistic plant life merged with the dominant trend in jewelry.

> *Voici les beaux jardins prédits by les Sibylles*
> *Feuillaisons d'émeraude et bleuets de saphir*
> *Les rubis, les bouquets de lys à fleurs mobiles*
> *Dont les gros diamants tressaillent au zéphyr.*[4]
> [Here the garden promised by the Sybil:
> sapphire the cornflower, emerald the leaves,
> with rubies and bouquets of lilies so supple,
> whose ample diamonds quiver in the breeze.]

Jean-Baptiste Fossin, an instigator of that trend marking the entire century, expressed his era's passion for plants by reviving, right from the Restoration, the art of bouquets practiced by eighteenth-century jewelers Lempeurer and Pouget. Women who emulated Empress Joséphine by taking an interest in botany, growing exotic species and developing gardens, then translated their new enthusiasm into decoration of the home and finery on the body. Coiffures of natural or artificial flowers, studded with jewels, produced a wonderful effect in the enchanting, ball-like atmosphere produced by sophisticated formal dress and a profusion of flowers enlivening every room. Noted at one society ball of 1834 were the coiffures of faithful Fossin clients such as Madame Baring, crowned in pansies and amethysts, the Duchess of Istrie, with tufts of Parma violet and red carnations, the Duchess of Montebello adorned in white roses, and the Duchess of Elchingen wearing a pink geranium tiara.[5] Devised by a few florists and manufacturers such as Fossin's famous neighbor, Batton, these fleeting creations inspired jewelers to craft parures that would make their clients sparkle at official receptions and gala events. The combination of imitation flowers and jewelry was highly appreciated. Madame d'Abrantès claimed that it was Princess Marie d'Orléans who launched the rage for garlands "in which a diamond and pearls were found in every flower."[6] Skillfully wed, the product of these two nature-inspired industries mutually enhanced one another. To this end Fossin mounted "little fragments of leaves or flowers and settings of brilliants to be used as pins with artificial flowers."[7]

In the wake of its early bouquets, Fossin's talents as designer and master jeweler led to the constant invention of new, lighter, and more natural models, thereby spurring imitators. By 1830 *La Mode* enthused that "everywhere topazes, emeralds, rubies, and diamonds were ingeniously combined and set by Fossin's inimitable art to reproduce the many diverse forms of garlands, flowers, bouquets, and bowknots."[8] The firm's international reputation won it fabulous orders for lavish jewelry as wedding gifts.

4   Théodore de Banville, "Le Palais de la Mode" (January
     1850), from *Le sang de la coupe*, in *Poésies complètes
     de Théodore de Banville* (Paris: Poulet-Malassis et de
     Broise, 1857), p. 363.
5   "Un raout chez la Mode," *L'Écho du commerce*

(September 28, 1834).
6   Laure Junot d'Abrantès, "Modes," *La Sylphide* (1840), p. 50.
7   Invoice ledger D, fol. 143, Chaumet Archives.
8   Quoted in Diana Scarisbricke, *Chaumet: Master Jewelers
     Since 1780* (Paris: Alain de Gourcuff, 1995), p. 85.

LEFT
Ary Scheffer (1795–1858),
*Princess Marie
of Orléans*, 1831.
Oil on canvas
Musée de la Vie
Romantique, Paris

FACING PAGE
*"Eglantine and
jasmine flowers" tiara*,
Jean-Baptiste Fossin
(1786–1848), c. 1830.
Gold, silver, and diamonds,
H. 8.9; W. 20.3 cm
Collection of the
Duke of Bedford

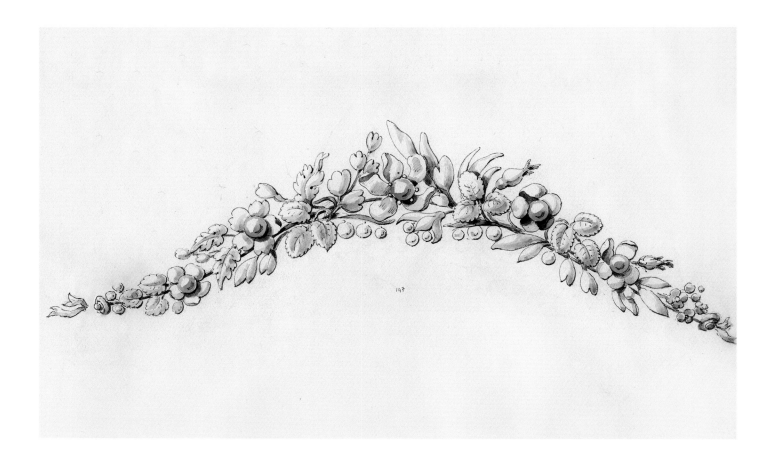

ABOVE

Design for a naturalistic tiara, c. 1830.
Graphite pencil,
pen and black ink,
ink and watercolor wash,
H. 28; W. 41.2 cm
Chaumet Paris Collection

"Large, bold sprigs of foliage" structured bandeaus, garlands, and opulent *sévignés*, whereas flowers and cluster of leaves ringed tiaras, culminating in a central motif.[18] The most highly requested types of foliage were chestnut, vine, and ivy leaves, whose jagged shapes were very decorative. In this respect, one unusual item was an imposing coiffure of two large mangrove branches of differing size, connected by a "shoot with buds and little leaves passing over the head"; it was made for Comte Bresson's wedding in 1842.[19] The wild leaves and creepers favored by some clients remain enigmatic, but an allusion to "crumpled leaves" testifies to a desire to display the entire life cycle of vegetation. There were many head ornaments featuring buds and leaves of roses or their wild cousin, eglantine. Whereas the Duke of Bedford chose a tiara that combined leaves and buds of eglantine with starry florets of jasmine, the Marquise of Alcañices preferred one entirely of jasmine, while the Marquise of Miraflores (wife of the Spanish ambassador) ordered a garland that generously included five eglantine flowers, fifteen buds, and eighteen large leaves, with smaller ones at the ends. Reeds were not only suitable for head ornaments, but their cylindrical tufts also suited other foliage in composite bouquets, notably in a popular large *sévigné* of "meadow flowers and leaves." Similarly, garlands and bouquets for the bust combined flowers with classical ears of wheat, thereby remaining aloof from the whims of fashion.

Unfortunately, very few of these pieces have survived, but preparatory drawings, along with invoice ledgers, confirm the popularity of the plant kingdom. A multitude of

18   Eugène Fontenay, *Les Bijoux anciens et modernes*
     (Paris: Société d'Encouragement pour la Propagation
     des Livres d'Art, 1887), p. 371.
19   Invoice ledger C, fol. 382, Chaumet Archives.

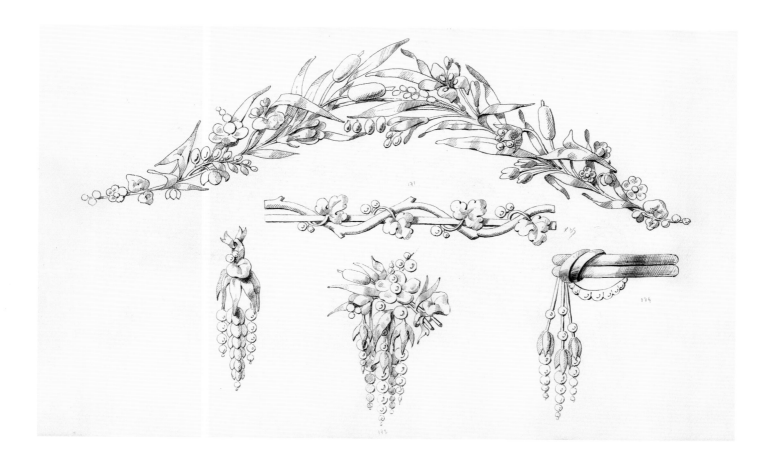

sketches provide precious examples of the infinite variety of the way motifs were arranged. Tiny variations occasionally reveal the skill of the designer, whose sure eye allowed his free hand to seek new harmonies of shapes. Having observed the specific character of each plant, the designer could exploit its least particularity, favoring its natural arrangement when composing and mutually underscoring combinations. The supreme art of these tiaras and garlands with their supple, intertwining vegetation lies in the fact that they could be broken down, so that their component parts could be used either individually (say, as a pin) or jointly in a new composition (corsage bouquet or side comb) that retained the original visual harmony.

Luxurious brooches gave blossom to many other flowers, executed in brilliants: convolvulus, daisy, campanula, fuchsia, hollyhock, cactus, heliotrope, and camellia. Most popular of all were ruby-and-diamond eglantines. Meanwhile, a purple-enameled violet of gold with a leaf of pavé-set brilliants from which dangled a briolette diamond was set on a pin for Prince Mikhail Galitzin in 1842, thereby merging the characteristics of exclusive jewelry and costume jewelry to highly realistic effect. Such was the goal sought by clients, as expressed by Madame Sieyès to Jules Fossin when she ordered a pair of pins, each of which was "to be a violet perfectly imitating nature."[20]

Costume jewelry employed the newly revived techniques of chasing and enameling, which, when combined with various other materials, produced works of

FACING PAGE

"Fuchsias" brooch,
attributed to Fossin,
c. 1840.
Silver, gold, diamonds
with briolette drops,
H. 6.5; W. 5; D. 1.5 cm
Private Collection

ABOVE

*Brooch and bracelet
from the "Bunch of
grapes" set,* c. 1850.
Gold, mauve pearls,
emeralds. Bracelet: H. 6.5;
W. 6.5; D. 2 cm. Brooch:
H. 2.8; W. 4.1; D. 1.8 cm
Private Collection

illusionistic naturalism. A large, hundred-petaled rose of stained ivory, lilies of the valley and orange flowers of white agate, convolvulus of white shell, and geranium flowers of opal testify to the ingenious resources employed to depict flowers blossoming on brooches, while enamel in a wide range of shades was used in much of the jewelry with foliate motifs. Fruit could yield delightful compositions, from sorb with coral berries to a golden orange with enameled leaves, used as an incense burner. Chestnuts had half-open burs, while strawberries and gooseberries nestled in their leaves, yet the most favored combination of fruit and leaves remained the vine, with grapes usually of pearls or garnets, ranging from a modest pin to the most magnificent tiara. Honoré de Balzac stressed their realism in his description of the coiffure worn by one of his characters in mourning: "In her hair she wore bunches of jet grapes, of the finest workmanship, part of a complete set of ornaments ordered at Fossin's.... The leaves were thin flakes of stamped iron, light as real vine-leaves, and the artist had not forgotten the little graceful tendrils that clung among her curls, as vine tendrils cling to every branch."[21]

The concern to convey faithfully the specificities of the plant kingdom extended to wood. Sometimes mention is made of the specific variety of wood, whose bark, knots, and sprouts supplied the motifs for bracelets of chased gold. Sometimes endowed with leaves, sometimes imitating a section of dead wood, composed of a single or two entwined

21   Honoré de Balzac, *The Government Clerks,*
trans. James Waring (London: Society of English
Bibliophilists, 1901), pp. 332–33.

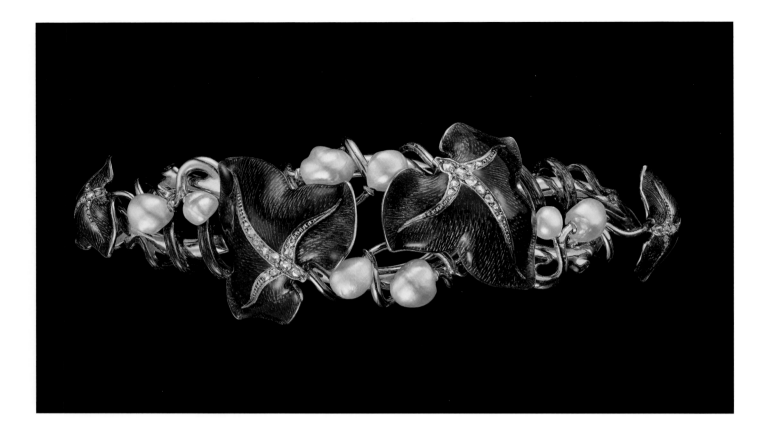

branches, these popular figures were among the most typical designs as the July Monarchy neared its end.

Draped in exuberant foliage and fronds, Romantic women willingly posed as modern Daphnes. Whereas the nymph Daphne physically fled Apollo's amorous embrace, Madame de Mortsauf, the protagonist of Balzac's *Lily of the Valley*, rejected Félix de Vandenesse's advances through the device of unusual bouquets of wildflowers, each of which had a symbolic meaning. Through them Balzac elaborated a poetic, sensual language of flowers unrelated to the traditional code found in fashionable magazines that listed the symbolism of flowers. His contemporaries, however, seeking to express their feelings via this sentimental botany—realized by jewelers at their request—focused their attention on a limited number of flowers of tried-and-true symbolic meaning. Ivy's association with "unshakeable attachment" explains its popularity, for it adorned both minor items and costly gems. The motto *Toujours la même* (Always the same) accompanying the pansy set in the middle of a medallion ordered by Baron Paulin sums up the significance of that flower. Likewise, it is no coincidence that Édouard Boucher asked Fossin to send two pins bearing forget-me-nots to his wife, who was abroad at the time.

This passionate interest in the plant kingdom crept into every nook and cranny of daily life, yet it represented just a small part of the vast palette used for expressing feelings or "sentiment."

ABOVE
"Ivy leaf" bracelet,
Fossin, 1847.
Gold, green enamel,
diamonds, and
fine baroque pearls,
H. 7; W. 7.8; D. 2.5 cm
Chaumet Paris Collection

FACING PAGE
Designs of bracelets.
Graphite pencil, pen
and black ink, gouache,
H. 37; W. 53 cm
Chaumet Paris Collection

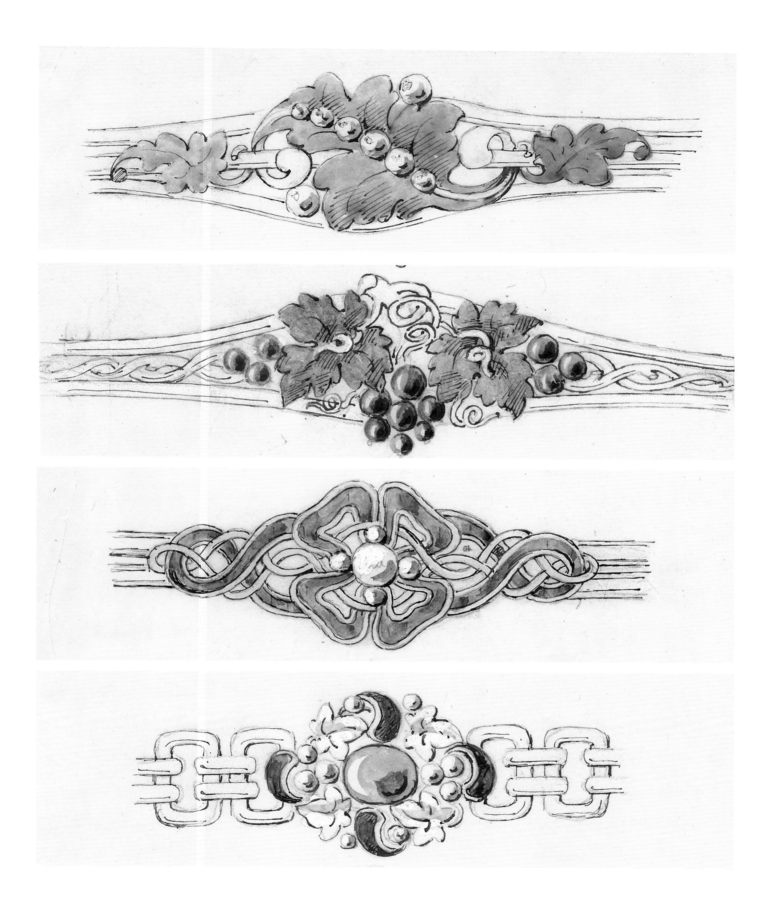

JEWELS OF SENTIMENT

Romanticism heralded the reign of heart and imagination, unleashing a powerful flood of feelings. Passion that remained unfilled due to adverse fate became a favorite theme of art, reviving famous pairs of star-crossed lovers such as Romeo and Juliet and Héloïse and Abélard. A long tradition of "jewels of sentiment" found fertile soil in the opinion that "of all countries, France is certainly the one where love, that science so useful and important to the happiness of men, has always been best understood and most encouraged."[22] Jewelers had the delicate task of crafting precious memorials to the attachments that mark an entire life. The emotional charge associated with these jewels reveals the power of the feelings that produced them. "I cannot dismiss an anxiety that my superstition makes all the greater. The turquoise fell off my ring yesterday, and this morning my pin broke. It would seem that all the signs of your affection are cracking," lamented a gentleman in 1816 to a beloved who sent him no news of herself.[23]

Gifts from thoughtful spouses were cherished above all. In 1849 Madame de La Faulotte had Fossin reset a jewelry set and bracelet made by the firm "because [her] husband had given them to [her] as a surprise," she wrote.[24] Judge Alexandre was also fond of ordering "little marital surprises" from Fossin.[25] Similarly, Alfred de Vaudreuil acknowledged that he "wanted to surprise" his wife but failed to keep the secret of a bracelet for her birthday in 1832.[26] In addition to the date of the event, the adoring diplomat wanted to have it inscribed with the motto on his ring, "Though far, not absent," suited to a profession that took him away from home. The completed bracelet, a joint symphony orchestrated by Fossin, found favor with the recipient and concretized the young couple's loving intimacy.

Dates, monograms, names, messages, dedications, Biblical quotations, and mottos are what turned these jewels into emblems of love, family, and friendship, sealed by fate. From a simple word etched on a ring—like the promise *Sempre* (Forever) carved on jasper— to the complex phrase adorning a bracelet, multiple variations reflected the wishes of highly diverse clients. The affliction accompanying the loss of a loved one might be transferred to a jewel, worn regularly (or constantly) in memory. *Nous nous reverrons* (We shall meet again) asserted one Aline Bocher, who had it engraved on the gold medallion that hung from a bracelet she ordered one month following the death of her younger son. She even designed the clasp, which expressed her sorrow (*Pauvre mère, que je souffre*—Poor mother, how I suffer) along with the place and date of death (*Passy 31 Mai 1849*).[27] The same inscription was engraved on the back of medallions given to the child's relatives and friends, whom she urged not to forget: *Frère souviens-toi* (Remember, Brother).[28] Such inscriptions might be chased, enameled, written in tiny diamonds, or simply engraved, especially when hidden from sight. The vast range of stones available to jewelers could on occasion replace inscriptions, imparting

22 Rey de Foresta, "De l'amour depuis la Charte," *La Mode* vol. 3, no. 12 (1830), p. 290.

23 Letter from Charles de Flahaut to Margaret Mercer Elphinstone, December 8, 1816. Flahaut Collection, Archives Nationales, Paris.

24 Correspondence 1849, Chaumet Archives.

25 Ibid.

26 Letters from Alfred Rigaud, Viscount of Vaudreuil, to his wife in 1832. Acquisitions Extraordinaires (acquisitions 1990–92), vol. 15, Archives du Ministère des Affaires étrangères, La Courneuve.

27 Correspondence 1849, Chaumet Archives.

28 Ibid., 1851.

messages through the combination of the first letters of their names. This technique, derived from poetic acrostics, combined the pleasure of rich colors with the keen appeal of a coded message; it was favored when indicating names, usually alone when applied to rings and pins, or conjoined when on a bracelet, such as one ordered by the Countess of Beaumont in 1840 to spell out the names of her three sons.

A jewel of sentiment was often designed to hold a commemorative item. Chevalier Longo wrote a message on a small piece of paper and had it set in a medallion whose sturdy chain and clasp he praised, because those tiny items were often used on an everyday basis. A Madame d'Anglade, when inquiring about the cost of a bracelet in plain gold, stipulated that it was "to be worn always" and must be "so arranged as to contain [locks of] hair."

"How delightful to run your fingers through the beautiful hair of a loved one's head!" exclaimed the author of an article on hair in 1830.[29] Admired for its color, texture, and opulence, hair has always been a wonderful sign of sensuality and seduction. Sturdy and imperishable, hair can also be braided and incorporated into much-appreciated pieces of jewelry. In 1850, the Countess of Hautpoul ordered a chain from Fossin for which she stressed that she had sent "enough hair for it to placed the entire length, as advantageously as possible."[30] Most orders, however, were for bracelets. The braid, given a clasp adorned with a sentimental motif or motto, often held medallions that contained more hair, as exemplified by an order from 1841: "bracelet large braid of hair, chased engraved padlock, five heart pendants that open with crystal interiors for hair."[31]

Indeed, the most common use of hair in jewelry came in the form of a lock of hair placed in the hollow of a ring, brooch, locket, or bracelet. Precious hair, which earned the same fond attachment whether it belonged to the living or the dead, was a good spur to business: Fossin met its clientele's wishes, seeking to devise suitable settings for these private marks of affection past or present. There emerged a multitude of models, from a sober "crystal brooch for hair" ringed with a double band of polished gold, to a lavish medallion-brooch crowned by a large bow of chased, engraved gold studded with emeralds, rubies, brilliants, and pearls, (the two crystal faces of the medallion held a portrait on one side and an lock of hair—bound by a tie of roses—on the other). In 1841 Prince Galitzin demonstrated his attachment to the person whose hair he obtained by having symbolic decoration of ivy leaves of chased gold surround the crystal enclosing the hair. Hair was cherished just as much as the loved one, having been part of him or her, which is why the loss of the deceased's hair due to a defect in the compartment earned Fossin bitter reproaches from a Madame Pinatel. After the accidental death of the heir to the throne, the Duke of Orléans, in 1842, Princess Adélaïde agreed to give a few of her nephew's "darling hairs" to the Countess of Flahaut in the name of friendship and in strictest secrecy, since "we do not give them to anyone."[32] She sent them in a little locket engraved with the initials FO (Ferdinand d'Orléans) accompanied by a portrait of the duke by Eugène Lami and an engraving of a portrait painted by Ingres. The death of a beloved relative or friend often also led to a quest for a depiction of his or her features done while still alive.

FACING PAGE, TOP
Study for an armorial wedding bracelet, 1844. Graphite pencil, pen and brown ink
Chaumet Paris Collection

FACING PAGE, CENTER AND BOTTOM
Studies for jewels of sentiment: bracelets with souvenir inscription and motto, bracelet made up of a series of rings. Graphite pencil, pen and black ink, gouache, ink wash
Chaumet Paris Collection

29   Auger, "De la chevelure," *La Mode* vol. 4, no. 5 (1830), p. 118.

30   Correspondence 1850, Chaumet Archives.

31   Invoice ledger C, fol. 337, Chaumet Archives.

32   Letters from Adélaïde d'Orléans to Margaret de Flahaut, August 20 and September 27, 1842. Flahaut Collection, Archives Nationales, Paris.

Miniature portraiture was thus a favored medium of commemoration, and played a historic role in the design of jewelry of sentiment. The large number of artists who exhibited this specialty at the Salons demonstrates the vigorous demand for it, which only declined as the century progressed, once it met competition from daguerreotypes and then photography.[33] Yet the art of miniatures long retained its aficionados. "Handled with great wit, it speaks to the heart and reflects personal feelings," which made a miniature the best ally of a piece of jewelry seeking the same effect. Furthermore, its "smallness enables even the untrained eye to grasp the most minute of details,"[34] favoring an attentive gaze that seeks to discern everything recalling the sitter's behavior, beyond mere physical resemblance. These portraits were commonly adapted to several types of jewelry, usually brooches and bracelets. Thus in 1842 the Count of Béarn ordered a bracelet whose central piece could be detached to form a brooch. It pivoted, showing on one side rose-cut diamonds set on a blue enamel base and on the other a portrait of a child, which could also be mounted on a brooch that had been ordered at the same time. The visibility of pictures could range from the ostentation of a bracelet bearing eight gold portrait frames held by two angels (made for a Monsieur Mignon in 1843) to the discretion of a very tiny portrait set in a ring and "surrounded by choice rose-cut diamonds," made for the Princess of Lieven in 1844. Sometimes the portrait was hidden from view. Like the locks of hair with which it was often associated, a miniature could celebrate an individual or an entire family.

Portrait cameos, especially engraved-shell versions, were an attractive alternative to a miniature portrait for many clients, although few seemed as enamored of them as the Countess of Toreno, who over a period of two months in 1841 had several—of various individuals and various sizes—set in no fewer than four brooches, two bracelets, and even a tortoiseshell comb adorned with foliage of rose-cut diamonds against pale blue enamel, in the middle of which stood a large portrait cameo ringed by brilliants.

As a vestige of a highly cherished bond, sometimes an item of jewelry becomes an object of special devotion. Evoking a private life, it is placed inside another jewel, which the owner can wear without exposing it to the eyes of others. The Count of Chardonnet therefore ordered a "ring with hinge containing an old wedding ring."[35] In the same spirit, Jules van Praet, minister in the royal Belgian household, ordered a "seal ring that opens to hold a turquoise ring that can be removed and worn separately."[36]

The inclusion of personal relics, fragments, and depictions supplied by the client immediately defines an item as a jewel of sentiment through the emotional relationship it embodies. That category also includes other things, however, resulting from the choice of symbolic motifs hallowed by tradition. First among them is the heart, which tradition views as the seat of affections and which has always had strong appeal. Many pendant-type lockets are heart-shaped. As an expression of love and marital happiness, hearts also adorn many wedding gifts. That was the case of a heart-shaped flaming-urn medallion, with its flame

33   Francis Wey, "Courtes réflexions sur l'exposition de   35   Invoice ledger D, fol. 311, Chaumet Archives.
        1850," *La Lumière* (February 9, 1851).   36   Ibid., fol. 55.

34   F. Miel, *Essai sur le Salon de 1817* (Paris: L'Imprimerie de
        Didot le Jeune), p. 328.

drawn in rose-cut diamonds against a blue enamel base, dangling from a bracelet composed of two strands of chain, bought by Héléna Fould in 1844. Conveying friendship as well as family ties, the heart shape was used for two pendants on which, in December of that same year, Countess Le Hon etched her own initials and those of her sister (Emilie Fontenilliat), then set them with flowers of rose-cut diamonds. The two pendants were attached to identical bracelets, suggesting that she intended to give one of them to her sister as a new year's present.

The snake was a latecomer to the sentimental repertoire, but quickly won lasting appreciation, whether it formed the perfect circle of *ouroboros* (a refined image of eternal love) or whether it entwined a companion to suggest the union of a couple (as seen on a chased gold ring owned by the Count of Kergariou, with two engraved dates, suggesting the anniversary of a meeting or a wedding).

More original, although based on ancient symbolism, was the declaration of love made by the Duke of Frias when in 1842 he ordered a pair of earrings set with a brilliant: from one ring hung a heart-shaped padlock, and from the other hung the key, both being pavé-set with rose-cut diamonds.

Steeped in a sentimentality that affected all artistic trends, the Romantic period favored the creative vitality of jewelry that expressed a range of emotions. Although these pieces bowed to the conventions of symbolic ornament, people of the day expressed powerful, sincere feelings when ordering them. Whether flaunted or hidden, gazed upon with delight or regret, given out of fondness or sometimes destroyed out of anger or despair, Romantic jewelry faithfully reflected the power of feelings and the importance placed on them, something that literature—another mirror of that intense epoch—depicted with the touch of truth.

Fossin and Literature

Romain Condamine

*"Before the sublime Fossin deigned to abandon tiaras and princely
crowns in order to set the pebbles collected by your daughter,
I had to do much begging and beseeching, often leaving
my retreat where I am trying to set wretched sentences….
Fossin is a King, a power, and when one wants things done well,
one must kiss the devil's claw known as patience."*

—Balzac, Letter to Madame Hanska, 1833

It is surprising to note the extent to which mid-nineteenth-century literature is dotted with references to Fossin, more than any other Parisian jeweler. Contemporaries were clearly fascinated with the work done by Nitot's successors, Jean-Baptiste and Jules-Jean-François Fossin, then located on Rue de Richelieu. For aesthetes, their jewelry was always synonymous with high standards of excellence, and seemed always connected, in the minds of both writers and readers, with a certain elitism, an image probably linked to the personalities of Fossin the elder and younger. That is what Balzac suggested in a letter he wrote to his lover, Countess Hanska, in 1833: "Before the sublime Fossin deigned to abandon tiaras and princely crowns in order to set the pebbles collected by your daughter, I had to do much begging and beseeching, often leaving my retreat where I am trying to set wretched sentences." Balzac added a lesson in perseverance for anyone who wanted to address the jeweler: "Fossin is a King, a power, and when one wants things done well, one must kiss the devil's claw known as patience."[1] In the minds of readers, the majestic Fossin was also the only jeweler who could legitimately distribute regalia and other symbols of power. Thus Countess Dash, who regularly collaborated with Alexandre Dumas, chose Fossin as the jeweler of the great and powerful in her 1863 novel *La Marquise sanglante (The Bloody Marchioness)*. There she had Fossin furnish the mark of sovereignty by delivering a coronet to Mademoiselle de Chamarante.

"Shortly before dinner, a clerk from Fossin brought a huge box, with orders to deliver it to Mademoiselle de Chamarante. She hastened to open it, and remained stunned before the most wonderful piece of jewelry ever seen…. 'Madness! Monsieur, the coronet of a marchioness! A real marchioness's coronet!' …"

"Her cousin, the young Count Robert de Chamarante added, 'You shall be, cousin, like the princesses of England at the coronation, with the coronet of your House on your head.'"[2]

The exceptional stature acquired by Fossin in reality as well as in literature made their jewelry the perfect lure for ladies, the present that any romantic suitor must give, accepting his

1   Letter from Balzac to Countess Ewelina Hanska, dated
     November 13, 1833. Spoelberch-Lavenjoul Collection,
     Bibliothèque de l'Institut de France, Paris.
2   Countess Dash (Gabrielle-Anna de Cisternes), *La
     marquise sanglante* (Paris: Lécrivain et Toubon, 1863), p. 3.

subjugation to feminine whims. That was the case of a poor Alfred de Musset character, Tristan, who sought to reconquer the indifferent Javotte by earnestly asking: "Tell me, will you permit me to go this very instant to Fossin, to buy a bracelet, or chain, or ring, whatever you like, whatever may please you ... according to your desire?"[3] The unlucky suitor, who had a turquoise-studded chatelaine delivered to Javotte, was killed in a brawl before he even received the young lady's reply.

In the theater, a play by Victor du Hamel called *Le bonheur chez soi (Happiness at Home)* has the character of Henri de Breuilpont attempt to seduce the young widow Cécile de Nervale with a bracelet by Fossin, "the perfect jeweler." It was chosen "from among countless items, true artistic masterpieces."[4] Baron de Neutitschein, the protagonist of Alphonse Royer's 1832 tale "Braunsberg le charbonnier" (Braunsberg the Coalman) did likewise when smitten by a young lady who was already betrothed. After having the pair of lovers followed, the baron "waited until the young man had left before sending the necklace, which Fossin had just set in a marvelous way. It had only two strands, but the stones were so beautiful, so dazzling, that their sparkle was probably unmatched even by the apple of Eden that tempted the first woman." Encountering yet another rejection by the lady,

the baron stubbornly persisted. "The next day Fossin delivered the necklace to the townhouse. A third strand of diamonds had been added to it. The stones in this strand far surpassed in size the ones in the first.... Their water was magnificent.... The baron smiled and sent his valet to the home of the young lady" who wound up accepting the gift—but only to send it back to the "famous jeweler" whose "honesty" she trusted, hoping to get "six thousand francs" for it so that she could pay a "debt of honor" contracted by her brother.[5]

Although literature usually presented the jeweler as a kind of deified sovereign lord whom common mortals must revere and praise, similarly turning Fossin's jewels into heaven-sent manna designed to seduce, it did not overlook the poetic naturalism of the forms fashioned by the firm. This naturalist style, developed by the Fossins and more extensively exploited by Joseph Chaumet at the turn of the century, was often identified and described with great accuracy, notably by Balzac. In the press, too, Balzac—defending Victor Hugo and his play *Hernani*—informed any classicists who wished to listen that the play "will prove true, for it has Monsieur de Vigny's trueness, a poetic trueness that must be orchestrated, resembling reality the way Fossin's floral gems resemble flowers in the field."[6]

3   Alfred de Musset, "The Secret of Javotte," in *The Complete Writings*, trans. Raoul Pellissier (New York: Edwin C. Hill, 1905), vol. 7, p. 168.

4   Victor du Hamel, *Le bonheur chez soi, comédie en un acte et en vers* (Paris: Charlieu, 1858), p. 12.

5   Alphonse Royer, "Braunsberg le charbonnier," *Revue des Deux Mondes* (Paris: Editions de la Revue des Deux Mondes, 1832), vol. 6, pp. 210–11.

6   Honoré de Balzac, *"Hernani ou l'honneur Castillant,* drame par Victor Hugo," *Le feuilleton des journaux politiques* (March 24, 1830), n.p.

ABOVE
Designs of bracelets. Graphite pencil, pen and black ink, gouache, H. 37; W. 53 cm
Chaumet Paris Collection

FACING PAGE
"Bunch of grapes" set, c. 1850. *Study for a centerpiece*, detail of a candelabra with vine stock and putti with bunches of grapes, design by Morel & Cie., c. 1845.

SECOND-EMPIRE ECLECTICISM

Karine Huguenaud and Isabelle Lucas

After having swept through the decorative arts during the Romantic period, the penchant for reviving historic styles became more intense, serving as a crucible in which all influences were mixed. Historicism became eclecticism. Jewelry was inevitably affected by this key artistic trend of the July Monarchy (1830–48) and Second Empire (1852–70). Jean-Valentin Morel's determination to rekindle the spirit of antiquity and to equal not only Renaissance masters but also those of the seventeenth and eighteenth centuries made him a worthy representative of this eclecticism. His enormous talents as goldsmith and stoneworker earned him the unflagging support of several enlightened patrons throughout his chaotic career. One such patron was the Duke of Luynes, who in 1853 commissioned a watch from Morel that was greatly admired at the Universal Exposition of 1855. Fossin, who delivered many items of jewelry to the future Empress Eugénie—including the wedding rings for her marriage to Napoleon III—recognized Morel's talents and ultimately transferred the firm to Morel and his son Prosper.

Jean-Valentin Morel, Inspired Goldsmith and Stoneworker

Karine Huguenaud

Jean-Valentin Morel devoted his entire career to advances in French precious metalwork, jewelry, and stonework. His was a life of sweat and passion designed to revive and perfect the luxury trades, transcending technical constraints and overcoming all difficulties of execution. "Morel has undergone every degree of apprenticeship, has practiced very known technique, has even rediscovered several that were lost and terribly mourned, and has thus become the most skillful goldsmith-jeweler France has ever had."[1] Those are the terms of praise used in the report of the French commission to the Great Exhibition held in London in 1851 to describe the man whose sole ambition was to make true works of art. The technical virtuosity and magnificence of the pieces that left his workshop—cups, ewers, and vases of precious materials—were the pride of the collections of the great aesthetes and patrons who supported him, such as Prince Mikhail Kotchoubey, the banker Henry Thomas Hope, and the Duke of Luynes. "True connoisseurs, the ones who can legitimately claim to be friends of the arts, have always come to me and kept me at work," Morel liked to say.[2]

Morel long worked for Fossin, being head of the workshop from 1834 to 1842. That is where he nurtured his ambition with respect to the precious metalwork and vessels of hardstone with enameled gold mounts that made his reputation. By studying masterpieces of the past, and through a desire to rival the English goldsmiths who were then dominating European decorative arts, Morel revived the repoussé technique in 1836 for a cup made for the Rothschilds. He and Fossin also crafted the hilt of the sword for the Count of Paris, a masterpiece of Paris goldsmithery made under the supervision of Froment-Meurice; the sword was given by the City of Paris to the eldest son of the Duke of Orléans, styled the Count of Paris, on the child's baptism at Notre Dame Cathedral on May 2, 1841.

An unfortunate partnership with Henri Duponchel led to Morel's exile to London in 1848, but he then began working even closer with Fossin, who trusted him enough to make him the manager of Fossin's London outlet. Later, in 1862, it was Morel's son Prosper who took over the business.

Chaumet's Archives boast several volumes of designs by Morel, containing his studies for sets of silverware and carved stone vessels. They include drawings for a monumental silver centerpiece made in 1846 for a Polish aristocrat, Prince Leon Radziwill. The various parts of the service, done in the revival taste of the day, combine a naturalist hunting scene with the depiction of a heroic deed that led to the ennobling of the Radziwill family in the thirteenth century. The incident took place in the depths of a forest in Lithuania when gamekeeper John Radziwill saved his sovereign prince Alexis from a charging boar, and was rewarded with a grant of all the land where his horn was heard. This centerpiece, which Morel considered the masterwork of his career, was admired by many people, including Tsar Nicholas II; it was composed of spectacular pieces such as six-foot-high candelabras in the form of pine trees and wine coolers decorated

1   *Exposition universelle de 1851: Travaux de la Commission française sur sur l'industrie des nations publiés par ordre de l'empereur* (Paris: Imprimerie Impériale, 1857), vol. 8, p. 209.
2   Comte Horace de Viel-Castel, "Conversation," *Le Constitutionnel*, March 19, 1854, p. 2.

FACING PAGE
Ewer,
Jean-Valentin Morel
(1794–1860) after Jean-Baptiste-Jules Klagmann
(1810–1867), 1856.
Silver,
H. 101; W.26; D. 46 cm
Musée du Louvre, Paris

with battling bears, which required the assistance of sculptors such as Alfred Jacquemart and Pierre-Alexandre Schoeneweerk. Other famous sculptors started out with, or worked for, Morel, notably Carrier Belleuse, Cain, Cavelier, Simart, and Barye, whose lion-with-snake paperweight was sold to Queen Victoria in 1849. It was with Jules Klagman that Morel produced the wine cooler depicting "drunken dreams," a key work shown at the Exposition des Produits de l'Industrie in 1844 and now in the Louvre; the original drawing by Jules Dieterle is in the Chaumet Collection. Klagman also worked on a large silver ewer of 1856. Morel

furthermore made many tea and coffee services that employed designs by ornamentist Jules Peyre and reflected the fascination with Oriental cultures—the Chinese, Turkish, Moorish, and Persian styles all heartily rivaled French classicism.

This particular chapter in the company's history, focusing on precious metalwork and artistic stonework during the July Monarchy (1830–48) and Second Empire (1852–70), continued, if less intensely, into the Belle Époque (1871–1914) under Joseph Chaumet. It was revived again in a modernist vein by designer René Morin in the second half of the twentieth century.

ABOVE

Chinese-style teapot
and cream jar,
Henri Duponchel (1794–
1868), Jean-Valentin
Morel (1794–1860),
gold and silversmith,
Jules-Constant-Jean-

Baptiste Peyre (1811–1871),
ornamentalist.
Teapot: c. 1848, H. 50;
W. 28 cm. Cream jar:
c. 1849, H. 12.5; W. 18 cm.
Gilded silver
Musée du Louvre, Paris

FACING PAGE

Cooling bucket model
from the Radziwill
centerpiece, bear fight,
Morel & Cie., c. 1846.
Graphite pencil,
H. 45; W. 30 cm
Chaumet Paris Collection

The Hope Cup

Isabelle Lucas

This imposing bloodstone cup is not just an illustration of a period taste for technical prowess and of Romanticism's encouragement of a revival of the art of fashioning precious materials. It is also Jean-Valentin Morel's most ambitious example of a magnificent work of semiprecious stone with lavish mount. It was the highlight of his display of jewelry, precious metalwork, and stonework at the Universal Exposition held in Paris in 1855. Morel strongly contributed to the rebirth of these arts, and this piece is the culmination of his patient rediscovery of old, forgotten skills. This son of a stonecutter got his start in the 1830s just as the Renaissance revival began to exercise its irresistible appeal on French artists. Reflecting the spirit of the times, Morel's determination to rival his predecessors of the sixteenth and seventeenth centuries drove him to interpret works freely, and to call upon brilliant colleagues who designed and executed the mounts for the vases and cups that Morel cut from jasper, agate, lapis lazuli, and rock crystal.

The large, spectacular Hope Cup—commissioned by English banker Henry Thomas Hope, an experienced collector and patron—flaunts a virtuosity worthy of the Renaissance even as it conveys a new vision through its careful development of a specific iconographic program (the story of Perseus freeing Andromeda) all across the enameled gold mount. Inscribed on a scroll held by a putto is the Hope family motto, alluding to steadfast hope, which perhaps influenced the choice of subject. Renaissance paintings on this theme surely influenced the style of these in-the-round figures. The design developed by Constant Sévin, full of nods in the direction of Louis XIV's collection of gems—held at the Louvre and a constant source of formal and technical inspiration to Morel and his associates (for example, the shell of the cup with its spout, the dragon that functions as the handle, the masks on the base)—eschews the whimsical decoration of historic examples in favor of a rational arrangement of motifs. The uniqueness of this masterpiece, produced in the final years of Morel's career, ensured that his name went down in the history of goldsmithery even before his protean œuvre was rediscovered.

*"This fine piece combines all the difficulties
of execution with all the exquisite delights
of elegance, good taste, and perfectly expressed ideas;
in a word, it is a work like those designed by Rosso
or executed by Benvenuto Cellini for Francis I."*

Count Horace de Viel-Castel, "Conversation," *Le Constitutionnel*, March 19, 1854, p. 1.

The Duchess of Luynes's Watch

Karine Huguenaud

Jean-Valentin Morel, who took over the Fossin business in the 1850s, earned a reputation for his enormous talent as goldsmith and stoneworker. This won him unflagging support from a few enlightened patrons throughout his chaotic career. One of those was Honoré-Théodoric-Paul-Joseph d'Albert, Duke of Luynes (1802–1867). Heir to an old family of the high French nobility, the duke was greatly respected by his contemporaries for his encyclopedic mind, and he became an enthusiastic collector of ancient art and coins, expressing his passion for antiquity through his studies on advances in archaeology. In 1862 he donated his collection to the Bibliothèque Nationale's Cabinet des Médailles; this, the largest donation in the nineteenth century, included 6,925 ancient coins, 373 ancient carved stones, cameos, and intaglios, cylinder seals and cones from the Near East, and nearly 200 pieces of Greek, Etruscan, and Roman gold jewelry uncovered at excavations in southern Italy, not to mention ceramics and sculptures.

The Duke of Luynes was not just a scholar but also had an exalted sense of beauty—he sought to revive the arts of precious materials in France by promoting techniques and skills of the past. His historical and perfectionist leanings found perfect expression in Morel. "Never will any professional obstacle stop Mr. Morel, never will he encounter one without solving it with every desired success," wrote the duke in a report he drafted for the Great Exhibition of 1851.[1]

A watch, now in the Chaumet Collection, ordered by Adèle Amys du Ponceau, Duchess of Luynes, was the product of this encounter between a demanding aesthete and a craftsman whose technical skills encouraged inventiveness. It began with preparatory drawings approved by the client, and was then apparently made in several stages. For even as the watch itself was being made, on October 4, 1853, the duke wrote a letter to accept an estimate dated September 30 for the execution of a chatelaine—or waist ornament with long chain—set with semiprecious stones and gems.[2]

A chatelaine was emblematic of a certain social rank, and was viewed as an indispensible accessory of daytime dress. It could be fixed to the waist by a pin. Several additional little chains ended in hooks for attaching all kinds of small personal items, such as keys, seals, lead pencil, scent bottle, scissors, miniature portraits, and so on. The Duchess of Luynes's matching set consisted of a brooch plus a chatelaine with three small chains holding her watch, key, and a seal, as well as the long, ornate chain of gold links, pearls, and hardstone spindle-links set with gems. The watch movement was made by Breguet, while the watch case, adorned with the duchess's monogram beneath a ducal coronet in diamonds, was a combination of bloodstone, rubies, and diamonds in a subtle composition of shapes and colors that prompted the enthusiasm of Count Horace de Viel-Castel, a famous Second Empire chronicler, when he saw it in early 1854: "We also admire a watch with its chain and hook, all set with semiprecious stones, a veritable masterpiece in which the number and variety of stones in no way diminishes its harmony."[3] These compliments from the ordinarily biting pen of Viel-Castel say much about Morel's reputation among cultivated society of the day, an admiration shared by visitors to the Universal Exposition of 1855, where the watch was exhibited.

Returned to Chaumet in the late nineteenth century for alteration, the duchess's watch and chatelaine were photographed, constituting the sole record in the company's archives of the complete, original design. The shell-shaped brooch and chatelaine no longer suited the fashion of the day, and disappeared to the benefit of the chain alone, converting the watch into a pendant more appropriate to Belle Époque taste.

1   "Industrie des métaux précieux par le duc de Luynes," Jury XXXIII, *Exposition universelle de 1851: Travaux de la Commission française sur sur l'industrie des nations publiés par ordre de l'empereur* (Paris: Imprimerie Impériale, 1854), p. 70, quoted in Isabelle Lucas *Vie et œuvre de Jean-Valentin Morel (1794-1860), orfèvre-joaillier,* Thesis for the École du Louvre, 1999, p. 58.

2   Chaumet Archives.

3   Count Horace de Viel-Castel, "Conversation," *Le Constitutionnel,* March 19, 1854, p. 2.

Watch and chain of the Duchess of Luynes and its preparatory design, Jean-Valentin Morel (1794–1860), 1853–54.

Gold, silver, rubies, sanguine jasper, diamonds, natural pearls, and enamel. Chain L. 38; D. 3 cm
Chaumet Paris Collection

Dessin de Montre

Madame la Duchesse de Luynes.

Empress Eugénie's "Clover"

Karine Huguenaud

In late December 1852, the French imperial court hummed with rumors. Napoleon III had fallen in love with a twenty-six-year-old Spanish beauty, Eugenia de Palafox Portocarrero de Guzmán, Countess of Teba, daughter of the Count and Countess of Montijo. For the past two years the young woman had been living in Paris, and the emperor wooed her assiduously with many gifts. Certain signs convinced him that they were fated to be together: during a stroll, had not their watches stopped at the same moment? Had not an exotic flower in the botanical gardens flowered for the first time since the wedding of Napoleon and Joséphine?

Charlemagne de Maupas, a prefect, personally witnessed and recounted an anecdote that was soon making the rounds.

One fine autumn morning the Emperor, accompanied by just a few people including Madame and Mademoiselle de Montijo, was strolling on the grounds of [the Château de] Compiègne. The grass was abundantly drenched in dew, and the rays of the sun gave every drop on the blades the shimmer and reflections of diamonds. Mademoiselle Eugénie de Montijo, with her highly poetic temperament,

ABOVE AND FACING PAGE

Édouard-Louis Dubufe (1819–1883), *Portrait of Empress Eugénie Wearing the "Clover" Brooch Given to Her by Napoleon III*, 1853. Oil on canvas, H. 149; W. 114 cm Musee national du Palais de Compiègne

delighted in admiring the magical, whimsical effects of the light. In particular she noted a leaf of clover so wonderfully graced with dewdrops that it looked like a real gem that had fallen from some larger jewel. Once the promenade was over, the Emperor took Baciocchi aside; a few minutes later Baciocchi left for Paris. The very next day he returned with a delightful jewel that was nothing other than a clover, each of whose leaves bore diamonds imitating dewdrops. Count Baciocchi, known for his refined taste, had commissioned an unusually perfect imitation of the clover admired by his future sovereign the day before; and shortly after his return the little clover, looking for all the world like an engagement ring, was seen on the elegant foreigner's fair breast.[1]

More precisely, it was during the Christmas lottery that Eugénie happened to receive the delicate jewel that she would henceforth wear on the middle of her chest on all occasions, as seen in a formal portrait painted by Dubufe in 1853.

The Chaumet Archives from the Fossin period contain many examples of highly fashionable three-leaf clovers made of enamel and diamonds. The clover's three leaves symbolized the Christian trinity. The devout Empress Eugénie was probably aware of this allusion but it was certainly the romantic aspect that prompted her to keep this little brooch to the end of her life. Although a modest present by the standards of the magnificent jewelry made by Chaumet for monarchs since the early nineteenth century, Eugénie's clover is a perfect embodiment of a "jewel of sentiment," for it wonderfully incarnates and expresses the charm of budding love. When, in 1906, Eugénie commissioned Chaumet to make the tiara she wished to wear at the wedding of her goddaughter, Victoria Eugenia of Battenburg, to King Alfonso XIII of Spain, she chose a highly fashionable Belle Époque design of two wings of diamonds flanking a central device that could be detached and worn as a corsage ornament—for which she chose a particularly cherished motif, namely a clover composed of three large diamonds.[2]

Eugénie's clover has come down to us via Countess Antonia d'Attainville,[3] who was the niece of the deposed empress, acting as her companion in her final years. Eugénie gave it to Antonia very late in life, perhaps upon Antonia's marriage to Pierre Lescuyer d'Attainville on June 7, 1900.[4] After her husband died in 1921, Antonia married Félix de Baciocchi-Adorno, the empress's private secretary from 1915 to 1920. In a strange twist of fate, Félix was related to the Count Baciocchi whom Napoleon III dispatched to Fossin in December 1852 to acquire the jewel conveying the emperor's feelings. Eugénie's clover brooch still belongs to their descendents.

1   Charlemagne Émile de Maupas, *Mémoires sur le Second Empire* (Paris: E. Dentu, 1885), vol. 2, pp. 16–17.
2   Invoice ledger 1905–6, folio 78; glass-plate negative no. 2906, February 24, 1906. Chaumet Archives.
3   The clover brooch excited imaginations right from the Second Empire. It has often been described as made of emeralds and diamonds, and several historians claimed that after the death in 1879 of her only son, Imperial Prince Napoleon, Empress Eugénie gave it to the Duchess of Mouchy.
4   Private archives.

ABOVE
"Clover" bracelet,
Jules Jean-François Fossin
(1808–1869), c. 1850.
Graphite pencil,
ink wash, watercolor
Chaumet Paris Collection

FACING PAGE
Empress Eugénie's "Clover"
brooch, Jules Jean-François
Fossin (1808–1869), 1852.
Translucent green
enamel and diamonds,
H. 3.7; W. 3.4 cm
Private Collection

Items Ordered by Napoleon III and Eugénie

Karine Huguenaud

Long a client of Fossin, the Countess of Montijo naturally took her daughter Eugénie—the future empress of France—to the jeweler. By an amazing coincidence, in 1851 and 1852 the two women resided at 12, Place Vendôme, in the same townhouse where Joseph Chaumet would later install the company in 1907. Among the orders recorded in the ledgers during those two years it is worth noting a diamond wreath of nine jasmine flowers, the supply of 169 pearls for a six-strand necklace, and a snake bracelet.[1] On January 6, 1853, the Countess of Montijo placed a more symbolic order for "two wedding rings of polished gold, in one Eugénie *Louis* Napoléon, in the other *Louis* Napoléon Eugénie."[2] A clover brooch purchased from Fossin on the eve of Christmas 1852 had betrayed the growing romance between Napoleon III and Eugénie and was perceived as a forerunner of engagement. And on the following January 15 he asked for her hand. Going against the tradition at European courts, Napoleon decided to marry for love. Despite hostility from his political entourage and the imperial family, who right up to the last minute advocated marriage to some royal personage, on January 22, 1853, Napoleon announced his betrothal in a famous speech delivered before senior imperial officials: "I prefer a woman I love and respect to an unknown woman with whom marriage would have had advantages mingled with sacrifices." The civil ceremony took place on January 29 in the Throne Room of the Tuileries Palace, while the religious service was held the next day, January 30, in Notre Dame Cathedral in Paris.

Witnesses noted that the empress, wearing a high gown with basques of white velvet and a tunic of Alençon lace beneath a veil and double wreath of orange flowers and brilliants, glittered with diamonds. "The tiara, the belt, etc., were indeed those worn by Marie-Louise at her coronation [*sic*], but the three great Parisian jewelers Fossin, Lemonnier, and Moïana completely altered them and added details that lent them new splendor even while retaining their overall style."[3] Wedding-related orders received by Fossin included bracelets, shoulder ornaments, corsage ornaments, and a parasol mount of green enamel studded with diamonds.[4] It was also Fossin who supplied the wedding missal that Princess Mathilde gave to Eugénie.

Despite such a promising start, Fossin remained faithful to the deposed Orléans family, and turned down the title of jeweler to the empress. He thus stood aside for Alexander-Gabriel Lemonnier (who made the monarchs' crowns) and Kramer. And yet Napoleon III continued to patronize Fossin for watches, rings, and bracelets designed to be given as gifts.

1   Invoice ledger G (1851–52), pp. 247 and 260, Chaumet Archives.
2   Ibid., p. 400.
3   Fulgence Girard, *Histoire du Second Empire* (Paris: 1861), p. 120. The Chaumet Archives contain no details on these alterations.
4   Folder on the emperor's marriage, O² 2301, Archives Nationales, Paris.

FACING PAGE

Chatelaine watch with Empress Eugénie's crowned cipher, Jules Jean-François Fossin (1808–1869), 1853. Gold, rose-cut diamonds, natural pearls, and enamel, H. 10.4 cm (watch and chatelaine); D. 3.1 cm (watch)

Musée national des châteaux de Malmaison et Bois-Préau
This chatelaine watch was a gift from Napoleon III to Empress Eugénie, who gave it to one of her ladies-in-waiting, the Countess de La Bédoyère.

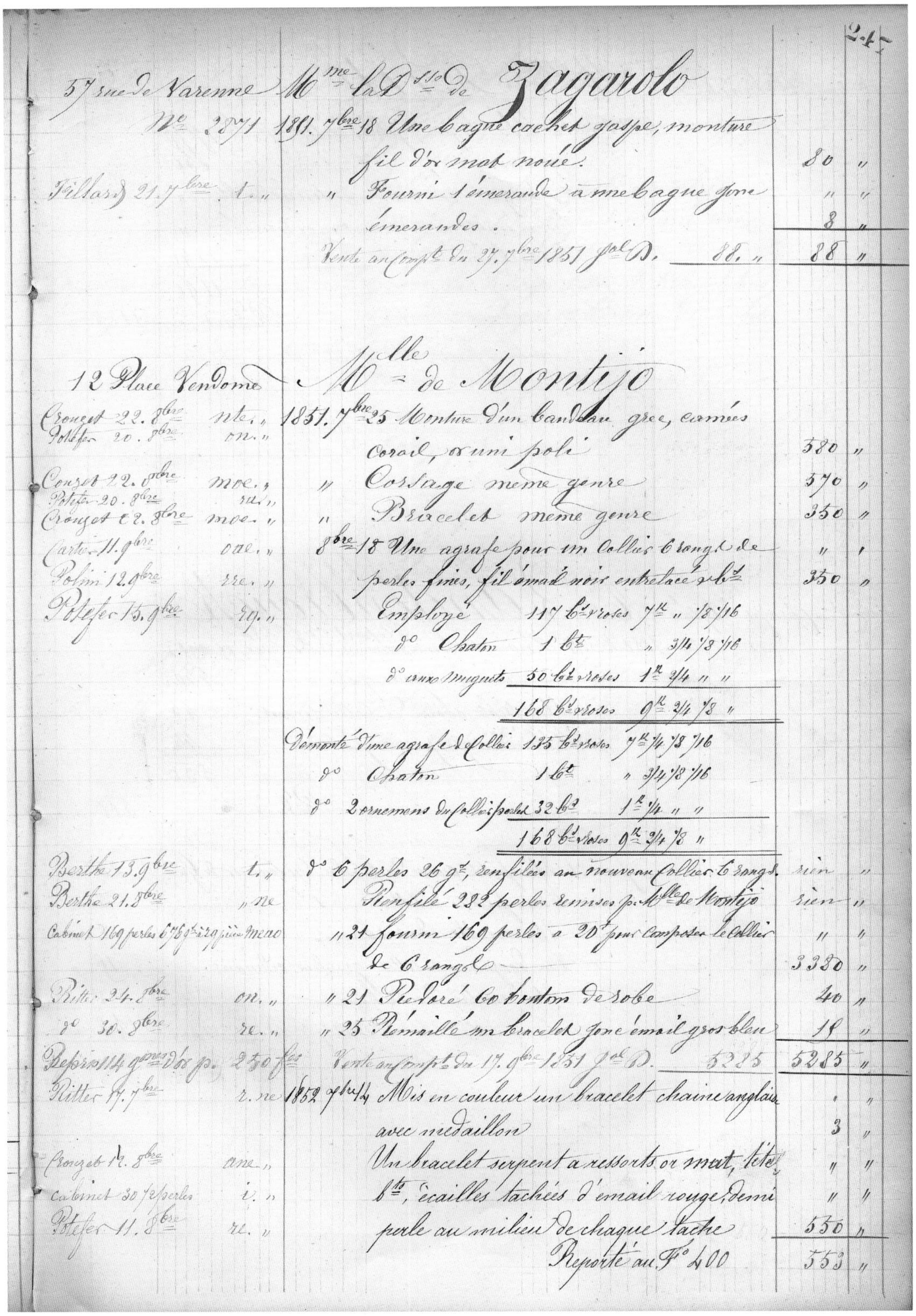

Items bought by
Mademoiselle de Montijo,
12, Place Vendôme,
September 25, 1851.
Invoice book G
1851–52, p. 247
Chaumet Archives

Items bought by
H.M. the Emperor,
Tuileries Palace,
January 3, 1853.
Invoice book G
1851–52, p. 470
Chaumet Archives

Sa Majesté l'Empereur

Aux tuilerie

N° 3504	1853 Jner 3 Un bracelet trois joncs or et brillants agraffe 3 emeraudes	2150
N° 3457	Un bracelet 7 saphirs et brillants biseau email bleu saphir	1600
N° 2668	Un bracelet trois opales anneaux email bleu turqse et bts	1850
N° 664	Un do gourmette rubis et bts	1600
N° 3086	Une epingle 8 chatons argent email noir	1600
N° 3187	Une do 8 chute bts arcades email noir	1900
N° 3198	Une do 8 chatons argent 4 griffes clous en roses	2100
N° 2785	Une do perle griffes en roses bts email turqse	230
N° 3079	Une epingle perle ronde brune	130
N° 311	Une epingle perle ronde strillé	200
Filard 4 Janvier nae "	Une epingle belle perle	650
N° 3399	Une bague perle entourée de brillants	350
N° 3832	Une do 2 rubis coeurs couronne bts	200
N° 3835	Une do beau rubis 2 bts montées a griffes	570
N° 3645	Une do beau rubis 2 kts bts ¾ ⅛ corps bts	1850
Filard 4 Janvier oan "	Une do turquoise entourée de bts	325
Filard 4 Janvier rge "	Une do perle 8 bts grains noirs	230
Ritter 31 Dbre ro	Une bague forme chapelet milieu christ	15 "
		17550 "
N° 1561	" " 25 Un bandeau grec rubis et brillants faisant	
N° 3228	plaque de collier et bracelets a volonté	
	Bracelets 7 81 bts 68 kts ¼ " 4⁄16	
	do 12 rubis 14 kts ¾ " .	
	Broche du milieu	
	36 bts 6 kts ⅛	
	1 rubis 3 kts " …	20,000 "
	" fevrier 20 7 perles rondes pour ressortir en collier	
	164 grains	6800 "

PART THREE

THE WORLD OF CHAUMET

1900: TRADITION AND INNOVATION

Philippe Thiébaut

There can be no doubt that in 1889, when Joseph Chaumet became the owner of the firm in which he had worked for some fifteen years, one of his goals was to participate in the major event on everyone's mind: the Universal Exposition to be hosted by Paris in 1900, which would mark the passage from one century to another.

The jeweler was fully aware of the stakes of these gigantic fairs that dotted the second half of the nineteenth century. Indeed, in a report he addressed in 1900 to members of the jury of the jewelry section, he used the term "serious harm" in reference to the absence of Morel & Compagnie at the 1867 Universal Exposition in Paris. This absence was in fact due solely to the scruples of Jules Fossin, who had agreed to chair the jewelry-section jury that year.

> He [Fossin] informed his successor of his desire that the latter not appear at the Exposition, so that he would not have to issue a judgment that might be suspected of bias. The abstention of Morel & Cie. caused great harm to the firm. The powerful stimulus that Universal Expositions give to the development of individual initiative would have been all the more useful in that the company's location in an apartment left it with no direct contact with public opinion. Despite Monsieur and Madame Morel's intelligent management, business became anemic; it directors realized that they would have to revive its weakened constitution by infusing it with new blood.[1]

1   *Exposition universelle de 1900. Classe 95. Joaillerie & Bijouterie. Notice sur l'origine et l'organisation actuelle de la maison J. Chaumet, successeur de Morel &* *Compagnie, présentée à Messieurs les Membres du jury,* typewritten document, undated, pp. 2–3.

Furthermore, the considerable boom in the popularity of jewelry was one of the lessons of the Universal Exposition of 1889, which had recently ended. The report on that year's jewelry section notably explained this expansion by the abundance of diamonds on the market. "Diamond jewelry, having become more affordable, is no longer the exclusive prerogative of the wealthiest classes, and affection for these gems is spreading among the middle classes; from there springs competition among jewelers."[2] Chaumet had no choice—despite an already large clientele whose loyalty he could count on, recognition in professional circles and the spread of his reputation among a wider public were dependent on his presence at the competitive exposition in the offing, where he hoped to win a prize.

Thanks to changes in the industry that gave him almost total autonomy of production by the late nineteenth century, Chaumet felt he was ready to face international juries. This fortunate decision was crowned by success, for his peers awarded a gold medal to the "new arrival." A grand prize—the supreme recompense in this kind of event—was within his grasp. And indeed in subsequent years the jeweler walked off with the grand prize on three occasions: the 1904 Louisiana Purchase Exposition in St. Louis, Missouri; the 1905 Universal Exposition in Liège, Belgium; and the 1906 International Exposition in Milan, Italy. In the meantime, the Russian government honored Chaumet with induction into the Order of Saint Anne for his involvement in the International Artistic Exposition held in St. Petersburg from December 1901 to January 1902. This event, organized by and for the benefit of the Russian Red Cross under the patronage of Her Imperial Highness Princess Eugenie of Oldenburg, featured the jewelry, precious metalworking, and enameling industries in particular.[3]

As soon as he began preparing for the 1900 exposition in Paris, Chaumet knew full well that it would be the scene of a confrontation between two camps. On one side were the partisans of Art Nouveau, the first inklings of which could be detected in the 1889 fair, notably in the kiln-related arts. On the other side were the upholders of tradition, constantly confronted by the pitfalls of pastiche and historical style. Jewelers found themselves in a particularly tricky situation in so far as the very essence of their art resides in the intrinsic beauty and financial value of the material they use—fine stones and pearls—enhanced by a setting that, however difficult to obtain, should display modesty and discretion. In contrast, the advocates of Art Nouveau jewelry felt that its beauty derived from an artistic vision in which the value of the stone was infinitely less important than the quest for a design that broke free of historical styles—a key path to that break, they felt, entailed a free and personal interpretation of nature.

For help in pursuing his reflections on the matter, Chaumet commissioned one of his employees, a designer named Wibaille, to draft a report. The handwritten, never-published document on eight large pages was delivered in July 1889.[4] It turns out to be of

2   *Exposition universelle internationale de 1889 à Paris. Rapports du jury international publiés sous la direction de M. Alfred Picard. Classe 37. Joaillerie et bijouterie.* Report by M. E. Marret, jeweler and goldsmith (Paris: Imprimerie nationale, 1891), p.25.

3   See Martial Bernard, "Exposition Internationale Artistique de Saint-Pétersbourg (1901–2)," *Revue de la Bijouterie, Joaillerie, Orfèvrerie* 22 (February 1902), pp. 345–69.

4   Recently recovered from the Chaumet Archives, this document was unavailable to Diana Scarisbrick when she wrote her authorative study, *Chaumet: Master Jewelers Since 1780* (Paris: Alain de Gourcuff, 1995).

FACING PAGE, TOP
Study for a "Naiads frightened by a sea monster" hair comb, c. 1900. Graphite pencil, pen and black ink, watercolor wash, white gouache highlights, H. 12; W. 18.8 cm Chaumet Paris Collection

FACING PAGE, BOTTOM
Study for an "Apple tree branches and snakes" choker, c. 1900. Graphite pencil, pen and black ink, watercolor wash, and gouache, H. 9.9; W. 35.5 cm Chaumet Paris Collection

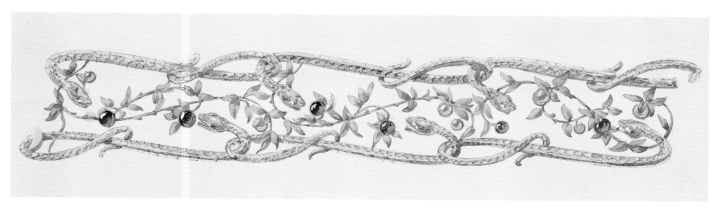

642

great interest for the objective look its author took not only at the situation of the Chaumet company but at the entire jeweler's trade at the close of a century concerned with improving life and lifestyles.[5]

Right from the start, Wibaille asserted the need to innovate. He acknowledged the pioneering role played by René Lalique in the movement toward reform:

> Five or six years ago, when the promoters of Art Nouveau—among them Lalique, who towered over them with his indisputable talent—were seeking their way and launching their first new pieces, there was a perfectly understandable stir upon the appearance of this cat among the excessively traditionalist pigeons. Indeed, the heads of jewelry firms, even leading ones, had been induced to espouse the so-called Classic style by the demands and traditions of their clientele, and did not want to hear of bold innovations, for they feared that if they strayed from their outmoded style they would upset the people who, from generation to generation, had displayed their trust by placing orders for things that are always fairly similar.[6]

Wibaille then pointed out the constraints inherent in the jeweler's trade. "[T]he range within this difficult specialty is highly limited, for the effects produced by usually similar stones are often the same, if not in shape at least in color (diamonds being the basis and principle of fine jewelry), the craftsman being obliged to use more or less the same techniques, needing to obtain the same effect by the same artifice."[7] This posed a dilemma, which Lalique's accomplishments threw into sharp relief:

> Lalique managed the exploit of creating original effects.... Everything is handled with an intense skill for effect—the line of the design is always pure, the whole piece lights up at a glance. Despite that, the fine jewelry component, properly speaking, is somewhat inferior; it would take much greater experience of this specialty to assimilate it and fully merge it into these depths of obscurity—to obtain with startlingly pure, white stones an overall effect that might be called sublime! This appears to be a dilemma, and yet it might be hoped that it could be obtained when, with aid of special tools, we will be able to reliably determine the degree of transparency of a diamond or other gemstone designed to adorn the jewel, and thus obtain, perhaps through surrounding, appropriately colored cloisons, the degree of receptiveness of beams whose power remains to be discovered.[8]

There was still no question, according to Wibaille, of imitating Lalique, but it was worth reflecting on a way of profitably riding the wave of reform he had unleashed. "It would

5   Wibaille, *Rapport adressé à monsieur Chaumet au sujet des différentes phases traversées par la Joaillerie, Bijouterie & Orfèvrerie depuis quelques années et du parti qu'il y aurait lieu d'en tirer*, dated July 12, 1899, Paris. Chaumet Archives.

6   Ibid.

7   Ibid.

8   Ibid., pp. 3–4.

FACING PAGE
Designs for a "Marsh Fairies" pendant, c. 1900. Graphite pencil, pen and India ink, ink and watercolor wash, H. 27; W. 12.4 cm Chaumet Paris Collection

PAGE 290
"Raiden, god of rain and thunder" Japanese-style brooch, c. 1900. Gold, opal, rubies, diamonds, emeralds, H. 8.5; W. 5.5 cm Chaumet Paris Collection

PAGE 291
"St. George defeating the dragon" pendant, c. 1890. Gold, cornelian cameo, diamonds, enamel, pearls, H. 12; D. 4.7 cm Chaumet Paris Collection

"The largest, most magnificent, most magical of all the jewelry
is the corsage ornament exhibited by Mr. Chaumet,
which owes its splendor less to the size and number of diamonds than
to the composition governing their use, making the water of the gems
shimmer like the waves of a waterfall, like shafts of light."

—Roger Marx

9   Wibaille, *Rapport adressé à monsieur Chaumet*, p. 6.

10   See Christie's London sale of *19th-Century Furniture and Sculpture*, November 1, 2001, lot 308. It should nevertheless be noted that whereas the head, arms, and feet of this lot are made of ivory, the list drawn up by Chaumet himself describes them as agate.

11   The list, comprising a corsage ornament, three tiaras, eight necklaces, two *plaques de cou* (choker plaques) and a brooch, figured in a report titled *Note sur les difficultés d'exécution des principales pièces exposées par M. Chaumet joaillier, subsequent to a Note sur*

l'origine et l'organisation actuelle de la maison J. Chaumet. Chaumet Archives.

12   *Note sur les difficultés d'exécution...*, p. 9.

13   *Ibid.*, p. 9. "No. 7. The waterfall corsage ornament overcomes the difficulty of imitating the lightness and movement of water in metal: the waves of water in brilliants are edged with caliber-cut emeralds to obtain watery reflections. No. 8. The waterfall tiara presents the same difficulty; the drops of water are represented by briolette-cut diamonds." The whereabouts of these pieces is unknown. Several photographs in the Chaumet

"Waterfall" corsage
ornament shown at the
1900 World's Fair.
Matte paper print from
gelatin silver bromide glass
negative, H. 30; W. 40 cm
Chaumet Paris Collection

be pointless, from every angle, to slavishly copy Lalique, as many of his denigrators have thought it necessary to do, but rather to profit from the new situation he has created almost without meaning to. Indeed, everything that appeared extremely bold—overly bold—a few years ago, now seems natural today. This situation would seem to indicate, in short, that it might be possible to find in so-called Art Nouveau documents many flattering arrangements from the standpoint of these special optics, above all independent of any specific style yet with a boldness that never excludes good taste, and whose new manufacturing techniques will facilitate the development of this new style." [9]

The quest for designs that would respect the craft's technical demands (which could in no way be compromised), while displaying a novelty arising from a rejection of allegiance to any given style, culminated in several pieces made for the Universal Exposition. Alongside a demonstration of astonishing skill in the form of five sacred and secular objets d'art, including the famous *Christus Vincit* and an allegorical figure of France,[10] the display of jewelry featured fifteen items that Chaumet himself drew to the attention of the jury.[11] The jeweler stated that his work was notable above all for the quality of its gems and pearls, for the lightness and refinement of its settings, and for its supple assembly.[12] It was certainly thanks to meticulous work on settings and assemblies that the design came to life, ridding the jewel of the weighty inertia specific to the pastiche of historical styles. A "waterfall" corsage ornament and tiara[13] were certainly the pieces the most emblematic of Chaumet's new approach, which observers appreciated. The official jury report, written by Paul Soufflot, mentioned "a waterfall corsage ornament and tiara of quite technical execution, another ribbon tiara, [and] a surprisingly flexible ruby-and-diamond choker, its flexibility obtained through numerous meshes."[14] Roger Marx, a civil servant and art critic who defended the Art Nouveau cause, viewed Chaumet as a reformer of the aesthetics of feminine jewelry: "The largest, most magnificent, most magical of all the jewelry is the corsage ornament exhibited by Mr. Chaumet, which owes its splendor less to the size and number of diamonds than to the composition governing their use, making the water of the gems shimmer like the waves of a waterfall, like shafts of light".[15] Meanwhile, the *Revue de la Bijouterie, Joaillerie, Orfèvrerie*, a recently launched magazine also keen on novelty, found Chaumet's jewelry to be the product of considerable effort but would have wished it to be "of a more modern, more unpredictable inspiration." The reviewer criticized certain pieces for their "lack of a sufficiently firm decorative stance."[16] However, it should be noted that these reservations, published under the female pseudonym of Maud Ernstyl, came in fact from the jeweler Henri Vever who, like Lalique, advocated the overthrow of the hierarchy of materials and the primacy of design.

Archives show the motif of waves of water on various other items—necklaces and corsage ornaments—but no chronology within this "series" can be established.

14 Paul Soufflot, *Exposition universelle internationale de 1900 à Paris. Rapports du jury international. Groupe XV. Industries diverses. Classe 95. Joaillerie et bijouterie* (Paris: Imprimerie nationale, 1902), p. 388.

15 Roger Marx, *La Décoration et les Industries d'Art à l'Exposition Universelle de 1900* (Paris: Delagrave, 1901), p. 74.

16 Maud Ernstyl, "La Joaillerie française à l'Exposition de 1900", *Revue de la Bijouterie, Joaillerie, Orfèvrerie* 5 (Septembrer 1900), pp. 13–14. Chaumet's jewelry was illustrated by a picture of a ruby-and-diamond Chimera necklace. Note that the same issue of the magazine provided readers with a list of twenty-three of the largest stones in the Exposition. Five Chaumet pieces were cited, notably the Chimera necklace for its 40-carat ruby and 23-carat old diamond, plus a strand of twenty-nine pearls.

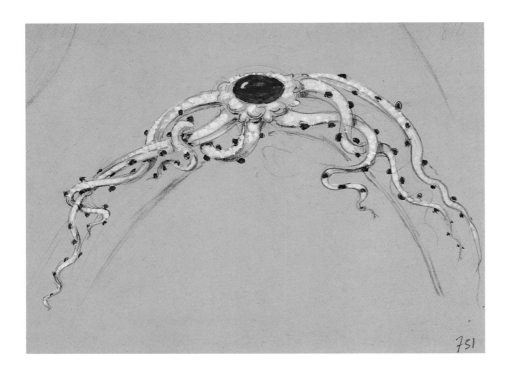

751

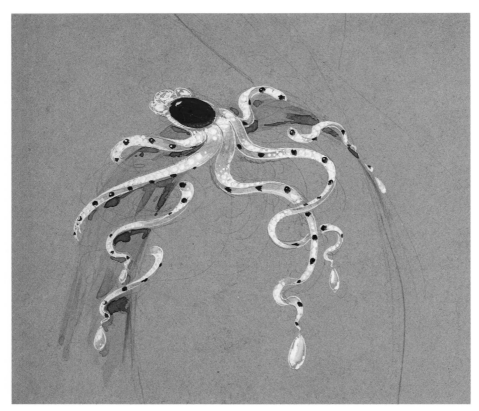

LEFT
*Two designs for
"Brittle star" shoulder
ornaments*, c. 1900.
Graphite pencil,
pen and India ink,
ink and watercolor wash,
H. 11.6; W. 15.6 cm and
H. 13.5; W. 15.3 cm
Chaumet Paris Collection

FACING PAGE
*"Chimera fight"
brooch*, c. 1890.
Gold, diamonds,
H. 4.6; W. 9 cm
Chaumet Paris Collection

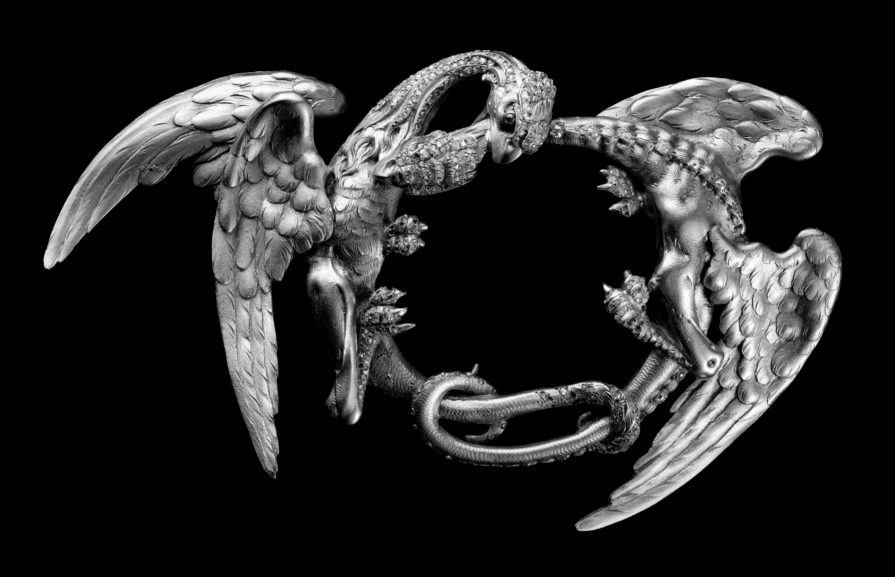

ABOVE

*Design for a "Lady's
slippers" tiara,* c. 1900.
Graphite pencil, pen and
ink, ink and watercolor
wash, H. 16.1; W. 25.4 cm
Chaumet Paris Collection

Yet it must be acknowledged that Chaumet's display of 1900, which sparked a certain reticence on Vever's part, did not demonstrate his commitment to the new ways of thinking. His Japanese-inspired brooch of chased gold studded with opals, rubies, and diamonds—which, with its cloud-like swirls and figures, evokes certain designs by Vever—stems more from a picturesque eclecticism based on a whimsical Far Eastern repertoire, as well as on anthologies of seventeenth-century and Renaissance ornamentation, which Chaumet had been drawing on for a decade, as seen in perfectly accomplished examples like a gold brooch depicting the combat of two chimerical birds, and a pendant based on a satyr's mask and two panther heads emerging from highly complex scrollwork.

This raises the question of the large collection of gouache drawings done on tracing paper and vellum, all of very high quality, now in the company archives. These drawings fully reflect an Art Nouveau style, not only through choice of motifs but in their free, flowing handling that underscores a simultaneously dreamy and organic quality. Sensuous lady-slipper orchids, wave-driven seahorses and serpent stars, web-spinning spiders, intertwined snakes, a mask of Melusina, an insouciant dream maiden, and nymphs alarmed by a sea monster are just a few of many suggestions for the making of corsage ornaments, chokers, rings, and combs. One question immediately springs to mind: were these very precisely drawn designs ever executed? The answer is to be sought in the thousands of

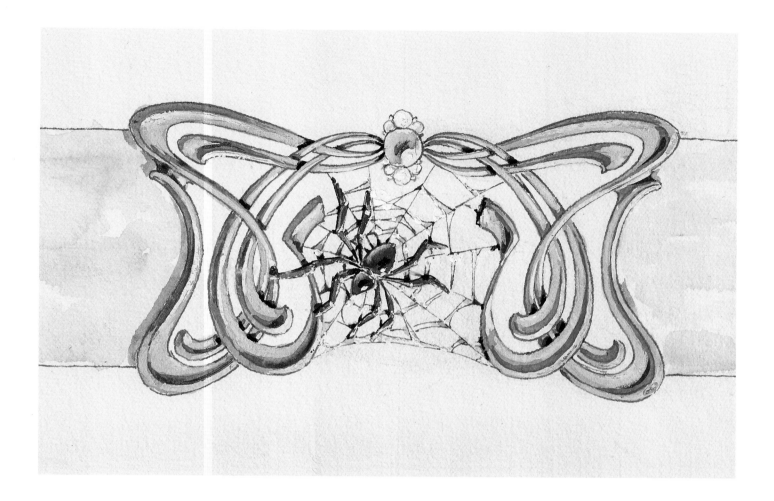

ABOVE

Design for a "Spider"
belt buckle, c. 1900.
Graphite pencil, pen and
ink, ink and watercolor
wash, H. 8.2; W. 13.5 cm
Chaumet Paris Collection

glass-plate negatives also found in the Chaumet Archives, documenting the jewelry that was actually made. Only once a complete inventory of these plates has been done will it be possible to assess the impact of Art Nouveau on Chaumet jewelry. However, this author's opinion is that very few Art Nouveau jewels actually saw the light of day. In his report dated July 1899—that is to say, less than a year before the opening of the Universal Exhibition of 1900—Wibaille made no mention of any concrete attempts in that direction, but merely advocated it. Furthermore, while Art Nouveau jewelry indisputably triumphed at the 1900 fair, notably thanks to the work of Lalique, Vever, and Georges Fouquet, that event might just as well have been its swansong. By 1902 already, signs of weariness were evident, and—of extreme significance—the fashion press seemed to be the leading herald of a loss of interest by the people most concerned, namely women of fashion. That was the year Gabriel Mourey, an expert commentator on his times who wrote a column in *Les Modes* and who endorsed a moderate Art Nouveau aesthetic, staged a dialogue by one such woman (an artifice often used by journalists in those days): "[T]he tune is becoming monotonous. When will there be an end to those peacock feathers, swans, irises, orchids, what-have-you? You'll see that people will be perfectly happy to return quite simply to the styles of yore, to exquisitely Louis XV or delightfully Louis XVI tastes, and even to the frigid Empire style that people would have found dreadful less than ten years ago."[17] Four years later, the jewelry exhibited at the

17   Gabriel Mourey, "L'art décoratif aux Salons de 1902,"
     Les Modes. Revue mensuelle illustrée des Arts décoratifs
     appliqués à la femme 12 (May 1902), p. 19.

LEFT

Studies for "Dragonfly",
"Butterfly", "Hummingbird",
"Beetle", and "Frog"
brooches, c. 1900.
Graphite pencil,
pen and India ink,
ink and watercolor wash,
H. 34; W. 41 cm
Chaumet Paris Collection

FACING PAGE

"Butterfly" brooch, c. 1895.
Gold, silver, rubies,
and diamonds,
H. 6.3; W. 6.6; D. 2.5 cm
Private Collection

International Exposition in Milan (where Chaumet made a brilliant presentation) signaled an undeniable return to the Louis XVI and Empire styles, sparking revived interest in the bow motif, of which Chaumet has consistently been a dazzling advocate.

There is every reason to think that Chaumet's "Art Nouveau" designs were limited to the very brief period when the style was at its height and yet already on the way out, 1900–1905. With respect to the repertoire typical of Art Nouveau jewelry, Chaumet made some very clear choices. His jewels featured no female figures and very few landscapes, symbolist motifs dear to Lalique, Vever, and Fouquet (the latter two even turning to artists for those types of composition).[18] On the other hand, there were many peacocks, reptiles, butterflies, dragonflies, and bats, not to mention flowers. From a technical standpoint, Chaumet used enamel sparingly, unlike other Art Nouveau enthusiasts, and continued to base his art on the setting of precious stones.

It would seem that Chaumet's Art Nouveau–tinged naturalism was most fully expressed at the World's Fair hosted in St. Louis, which provided him with another opportunity to display *Christus Vincit* alongside another masterpiece of the same type, *La Via Vitae*. The French report on national participation ended its section on jewelry with strong praise for Chaumet's display. "Everything was truly of rare perfection: the wealth of pieces on show, the beauty of the gems, the luster of the pearls, the refinement of the cutting, the skill of setting, the delicacy of assembly, the finish of the work, the purity of style, the novelty of design." Among the most remarkable pieces underscored by the report were a tiara "whose platinum setting could be considered a model of lightness," an elegant butterfly with "wings edged with carved rubies," and a plaque "of incredible lightness, composed of dragonflies of brilliants and carved emeralds."[19] Novel design, light settings, butterflies, dragonflies: all this terminology evokes the world of Art Nouveau and effectively conveys Chaumet's goal as he summed it up in a note written for the members of the jury in St. Louis: "By taking these objects in hand, Sirs, you may observe the suppleness we have imparted to each item as well as the lightness of settings and the harmony of lines."[20] The same note reveals that the dragonflies, butterflies, and a "wing brooch" all had spring settings that "set them aquiver at the slightest movement." This is the first reference to jewelry based on the wing motif, a theme that would become highly popular after World War I, as witnessed by many surviving versions. One of them was specially ordered in 1910 by the extremely wealthy, whimsical Mrs. Harry Payne Whitney, née Gertrude Vanderbilt.

This was clearly Chaumet's new image: the airy quality of the designs on paper were realized thanks to a constantly refined technique that focused special attention on the execution of settings. Turn-of-the-century jewelry, in fact, is characterized by the fineness of settings, in which gold and silver were steadily replaced by platinum, even if that option did not figure in Wibaille's recommendations nor in Soufflot's jury report of 1900. Platinum's intrinsic qualities lent greater flexibility to the assembly, and given its strength it could be

FACING PAGE
Félix Tournachon, known as Nadar (1820–1910), *Baroness Gustave de Rothschild, a Chaumet Customer.* Print from gelatin silver bromide glass negative Médiathèque de l'Architecture et du Patrimoine, Charenton-le-Pont

PAGES 302–303
Study for a "Butterfly" tiara. Graphite pencil, watercolor, and white gouache highlights, H. 14.3; W. 21.7 cm Chaumet Paris Collection

18　Eugène Grasset worked for Vever, Alfons Mucha for Fouquet.
19　Elie Weil, *Exposition internationale de Saint-Louis U.S.A. 1904. Section française. Rapport du groupe 31* (Paris: Comité français des expositions à l'étranger, 1905), pp. 17–18.
20　See *Exp on St Louis/9 Xbre 1904*, typewritten document. Chaumet Archives.

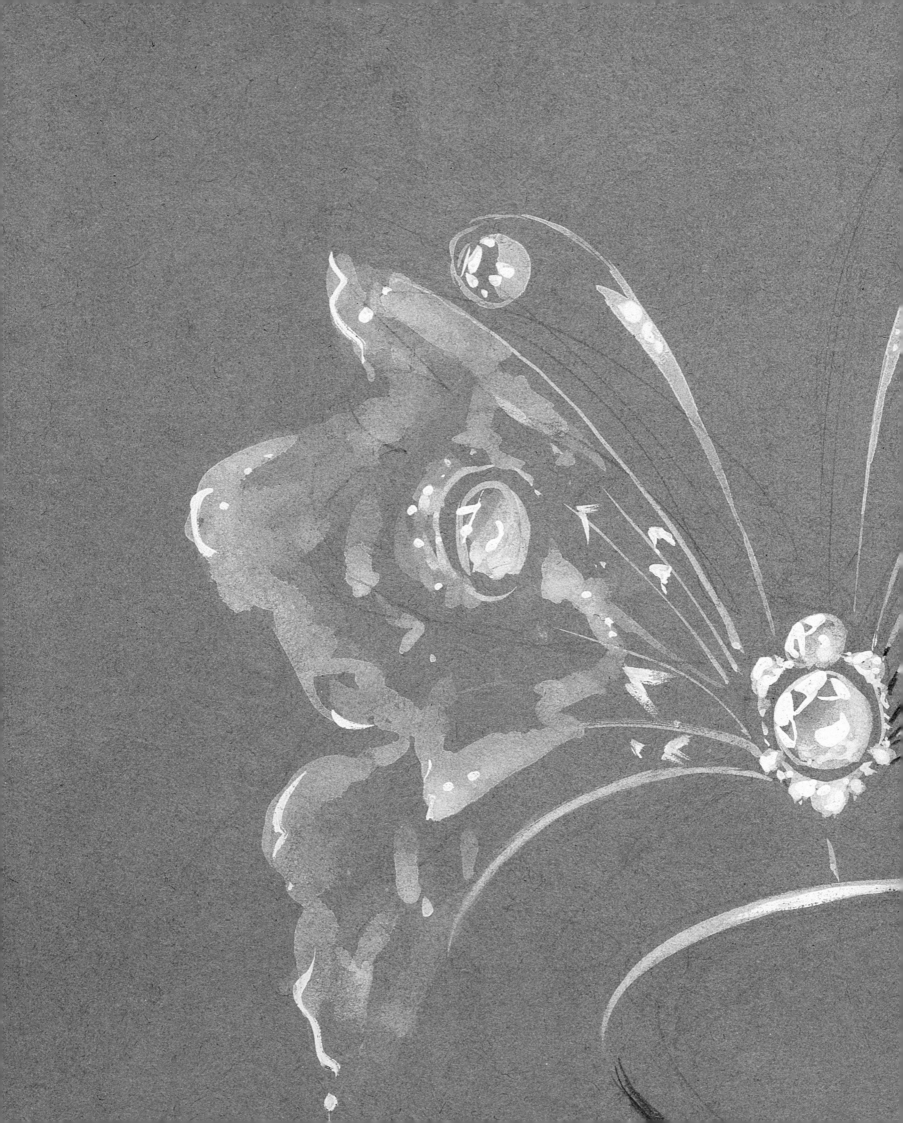

ABOVE

Study for a "Wings"
aigrette tiara.
Graphite pencil,
pen and India ink,
ink and watercolor wash,
H. 15.5; W. 25.5 cm
Chaumet Paris Collection

FACING PAGE

AND PAGES 306–307

"Wings" aigrette tiara
(detail) of Mrs. Payne
Whitney, born Gertrude
Vanderbilt, 1910.
Platinum, diamonds, enamel,
Left: H. 4.7; W. 15 cm;
Right: H. 4.7; W. 16 cm
Private Collection

Bought in New York on 6 July 1910 by one of the
most influential American figures of the early 20th
century, Mrs. Payne Whitney, born Gertrude Vanderbilt
(1875–1942), this pair of wings adorned with 566
diamonds and 708 rose-cut diamonds is worn as a tiara
mounted on a frame. Gertrude's marriage to Harry
Payne Whitney in 1896 has brought together the
wealth of the Vanderbilt family and the fortune of the
Standard Oil company, thus giving the couple almost
unlimited financial resources. Passionate about jewels,
this great patron and founder of the Whitney Museum
of American Art, New York, was among the clientele
of American billionaires rushing to Chaumet's salons
during the Belle Époque.

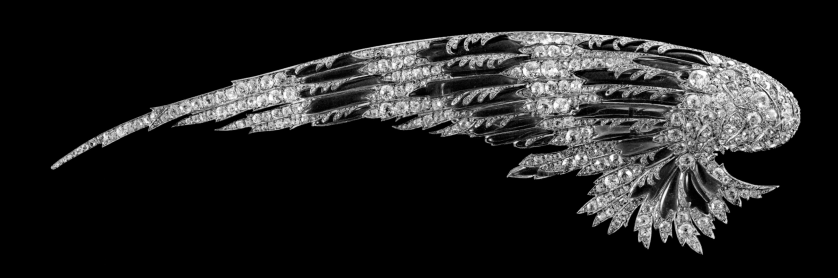

FACING PAGE

*"Hummingbird" aigrettes
convertible into
brooches*, c. 1890.
Gold, silver, rubies,
diamonds, demantoid
garnets, H. 4; W. 4 cm
Chaumet Paris Collection

RIGHT

*Design for a "Hummingbird"
aigrette*, c. 1890.
Graphite pencil, pen
and India ink, gouache,
H. 17.6; W. 12 cm
Chaumet Paris Collection

ABOVE

"Daisies" tiara ordered by Mademoiselle de Chaponnay, 1905. Print from gelatin silver bromide glass negative, H. 18; W. 24 cm Chaumet Paris Collection

used in smaller quantities. Furthermore, when worked in a technique as traditional as a millegrain setting, its naturally shiny surface lights up with a multitude of reflections that increase the sparkle of gems tenfold. Chaumet's very fine metal frames—called *fil de couteau* (knife edge)—allowed the naturalistic motifs of tiaras to scatter throughout the hair. The effect was all the more striking in so far as Chaumet mastered the cutting of modestly sized gems. The upshot was great precision in delineating the design, whether a branch, a leaf, a flower, or even an insect or bird. The suppleness of these new settings allowed the stones to oscillate with much greater freedom than those set in rigid assemblies.

One compositional principle that Chaumet only rarely ignored was symmetry. Thus when it comes to tiaras, whatever the naturalistic motif—ivy, holly, clover, daisy, reeds—symmetry took the form of two clusters meeting above the forehead. One of the most elegant is probably a carnation-themed tiara done in 1907 at the same time as a corsage ornament for the wife of industrialist Henri de Wendel. In addition, the lightness and flexibility of these settings certainly made it more comfortable to wear the chokers in which diamonds took the form of meshwork, scrollwork, or even stalactites.

Proportion was another skill mastered by Chaumet. Concerned to make often highly complex designs legible, artistic jewelry tended to grow in scale, making an item hard to wear precisely because of its size and weight. This not insignificant inconvenience was stressed several times during the Universal Exposition of 1900, beginning with the official report, which noted: "In several display cases we saw jewels of various kinds—tiaras, necklaces, plaques, and corsage brooches—made in abnormal sizes. It is incontrovertible that, in these conditions, the jewel will strike the beholder's eye more strongly, even as the design, given the scope of these pieces, displays sharp lines that accentuate its nature and make it easier to grasp.... If you reduced these jewels to their normal dimensions, that is to

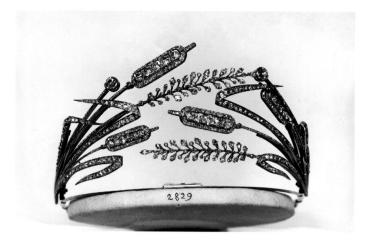

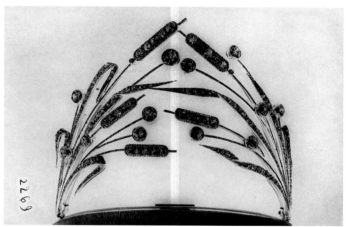

TOP, LEFT

*"Mistletoe" tiara
ordered by the Count of
Guébriant, before 1904.*
Print from gelatin silver
bromide glass negative,
H. 18; W. 24 cm
Chaumet Paris Collection

TOP, RIGHT

*"Reeds" tiara
ordered by Count Louis de
Clermont-Tonnerre, 1905.*
Print from gelatin silver
bromide glass negative,
H. 13; W. 18 cm
Chaumet Paris Collection

CENTER, LEFT

*"Reeds" tiara,
before 1904.*
Print from gelatin silver
bromide glass negative,
H. 18; W. 24 cm
Chaumet Paris Collection

CENTER, RIGHT

*"Foliage" tiara
ordered by
Mr. Vanderbilt, 1907.*
Print from gelatin silver
bromide glass negative,
H. 18; W. 24 cm
Chaumet Paris Collection

BOTTOM, LEFT

*"Foliage" tiara
ordered by Baron Gustave
de Rothschild, 1907.*
Print from gelatin silver
bromide glass negative,
H. 24; W. 30 cm
Chaumet Paris Collection

BOTTOM, RIGHT

*"Reeds" tiara
ordered by the Viscount
of Saint-Trivier, 1910.*
Print from gelatin silver
bromide glass negative,
H. 18; W. 24 cm
Chaumet Paris Collection

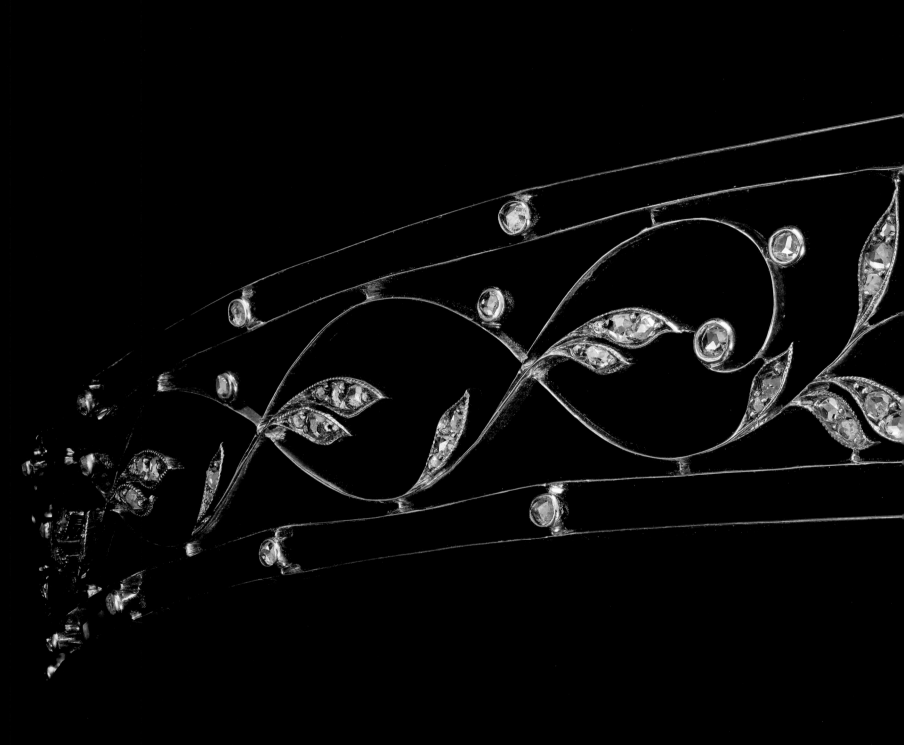

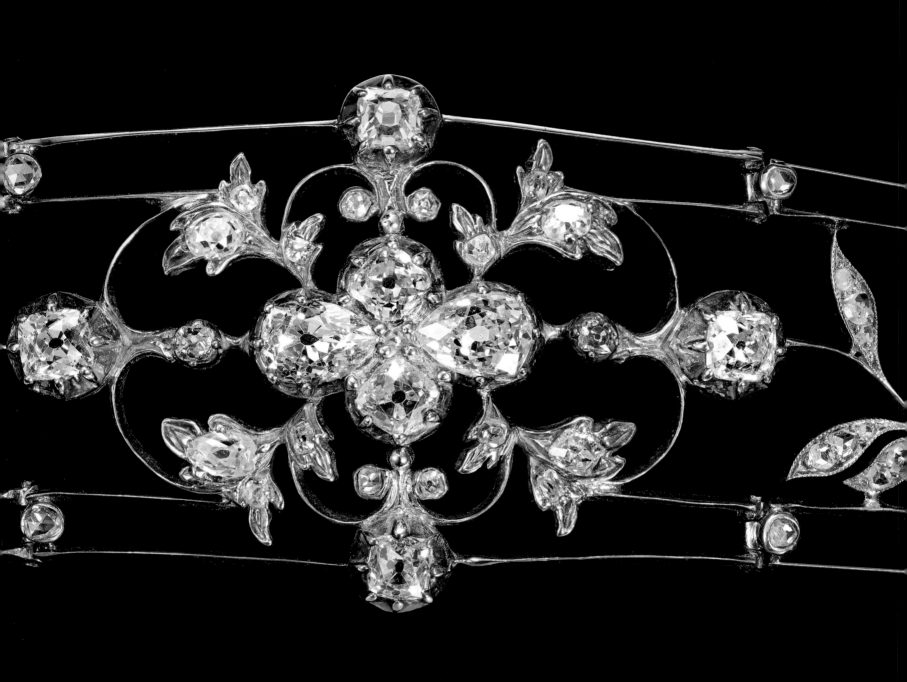

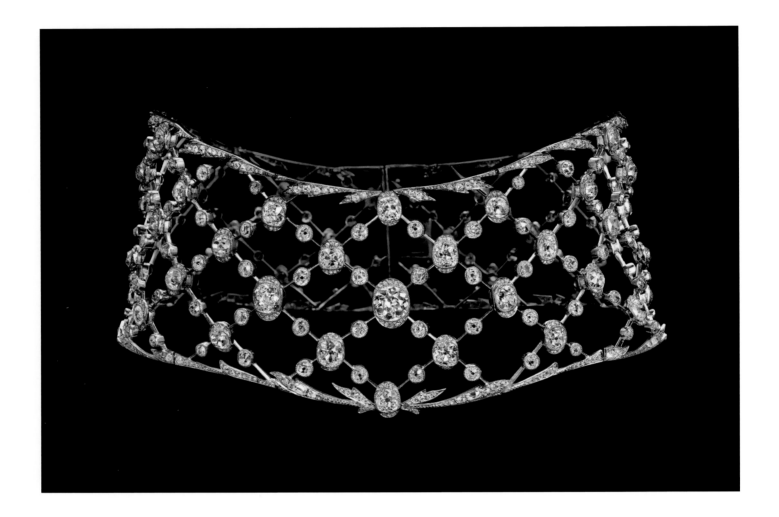

PAGES 312–313

*Articulated "Foliage"
bandeau tiara*, c. 1918–20.
Gold, silver, diamonds,
H. 3.5; W. 32 cm
Chaumet Paris Collection

ABOVE

*Articulated choker, known
as "Rohan" choker*, 1906.
Platinum and diamonds,
H. 6; W. 33 cm
Chaumet Paris Collection

FACING PAGE

Félix Tournachon, known
as Nadar (1820–1910),
*Madame Escandon,
a Chaumet Customer.*
Print from gelatin silver
bromide glass negative
Médiathèque de l'Archi-
tecture et du Patrimoine,
Charenton-le-Pont

This choker was ordered by the Duke of Rohan in 1906
as a wedding present for his daughter. Fully articulated
in order to perfectly follow the curves of the body, this
jewelry lacework is the result of continuous technical
improvements by Joseph Chaumet, who paid particular
attention to the manufacturing of the frames. The
delicate latticework trimmed with diamonds was made
possible by the use of the *fil de couteau* technique, as well
as of platinum, a metal whose intrinsic qualities allow
the creation of intricate designs. Combining lightness
and flexibility, the *fil de couteau* technique lit the fire of
creativity at Chaumet, as shown by the "Foliage" tiara
(pages 312–13) and the "Fuchsias" tiara (page 317).

say the usual size for the use for which they are intended, then they would certainly lose some of their qualities."[21]

Display jewelry held little interest for Chaumet, who much preferred finery made to be worn. That prompted him to take fashion into consideration, and to adapt to the practices of the day. Several drawings reflect this concern, showing a few designs on the figure of a woman's torso. There is not enough space here to develop the instructive parallel between Chaumet's jewelry and trends in turn-of-the-century fashion as presented in illustrated woman's magazines.[22] However, we should recall that bracelets were scarcely worn in those years due to the rage for long sleeves, that dangling earrings were despised (at least until 1907–8), and that pendants were preferred over brooches because they brought sparkle to the lace lining the scooped neckline. The top of the hierarchy, meanwhile, was occupied by the hair ornaments indispensible to high-society gatherings (hair, at that time, signifying woman as the object of male desire) and by corsage ornaments. Corsage ornaments might range from a veritable stole of pearls and diamonds falling in cascades from shoulder straps or brooches to a single gem pinned to the middle of the cleavage. Such finery was displayed only at grand dinners, balls, and the opera. Chaumet's art fully blossomed in this sphere, where a woman's rank in society was flaunted. Yet it also retained a certain sense of practicality, seeking to find ways of transforming a jewel so that it could be adapted to different outfits.[23] Thus the front of a necklace could be converted into a tiara, or the bars of a choker transformed into independent brooches (the choker itself becoming a bandeau), while an aigrette detached from its tuft of plumes could be worn as a brooch. In December 1897 Princess Brancovan bought "a foliate bandeau of rose-cut diamonds with diamond thistle centered on an emerald, the bandeau being easily detachable to become a corsage ornament," while Marino Valgia opted in September 1899 for a "gold and enamel *plaque de cou* [choker plaque] forming a hair comb, easily transformed into a necklace with five gold chains." When, in March 1901, the Baroness of Pertuis bought a "bat-wing tiara with aigrette in the center," it was explained that "the two wings can also be worn as brooches."

As the twentieth century dawned, Chaumet jewelry was exhibited at all the world fairs, and from 1907 onward it had a magnificent shop window on Place Vendôme in Paris, where sets of wedding presents were regally displayed. It was certainly marriages—whether cementing alliances among ancient families or forging new ones with fortunes born of industry and finance—that brought Chaumet its largest orders. The firm was often requested, however, to make greater or lesser use of family-owned stones. The task of the jeweler (who for that matter was often charged with safely storing family jewels) then involved taking stones from old pieces and resetting them in up-to-date designs for the bride. From this practice sprang some of Chaumet's most glamorous creations, one of the last examples being the "Fuchsias" tiara ordered in 1919 by the Duke and Duchess of

"Fuchsias" tiara, known as "Bourbon-Parma" tiara, 1919. Platinum and diamonds, H. 7; W. 18 cm Chaumet Paris Collection

21   Soufflot, *Exposition universelle internationale de 1900 à Paris...*, p. 380.

22   Worth mentioning are *Les Modes* (1901–37), *Femina* (1901–17), *Mode-palace* (1901–9), *Mode et Beauté* (1901–15) and *Le Figaro-modes* (1903–6).

23   The client would be supplied with the little tools required for these conversions, and lady's maids were taught to use them.

Pendant featuring
a swan, 1910.
Platinum, diamonds,
colored enamels,
D. 5.5 cm
Private Collection

Doudeauville for the marriage of their daughter Hedwige de la Rochefoucauld to Prince Sixtus of Bourbon-Parma. Wedding presents—costly gifts to the young bride—would be exhibited either on the day the marriage contract was signed or on the day of the church wedding under the watchful eyes of liveried servants who officiated at the bride's home. The jewels would be accompanied by a little card with the name of the giver, and a more or less detailed list would be published in the society pages of *Le Figaro* or *Le Gaulois*. The most impressive of such lists was surely the one for the wedding celebrated on November 12 and 14, 1904, of Elaine Greffulhe, daughter of the famous Countess Greffulhe who served as the inspiration for Marcel Proust's characters of the Duchess and Princess of Guermantes, and who was also a faithful Chaumet client.[24] Elaine married Armand de Gramont, Duke of Guiche, some of whose features Proust borrowed for the character of Robert de Saint-Loup. On November 14 *Le Figaro* ran the event on its front page with the title "A Grand Wedding," and the next day the newspaper devoted three columns to a list of wedding gifts. Chaumet's name was never mentioned in those articles, but the Chaumet Archives provide the details of the correspondence between Joseph Chaumet and the Duke of Gramont concerning a wedding order for a foliate tiara with nine pear-shaped diamonds and a three-strand diamond necklace.[25]

The social and economic upheaval following World War I delivered a fatal blow to such traditions, even as trends in fashion led to major changes in the forms and uses of lavish finery. In the early 1920s, corsage ornaments and crown-like tiaras fell into disuse. They were old-fashioned items that no longer accorded with the new female image forged by Paul Poiret ten years earlier. But this was not necessarily a problem for Chaumet. It is probable that the jeweler was less distraught than he had been by the emergence of Art Nouveau, especially since in the pre-war years many of its designs met the criteria of the new style laid down by André Véra in his famous manifesto of 1912.[26] Véra urged artists to react against the style of 1900 and to revive the French tradition allegedly characterized by "order, clarity, and harmony." An elegant pendant made by Joseph Chaumet in 1910, featuring a swan swimming in a pond flanked by porticos and fountains in a serene, classic arrangement, is perhaps emblematic of the new direction in taste sought by the younger generation. At the same time, the emergence of ever more compact, ever more geometric forms highly conducive to strict alignments of pearls and stones enabled fine jewelry to reclaim with a splash—during the international Art Deco Exposition of 1925—the leading role it had briefly conceded to costume jewelry.

24 Between March 1902 and March 1904 no fewer than ten purchases were recorded for a sum totalling more than 50,000 francs (one tiara, one choker, one bracelet, two rings, two brooches, two hair pins, and one hat pin).

25 Invoice ledger "N" and register of visits, July–November 1904. Chaumet Archives.

26 André Véra, "Le Nouveau Style," *L'Art décoratif* (January 1912), pp. 21–32. Garden designer André Véra was the brother of decorative painter Paul Véra.

Jewelry Owned by Princess Henckel von Donnersmarck

Philippe Thiébaut

Following the death of his first wife, the famous courtesan Thérèse Lachmann, better known as the Marchioness of Paiva (who died in 1884 in the palace of Neudeck, Silesia), the industrial magnate Count (later Prince, 1901) Guido Henckel von Donnersmark (1830–1916) remarried a young Russian noblewoman in 1887. Katharina Wassilievna of Szlepsowz (1862–1929) was enamored of gemstones and had a collection of jewelry that rivaled that of monarchs of the day. The prince placed numerous orders with Chaumet, several of which have survived to the present.

In chronological order, they are:

– In 1889 a diamond corsage ornament composed of laurel leaves stretching from one shoulder to the other, from which hung two diamond lizards with ruby eyes. In 1902, at the prince's request, Chaumet enhanced the piece by inserting a 34-carat ruby between the two reptiles.

– In 1896, a crown-like tiara set with fine large emeralds, plus a diamond necklace with pearl-shaped diamonds.

– Circa 1900, a tiara composed of eleven pear-shaped emeralds, traditionally said to come from Empress Eugénie's collection, dispersed at auction in London on June 24, 1872.

– Circa 1905, a choker necklace composed of fine diamond scrolls holding seven turquoises, in a splendid example of the lightness and flexibility achieved by Chaumet in the early twentieth century.

Tiara of Princess Henckel von Donnersmarck, c. 1900. Diamonds, emeralds Qatar Museum

FACING PAGE

*Portrait of Princess
Henckel von
Donnersmarck Wearing
the "Lizards" Corsage
Ornament*, c. 1900.
Pastel
Private Collection

TOP

*Study for a corsage
ornament with a
lizard motif*, 1889.
Graphite pencil, pen and
black ink, ink wash, and
white gouache highlights,
H. 14; W. 20.5 cm
Chaumet Paris Collection

CENTER

*"Lizards on a branch"
corsage ornament of
Princess Henckel von
Donnersmarck*, 1889.
Montage of two prints
from gelatin silver bromide
glass negatives,
H. 24; W. 30 cm
Chaumet Paris Collection

BOTTOM

*"Lizards" corsage
ornament of Princess
Henckel von
Donnersmarck*, 1889.
Remounted with
rubies in 1902
Gold, diamonds, and rubies
Private Collection

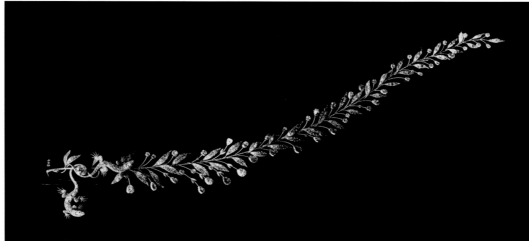

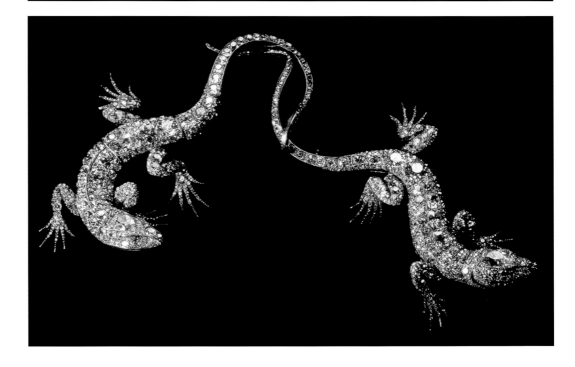

Goldsmithing

Philippe Thiébaut

Joseph Chaumet's work as a goldsmith is relatively tricky to appreciate. Wibaille, in his report of 1899, was somewhat condescending toward precious metalwork and was not surprised at the lack of initiative in "an art that consists only in making as quickly as possible an enormous quantity of spoons, forks, knives, and other everyday objects whose form hardly varies. Only from time to time does a salutary centerpiece or blessed candelabra come along to draw the sedentary goldsmith from his torpor!"

The precious metal workshop seems to have been highly dependent on the firm's other departments, at least at first. This secondary role appears confirmed by the adjectives "modest" and "devoted" used by Chaumet himself with respect to the head of the workshop, Rocher, when Chaumet solicited a gold medal for Rocher at the St. Louis World's Fair of 1904. A dip into the sales ledgers around 1900 reveals that Chaumet was subcontracting orders for dinner services at that time (one of the largest orders was placed by the Marquis of Brantes in June 1898 for "72 forks, spoons, sauce boats, vegetable dishes, 48 dessert settings, salt spoons, [and] platter engraved with coat of arms"); he turned to Christofle and above all to Tabouret-Puiforcat, the firm that attained fame in the 1920s under the resolutely "modernist" guidance of Jean Puiforcat.

Things evolved, however, because in 1918 the upper floor of the Place Vendôme premises hosted the display of a dinner service of thirty-eight place settings with centerpiece and dishes ordered by the Bolivian tin magnate Simón Iturri Patiño, who had moved to Paris in 1912. The forms and decoration—hunting trophies, fish, reeding, and vegetables—harked straight back to the great eighteenth-century French tradition epitomized by François-Thomas Germain.

Several highly finished drawings in the Chaumet Archives, bearing Patino's name on the back, feature Art Nouveau–influenced designs, notably indebted to the pieces Ernest Cardeilhac had displayed to wide acclaim at the Universal Exposition of 1900. The current state of research does not reveal whether the Art Nouveau service was ever executed, or whether these designs were presented alongside the eighteenth-century proposals for Patino's approval.

Study for a soup tureen and its platter, c. 1900.
Graphite pencil,
pen and black ink,
ink and watercolor wash,
white gouache highlights,
H. 43.5; W. 31 cm
Chaumet Paris Collection

Dessous
et
Soupière.

ART DECO AND THE INTERWAR PERIOD

Alain Stella

The Art Deco movement emerged at the beginning of the twentieth century, flourished after World War I and peaked in 1925. In fashion and jewelry, it shaped the look of the 1920s *garçonne* (flapper) in France. From 1905 and over a quarter of a century, Chaumet invented all sorts of jewelry designs in this multifaceted style dominated by clean, geometric lines and the vibrant, contrasting hues of precious stones, which was influenced by exotic decorative motifs. During the more somber days of the 1930s, Art Deco underwent a transformation, with greater emphasis on white, gold, and femininity.

THE BIRTH OF A MODERN STYLE

The pioneering manifestations of the emblematic style of the Roaring Twenties that was dubbed "Art Deco" from 1925 in fact appeared quite a bit earlier, between 1905 and 1910, in the applied arts, be it architecture, interior decoration, fashion, or jewelry. Art Nouveau, which emerged in the early 1890s, breaking with the continual repetition of the historical styles, was at its peak at the time in these creative spheres. But the ornate, organic, sometimes mannerist forms of Art Nouveau, its curves and swirling lines and precious symbolism, rather than sowing the seeds of change had brought about its decline. In reaction to this excessive ornamentation, which the Austrian architect Adolf Loos criticized in 1908 in his seminal essay *Ornament and Crime*, the first works in a pared-down, geometrical, abstract style began to appear. While Loos caused a scandal with the extremely plain building that he designed for Vienna's Michaelerplatz, the German architects and interior designers of the Deutscher Werkbund were calling for the rigor of a highly structured, "industrial" aesthetic, seen as synonymous with modernity. Their ideas went on display at the 1910 Salon d'Automne in Paris, on the invitation of the Société des Artistes Décorateurs, and rapidly spread in France. The work of the French architects Francis Jourdain, Auguste

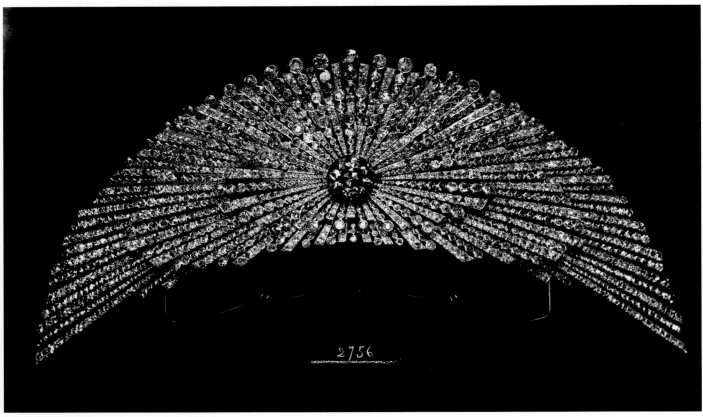

Perret, and Robert Mallet-Stevens, among others, reflected this trend even before World War I. In 1912, the garden designer André Véra published his manifesto *Le Nouveau style* in the journal *L'Art décoratif*, advocating geometrical layouts, symmetrical effects, and stylized motifs. These same years saw the early work of the German Walter Gropius, founder of the Bauhaus movement in 1920, while in the Netherlands, geometric abstraction, as illustrated by the painter Piet Mondrian, was influencing the interior designers and architects grouped around the journal *De Stijl*. In the United States, the Chicago School architects had started to favor rational design and modern materials such as reinforced steel and glass as early as the 1880s. Frank Lloyd Wright, who was connected to this school but more radical in his approach, influenced in his youth by the Japanese tradition, completed his first house design in 1889. He became famous in Europe after exhibiting some of his works in Berlin in 1910.

The same desire to break with Art Nouveau and forge a relationship with technical and industrial modernity inspired the main pictorial currents that appeared around 1910: geometric abstraction, cubism, and futurism celebrated the vitality and dynamics of structured, geometrical elements dominated by the straight line.

While he did not care much for Art Nouveau, Joseph Chaumet was drawn from an early date to this modern style that was emerging at the beginning of the twentieth century, while remaining true to the classicism of the Louis XVI and Empire styles. As numerous drawings and several glass-plate negatives show, the first jewelry pieces influenced by, or at least resembling this style, appeared in 1905, and became an enduring part of the jeweler's aesthetic vocabulary. The oldest one in the archives, dating from 1905, is a hair clip with diamonds bordering its slim rectangle and a faceted sapphire in the center surrounded by diamonds to form a circle. This hair clip already demonstrated the fascination exercised by simple, geometrical design when transfigured by the magic of precious stones—the principal characteristic of Art Deco jewelry, along with depth and elegance—twenty years before the modern style reached its height. Proof, perhaps, of its novel design, the piece was apparently not sold until 1913, the date of its photograph.

In 1906, Chaumet, the master of tiaras, did it again, with an impressive "Sun" tiara. It was commissioned in London by a wealthy aristocrat, William George Cavendish-Bentinck, and his wife, Elizabeth, for their daughter, Mary Augusta, for her wedding in November with the diplomat John Gorman Ford, First Secretary at the British Legation in Rome at the time. The various stages in the sale of this tiara, as recorded in the Visitors Book in the Chaumet Archives, provides a remarkable insight into the lengthy dialogue that could take place between jeweler and customer. The transaction began on June 9 with a visit by Elizabeth Cavendish-Bentinck, who wished to be "presented also with a choice of tiaras & prospective tiara designs according to her instructions," and was only completed on October 27 with the delivery of the piece—one week before Mary Augusta's wedding. In the meantime, in the course of a dozen visits to the London shop, a model of the piece was made, fitted, and approved by the young woman, often in the presence of her fiancé. The customers then requested a number of modifications, mostly concerning the size of the stones and the addition of a yellow diamond in the center.

The Cavendish-Bentincks had good taste, and were evidently bold in their choice, for the splendid Sun tiara was an eminently modern piece. Of course there

was nothing new about the sun motif, a preeminent symbol of the French *Grand Siècle* (seventeenth century). But Chaumet infused it with an unusual power and energy, creating the impression of a continuous outpouring of light from a large yellow diamond of more than 13 carats. These formal dynamics would be one of the major themes of Art Deco. The jeweler achieved the effect through long, geometrically arranged diamond rays that flared out almost imperceptibly from the core to the edge, intermingled with other rays in the form of lines of round diamonds to enhance the sparkle and overall impression of a cloud of light.

Many other pieces reflected the "modern" taste of Chaumet even before World War I, including, in 1906 again, a bracelet that could be converted into a bandeau (head band). Its central motif, a hexagon of diamonds and rubies, surrounded a rosette of pear-shaped rubies radiating out from a pearl. There were also several tiaras and bandeaux with a meander decor (an ancient geometric motif often used in Art Deco), earrings in the form of diamond hoops containing a ruby pendant (for Prince Henri Amédée de Broglie in 1911) and, the same year, a tiara made up of interlinked diamond rings.

JEWELRY FOR THE ROARING TWENTIES

The Exposition Internationale des Arts Décoratifs et Industriels Modernes, which took place in Paris from April to October 1925, was a major event in the history of art and taste, and yet lauded a style that had emerged twenty years previously. It was in fact the culmination of a project originally developed for 1911, and then postponed to 1916. Chauvinism, animosity between nations, the tragedy of the Great War, and the physical and psychological injuries that needed time to heal had delayed the celebration of what was now called "Art Deco." It was a global event: covering an area of over 20 hectares on the banks of the Seine between the Eiffel Tower and the Champs Elysées, hundreds of creatives from twenty-one countries presented their works, many of them especially produced for the occasion. The French offered a new vision of their tradition of elegance and luxury, one that was resolutely modern, dynamic, adapted to new lifestyles—women's liberation, tourism, sports—and open to the arts of the world. Steeped in jazz and the dreamlike fantasies of surrealism, the optimism of the Roaring Twenties—*les Années folles*—reflected modernity's promise of a bright future.

At the Exposition, the work of the jewelers, among all the artists present, reflected a truly new phenomenon that had emerged just after the war: the advent of the emancipated woman, dubbed the "*garçonne*" in France in a popular 1922 novel by Victor Margueritte. During the war, women had replaced men who had been called up, in factories, workshops, and offices, thereby acquiring a new independence and thus more freedom. City-dwelling women worked, played sports, smoked, and applied their makeup in the street. Fashion designers such as Jean Patou, Jeanne Lanvin, Coco Chanel, and Madeleine Vionnet designed a new look for them. It seemed an androgynous one at first glance, but in fact it made women more feminine: corsets were dispensed with, slimness was de rigueur, hair was worn short, dresses were straight and low-waisted, falling to the knee, and often featured low necklines and bare arms. The first women's pants were invented, and Coco Chanel brought in a classic fashion item: the "little black dress."

Princess Yusupov wearing a "Sun" tiara made by Chaumet, 1914.

—

A very fashionable model at the outbreak of World War I, the articulated sun tiara worn by Princess Irina of Russia, niece of Tsar Nicholas II, was made on the occasion of her marriage to Prince Felix Yusupov in February 1914.

This new silhouette needed jewelry to go with it, and Joseph Chaumet—who remained at the helm of his house until his death in 1928—and his designers set about providing it. The fashion for short hair influenced head ornament design: the tiara was replaced by the bandeau, worn low on the forehead. The flapper hair style was also conducive to wearing drop earrings. Chaumet designed many at the time: those chosen by Baroness Blixen in 1922, those acquired by Alexander I, King of Yugoslavia, the same year, and those now in the Victoria & Albert Museum in London are magnificent examples, known to us either from old photographs or because they still exist. The tube-shaped dress prompted the design of long necklaces (*sautoirs*), one variation being the *chaîne d'huissier* (literally, bailiff's chain) featuring geometrical diamond links, and the *garçonne* adorned her bare arms with numerous bracelets. Bare shoulders and low necklines led to the development of original jewelry pieces, such as necklaces that were worn on the back as well as on the chest, and shoulder jewelry or epaulets. The Chaumet Archives contain some very fine drawings of these new evening wear designs popular with the flappers.

The women of the Roaring Twenties were liberated, flirtatious, and loved wearing makeup. Cosmetics were all the rage, and Elizabeth Arden and Helen Rubinstein made a fortune. Women went out, had jobs, and needed to look good from morning to evening. They would apply makeup wherever they found themselves: in the street, at the office, or in their car, so jewelers came up with makeup or vanity cases with magnificently decorated lids or bases, often containing a tube of lipstick. The Grand Duchess of Luxembourg purchased three Chaumet vanity cases in 1926 at Place Vendôme. And because flappers also smoked wherever they went, they also needed feminine cigarette cases. Some of the sumptuous designs produced by the jeweler can be admired in the Chaumet Collection.

The jewelry and precious accessories of the Roaring Twenties usually served a specific purpose, be it to adorn exposed areas of the body, complement the clothing fashions, or suit the new lifestyles. In this, they were already echoing a certain conception of modernity that had been developing in the applied arts since the beginning of the century. But most of all, they made delightful use of the various facets of the Art Deco style—the straight line, geometrical forms, a clean, spare design. These characteristics gave the jewelry of the 1920s a restrained elegance and purity of line that imbues them with timeless appeal. Besides the large number of drawings that have come down to us, the glass-plate negatives provide a generous insight into this aesthetic approach, where the jewel's description often contains the word "line," such as the *diadème ligne* (line tiara) acquired by the Marquise of Lillers in 1920; the *diadème trois lignes diamants* (diamond three line tiara) for the Count Louis de Boisgelin in 1925; the *bracelet ligne diamants et ligne rubis* (diamond line and ruby line bracelet) and the *bracelet rigide ligne saphirs et diamants* (sapphire and diamond line bangle) chosen by the Baroness Gourgaud (née Eva Gebhard, the American wife of the great art collector Napoléon Gourgaud) in 1925 and 1926; the *bracelet diamants ligne émeraudes au centre* (central emerald line diamond bracelet) acquired by the Count of Cambacérès in 1927; and the *bracelet ligne rubis* (ruby line bracelet) belonging to the Princess Murat, which dates from 1930. All these pieces—whose buyers give us an idea of the French clientele of 12, Place Vendôme at that time—have in common an extremely spare design. The last four items featured stones caliber-cut into a square or "emerald" (rectangular) shape to fit the design of

Lady Wimborne wearing a Chaumet set, Photo: Cecil Beaton (1904–1980), 1925.

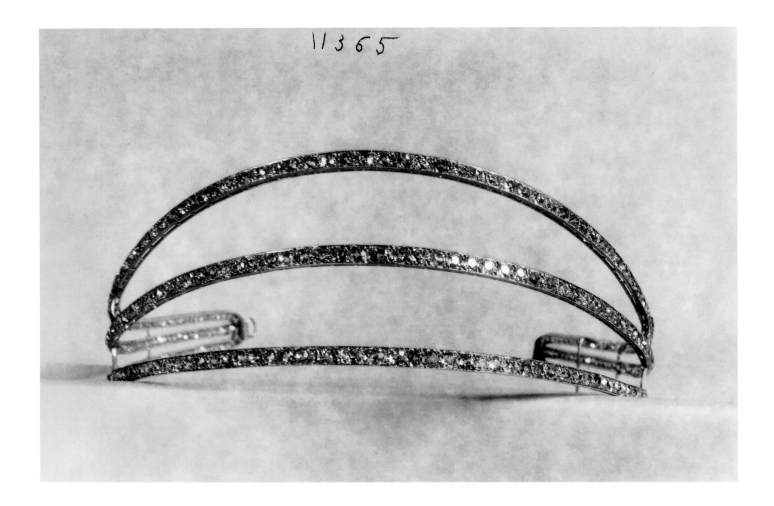

ABOVE

*Three-row tiara
ordered by Count Louis
de Boisgelin*, 1925.
Print from gelatin silver
bromide glass negative,
H. 24; W. 30 cm
Chaumet Paris Collection

the piece. Another square-cut shape common in Art Deco jewelry, specially for diamonds, was the "baguette cut" (a long, slim rectangle), present in a great number of Chaumet jewelry pieces and watches, often combined with other diamond cuts in a subtle play of forms. For example, two pairs of earrings, one purchased in 1928 by the steel industrialist Maurice de Wendel, and another acquired ten years later by the Countess Guy du Boisrouvray, daughter of the Bolivian "Tin King" Simón Iturri Patiño and sister of Antenor Patiño, one of the greatest art collectors of his time and a loyal Chaumet customer. A similar but more complex combination of diamond cuts appears in the wide cuff bracelet edged with a swirling Indian-style motif: dating from 1928, it was one of the first pieces executed under the direction of Marcel Chaumet, who had succeeded his father that year. It was not the jeweler's first cuff bracelet: the previous year, *Vogue* magazine had recommended for the "chic woman's wardrobe … jarred and bored by the jangling of many bracelets, one single cuff made for her by Chaumet—a thing of beautiful and intricate design."[1] There are a great many cuff bracelets among the drawings archived today, particularly in an Indian or Persian style, and it is likely that several of them were produced.

1 Roselyne Hurel and Diana Scarisbrick, *Chaumet Paris: Two Centuries of Fine Jewellery*, trans. Charles Penwarden (Paris: Paris-Musées, 1998), p. 137.

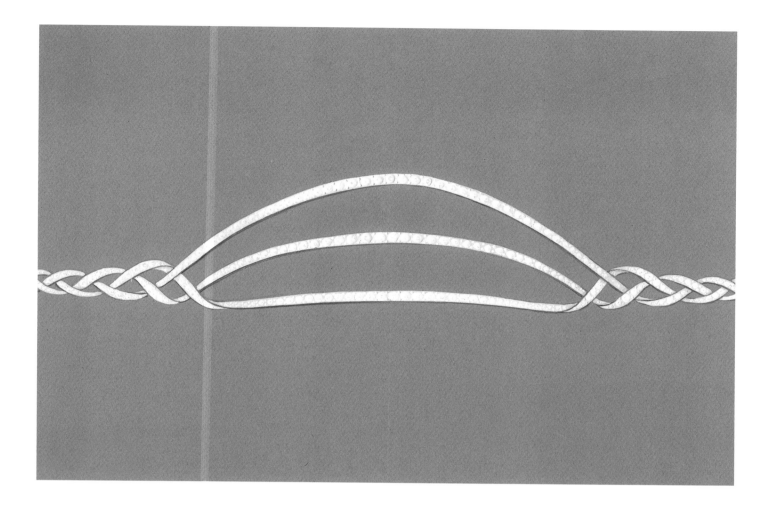

The use of strong, sharply contrasting colors was another characteristic of flappers' jewelry, which shunned any "soft" notion of femininity. Chaumet favored certain color pairings, including green and blue, sometimes called "peacock" because they suggest the bird's plumage. Precious and semiprecious stones might contribute to this bold combination, often present in Eastern-inspired pieces. A "peacock cigarette case" created in around 1925 was made with lapis lazuli and green aventurine, while a hexagonal "vanity case with a Chinese decor" from the same period contained lapis lazuli and nephrite, one of two kinds of jade (jadeite being the other). A number of spectacular pieces featured a combination of orangey-red coral and black onyx that contrasted with the whiteness of diamonds, such as a brooch with a pendant acquired by the Baroness von Schroeder in 1923 or the "½ circle brooch" made for Lady Henrietta Davis in 1932.

The most frequent contrast, however, is the most striking and most elegant one for the evening: black and white, often produced by a combination of onyx and diamond. In 1926, the magazine *Femina* described its purpose and effect: "Onyx has so many advantages it would seem impossible to do without it. Its somber sheen makes a pavé diamond ground

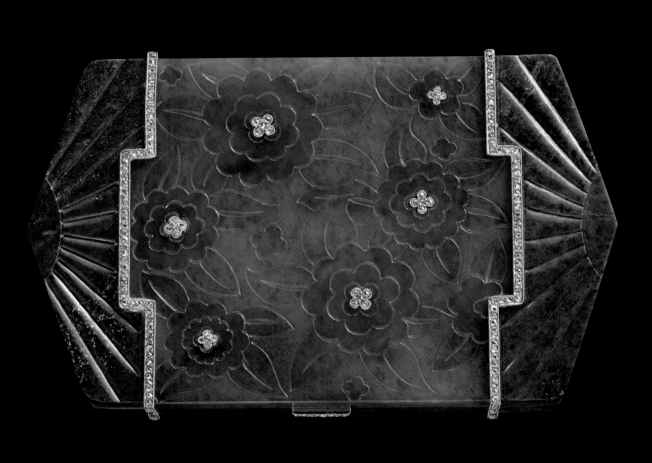

shine more splendidly, more brightly." Among Chaumet's splendid "black and white" pieces was the onyx and diamond bandeau created in 1924 for the Duchess of Alba, lady-in-waiting to Victoria-Eugénie, Queen of Spain, featuring an ancient Greek-style "wave" motif typical of Art Deco. The above-mentioned earrings belonging to Baroness Blixen, dating from 1922, were diamond hoops bordered with onyx, suspended from a line of diamonds. The incisive design of a "pendant with three drop beads" created circa 1920 for the American painter Romaine Brooks—with its broad surfaces of onyx, square links, and diamonds, and drop beads sharpened like claws—was one of Chaumet's most original jewelry designs at the time. The wealthy heiress Brooks, companion of the novelist Nathalie Barney for over half a century, wore this pendant suspended on a simple black silk cord known as a "rat's tail," which showed it off to perfection. And 1925 saw the creation of a "dolphin brooch" in which stylized natural and Greek-inspired motifs and geometric lines were blended in a beautifully harmonious and masterly composition. Here, sparkling diamonds contrast with the black onyx and the mat white of the frosted rock crystal plaques against which much of the motif stands out. Further developing that supremely elegant color combination, Chaumet also produced numerous bandeau bracelets with geometric motifs, drawings of which remain in the firm's archives.

In 1926, the prestigious journal *La Renaissance de l'art français et des industries de luxe* devoted a long retrospective article to jewelry at the 1925 Exposition International des Arts Décoratifs. A plate showed four of the pieces that Chaumet presented at the exhibition, where it had been awarded a Grand Prize. One of the four may have been withdrawn at the last minute: a ring-shaped brooch in diamonds, amethyst, and enamel, sold in December 1924 to the wife of the English politician and industrialist Sir Weetman Pearson, 1st Viscount Cowdray, a prominent Chaumet customer in London. This Indian-inspired brooch, which was shown at the Chaumet exhibition at the Musée Carnavalet in 1998, now belongs to a collector. We have lost trace of the three other items—a necklace pendant, a chain with a pendant, and a shoulder ornament.

The style of these four magnificent pieces is striking. They are all of "exotic" inspiration, featuring, for example, stylized palm frond or lotus motifs; precious stones in the form of round beads or raw and uncut; and a ruby and emerald combination characteristic of Indian ceremonial jewelry: everything was sumptuously evocative of the Arabian Nights. Similarly, a report entitled *1925–Exposition des arts décoratifs*, kept in the Chaumet Archives, contains mostly drawings of Indian- or Persian-inspired jewelry.

The stylized decorative motifs of Eastern and African civilizations were a major theme in Art Deco, as were those of antiquity. But this inspiration was not new in the applied arts. In the twentieth century alone, the 1900 World's Fair and the *Exposition des*

FACING PAGE
Studies for bracelets,
1925–30.
Graphite pencil,
gouache, and ink wash,
H. 16; W. 23 cm
Chaumet Paris Collection

PAGES 340–341
Seven-ruby bracelet
(detail), 1930–35.
Diamonds, rubies,
platinum, H. 2.7;
W. 18 cm (without clasp)
Private Collection

CHAUMET

CHAINE CONSTITUÉE
PAR DES BOULES
ÉMERAUDES ET DES
RUBIS, PENDANT
GROSSE ÉMERAUDE.

CHAIN MADE UP OF
EMERALD BALLS AND
RUBIES PENDANT,
BIG EMERALD.

ORNEMENT
POUR ÉPAULE
DIAMANTS, RUBIS
ET ÉMERAUDE.

SHOULDER
ORNAMENT
DIAMONDS, RUBIES,
AND EMERALDS.

PENDANT.
GROS DIAMANT
JONQUILLE
ENTOURÉ DE
DIAMANTS AVEC
MOTIFS
AMÉTHYSTES.

PENDANT.:
BIG JONQUIL
DIAMOND
SURROUNDED WITH
DIAMONDS WITH
AMETHYST
MOTIVES

BROCHE DIAMANTS
ET AMÉTHYSTES.

DIAMOND AND
AMETHYST BROOCH.

Arts Musulmans held by the Musée des Arts Décoratifs in 1912 generated a good deal of curiosity and influenced numerous designers. During the same period, in the fields of clothing and jewelry, the "Persian" fashion, for which the couturier Paul Poiret was famous, became popular in Parisian society evening events, in the wake of the successful production of *Scheherazade* by the Ballets Russes performed at the Opéra de Paris in 1910 and starring Ida Rubinstein and Vaslav Nijinski. Sultanas wearing turbans or a bandeau with a graceful aigrette on their forehead danced the tango at "Persian balls." In these pre-war years, Chaumet was already a great designer of Oriental-inspired aigrettes featuring precious stones or feathers. Among them, the splendid "sapphire and diamond sun" aigrette made in 1910 for the daughter of Count Charles de Boisgelin, Aliette, on the occasion of her marriage to Pierre-Henry de Vienne, and the "sun aigrette" with a central emerald, created in 1914, which is now in the Chaumet Collection.

The Arab-Persian world and the Indo-Persian world of the Moguls provided a rich source of elegant, stylized motifs adopted by Art Deco. In this period, Joseph Chaumet and his designers came up with numerous creative variations of them in all their jewelry pieces. The bandeau made for the Duke of Brissac in 1924 featured a square central 11.54 carat emerald and a pear-shaped pearl drop that could be detached to wear as a pendant. The one acquired by the Count of Fleury in 1926 had Persian *buta* or cashmere (paisley) motifs in diamonds. Perhaps the most impressive head ornament of this kind was the tiara designed for the Grand Duchess of Luxembourg, in 1926. While its overall form is inspired both by the Russian *kokoshnik* headdress, the impressive 43.42 carat emerald cabochon in the center gives it a distinctly Indian look. It was composed with a set of stones and jewels sent to Chaumet by Prince Felix of Bourbon-Parma, as a gift for his wife, Charlotte. The grand duchess collected it on November 6, and wore it four days later at the wedding of Leopold, Crown Prince of Belgium, and Princess Astrid of Sweden. She would remain very attached to this tiara, as many photographs show.

Chaumet created other items of jewelry in the same style, including brooches—notably one made with diamonds and rubies given by Prince Mdivani to his wife, the wealthy heiress Barbara Hutton, in 1934—bracelets, and necklaces. Some of them were executed after a highly original design, such as the diamond, rock crystal, and sapphire necklace acquired by the Belgian aristocrat Charles de Wouters d'Oplinter in 1928, probably with a view to his marriage with the daughter of Count Charles du Luart in April of the following year. The piece could be converted into two bracelets and a brooch. Another magnificent necklace of Indian inspiration was created in 1928. It featured carved rubies and emeralds in the Mogul tradition sourced from India, imparting its exotic touch, with diamond and baguette-cut diamond pavés tracing numerous geometric motifs. The necklace could be transformed into a brooch and a pair of bracelets. This piece is akin to a brooch that was created the same year: forming a geometric cascade, it is set with three large carved emeralds and fifty-six caliber-cut rubies, contrasting with pavés of 115 old-cut diamonds.[2] In 1930,

FACING PAGE

Jewels shown by Chaumet at the 1925 World's Fair. "The jewelry set at the Exhibition of Decorative Arts," *La Renaissance de l'art français et des industries de luxe* (The Renaissance of French Art and the Luxury Industries), 1926.

PAGES 344–345

"Rising sun" aigrette, 1914. Gold, platinum, emerald, and diamonds, H. 5.5; W. 13 cm Chaumet Paris Collection

2   Acquired at the time by the American businessman Frank J. Lauerman Jr. as a gift for his wife, Monica, it was sold at auction in Boston in 2011 for USD 385,500 to a collector, Skinner sale, December 6, 2011, no. 750.

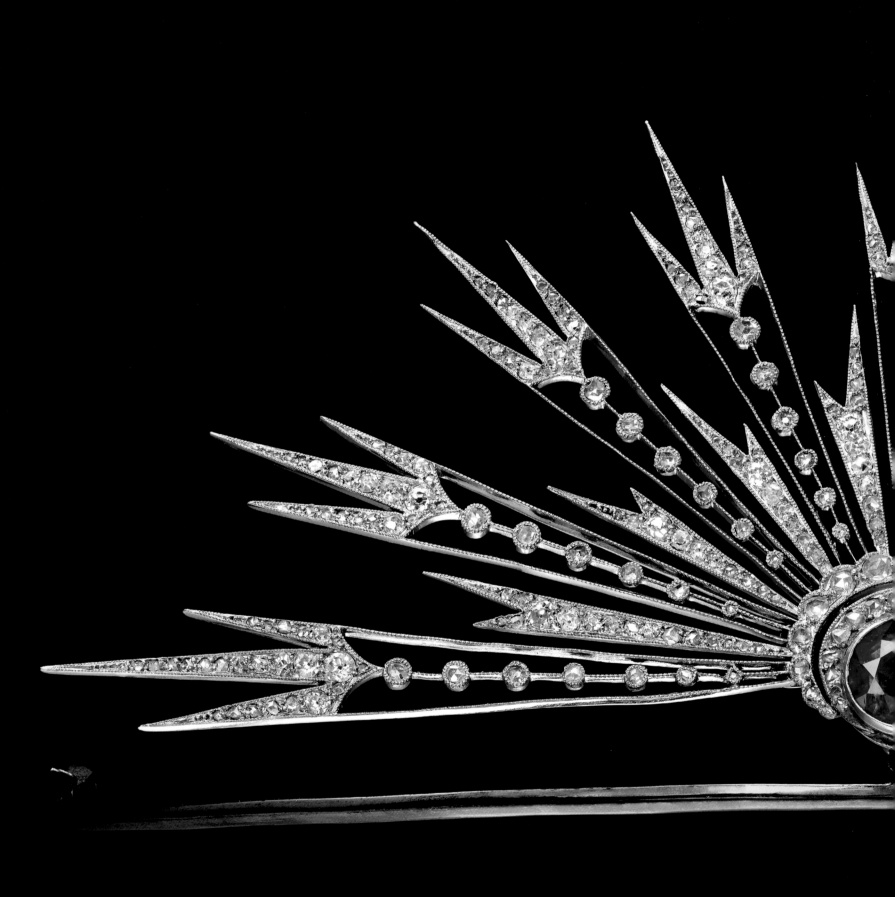

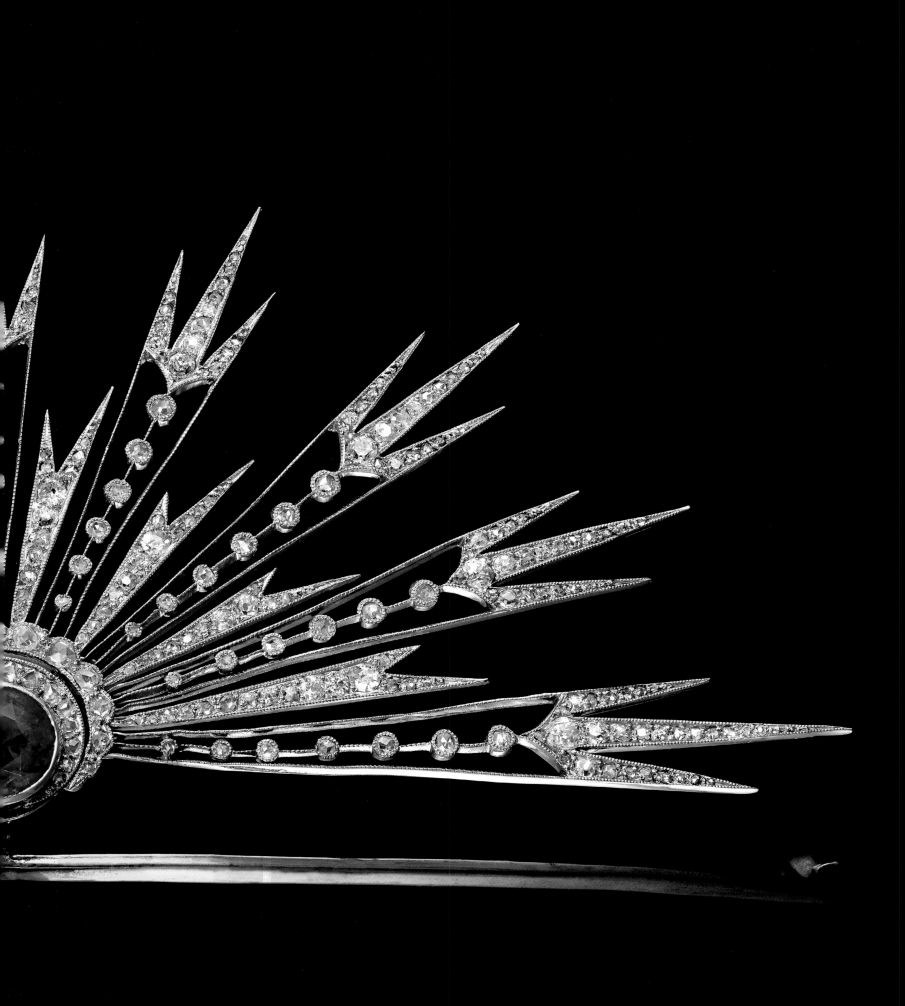

ABOVE
*Study for two "Egyptian"
head ornaments*, 1925.
Graphite pencil,
gouache, and ink wash,
H. 24; W. 32 cm
Chaumet Paris Collection

Mogul-style precious stones also inspired Chaumet to create a bandeau bracelet composed of a large number of these stones—emeralds, sapphires, and rubies—carved with plant, foliage, and berry motifs with stalks formed by small diamonds. The piece was acquired by Sacha Guitry, probably for his wife at the time, Yvonne Printemps.

A further variant of the Indian-inspired necklace, the *bayadère* (from the French word for a Hindu dancing-girl) was one of Chaumet's commonly produced creations during the Roaring Twenties. This long necklace with multiple strings of small natural pearls, sometimes twisted, sometimes including precious or semiprecious stones, often featured two "tassel" pendants made with strings of pearls topped with a precious ornament. The ornament crowning the tassels of the *bayadère* sold to one Madame Baumann in 1924 was in platinum set with sapphires and diamonds.

A second major source of inspiration for Art Deco designers was the Chinese artistic tradition, reflecting the continuing popularity of "*chinoiseries*" dating back to the

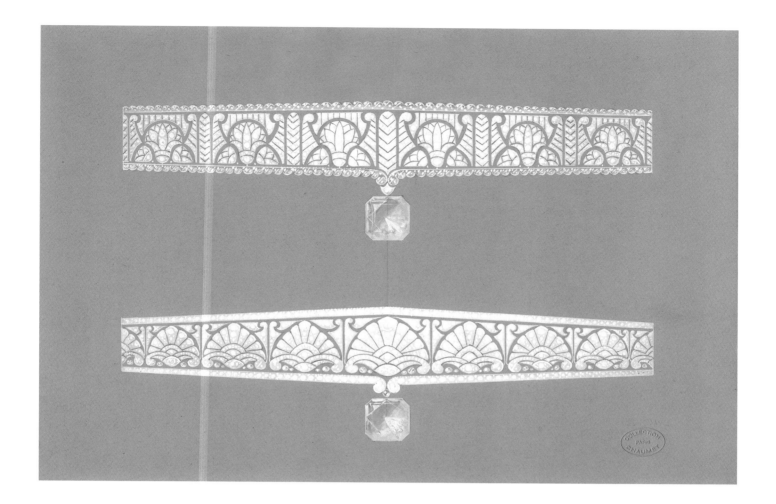

Renaissance. The first known piece by Chaumet obviously inspired by China, dating from about 1918, was a tassel of natural pearls topped with an ornament in platinum, onyx, and jade. This type of jewel was suspended on a simple chain, or a "rat's tail" cord, and it was fashionable to wear it thrown over the shoulder onto the back.

Jade, whether delicately carved or engraved, shaped into a pearl or disc, was the classic Chinese-style stone in jewelry. Chaumet showcased it in elegant pieces, particularly pendants and brooches. The refined pendant chosen by Queen Victoria-Eugénie of Spain in 1924 featured the "peacock" combination with a traditional sculpted motif in jade and three elongated pear-shaped blue stones; it was a fine example of the delicate and profoundly elegant style of the jeweler. In a different register, brooches occasionally featured a plaque of jade carved with a figurative motif, one example being a rectangular brooch with a border of caliber-cut onyx stones surrounding an imperial jade plaque depicting a junk, over a background of diamond clouds. This piece dates from circa 1925 and is now in the Chaumet

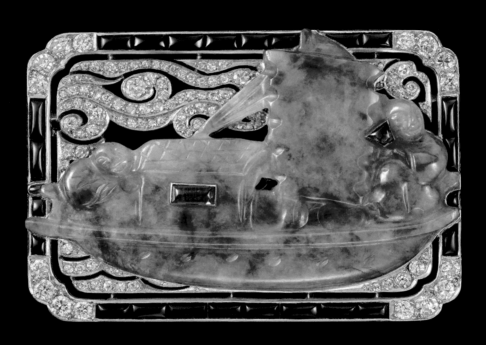

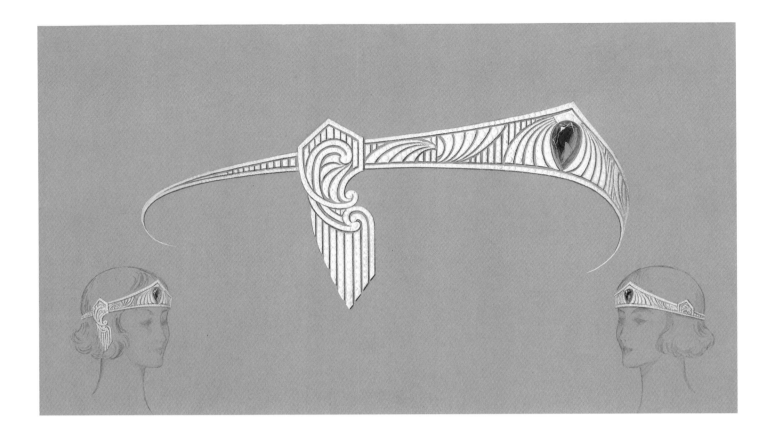

Collection. A similar style of brooch portraying a Confucius in jade over a geometric composition of onyx and diamonds was sold to Antenor Patiño in 1931. Another example, featuring a rectangular jade plaque delicately carved with a more stylized plant motif, was simply adorned by Chaumet in the 1920s with two vertical lines of diamonds. This precious brooch is now in the Tudor Place jewelry collection, Washington.

Because of their size, these large jade plaques were suitable for use as decorations for boxes, cigarette cases, and vanity cases. Chaumet designed and produced a large number of these precious "Chinese" accessories during this period, such as the above-mentioned hexagonal vanity case in lapis lazuli and nephrite, and a "vanity box with a Chinese decor," produced circa 1925, featuring a jade plaque framed with a Chinese motif in diamonds. But the Chinese inspiration could also manifest itself more allusively: a carved disc of jade placed in the center of a red enamel cigarette case created an equally exotic look. In certain accessories, it was suggested in traditional enamel motifs, an example being a small pocket watch with shutters in red and white enamel, featuring a diamond clasp and a movement by the great watchmaker Patek Philippe.

Aside from ancient Greek decorative motifs, other exotic or historical influences of Art Deco, notably black Africa and ancient Egypt, are practically absent from the Chaumet repertoire in this period, going by the archives and pieces that have come down to us. Among these there are only two brooches "with Egyptian warriors," with motifs directly inspired by ancient bas-reliefs. They were made for Chaumet by the studio of the brothers John and Robert Rubel in 1924. And among the firm's archived drawings, there is a single Egyptian-inspired piece: a bandeau with a stylized winged beetle in its center. Evidently, Joseph Chaumet was not particularly interested in the "Egyptomania" boosted by the discovery of the tomb of Tutankhamen by Howard Carter in 1922.

PAGE 348

*"Chinese junk"
brooch*, Lacloche for
Chaumet, c. 1925.
Platinum, imperial jade,
rubies, diamonds, onyx,
H. 3; W. 4.5 cm
Chaumet Paris Collection

PAGE 349

*Chinese-style
pendant*, c. 1925.
Platinum, diamonds, jade,
onyx, and natural pearls,
H. 12.5; W. 2.5 cm
Chaumet Paris Collection

ABOVE

*Study for a tiara
featuring an emerald
cabochon*, 1925.
Graphite pencil, gouache,
and sanguine wash,
H. 26; W. 45 cm
Chaumet Paris Collection

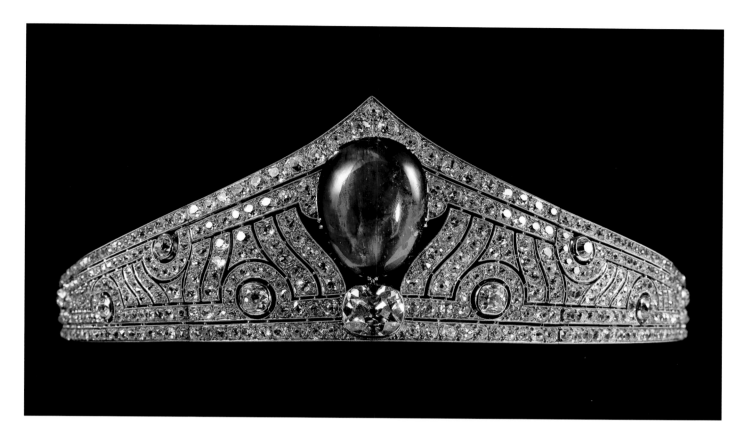

ABOVE

Tiara belonging to Charlotte, Grand Duchess of Luxembourg, 1926.
Platinum, cabochon emerald, and diamonds
Collection of the Grand Ducal Family of Luxembourg

RIGHT

Charlotte, Grand Duchess of Luxembourg, wearing a tiara made by Joseph Chaumet in 1926.

THE 1930s

The Roaring Twenties ended with the Great Depression, triggered by the Wall Street Crash of October 24, 1929. After taking its toll in the United States, the economic crisis hit Europe in the early 1930s, becoming a breeding ground for extremism and a major cause of World War II. The mood was neither festive nor eccentric. Flappers morphed into reassuring homemakers and fashions became more feminine. Crowned heads and wealthy aristocrats saw their power and privileges threatened, while middle-class socialites toned down their lifestyle and adopted more discreet behavior. Marcel Chaumet had to cut back staff in his Paris studios from eighty to fifteen employees.

The applied arts were affected by new lifestyles and the cost of certain materials, and Art Deco gradually waned during these somber years. Chaumet found itself with fewer customers who could afford luxurious jewelry with precious stones. A fair number of the sumptuous pieces produced by the firm at the time were made with family jewels provided by the customer, such as one of three pieces executed in 1936 for the wedding of Princess Alicia of Bourbon-Parma and the infante of Spain, Prince Alfonso of Bourbon-Two Sicilies. Still in the Art Deco style, with its geometric play of line and form, India-inspired motifs, and powerful contrast of red and white, the ensemble consisted of a bracelet, a pair of earrings, and a brooch paired with a chain, which together could be converted into a necklace with pendant and a bracelet. The rubies and diamonds were inherited from the groom's maternal grandmother, Maria Christina of Austria, queen consort of Spain. The previous year, the groom's uncle, King Alfonso XIII, purchased a brooch from Chaumet: of Indo-Persian inspiration also, and adorned with rubies and baguette-cut diamonds and brilliants, with matching drop earrings. These customers, who were still well off, enabled the jeweler to keep the business going at a minimum level.

Art Deco and its powerful contrasts of strong colors began to soften into a more feminine white. In architecture, the works of Le Corbusier and Robert Mallet-Stevens and that of interior designers such as Jean-Michel Frank and Arbus, the use of straw, parchment, and white fluffy fabrics heralded the end of the movement, while at the same time figurative representation was making a discreet comeback. In jewelry design, white was present in compositions in which platinum and diamonds formed motifs that were less geometric and more inspired by the natural world. Chaumet's designs included pieces in platinum and diamonds, sometimes rock crystal, which were either relatively discreet, such as a brooch with flame motifs acquired by the Marquis of Bourg de Bozas in 1934, or much more spectacular, for example the tiara made in 1931 for the Countess of Bessborough, born Roberte de Neuflize, on the occasion of her husband's appointment as Governor General of Canada. The design's motif of long, overlapping leaves of grass centered on a splendid navette- or marquise-cut diamond, a gift to the count from De Beers company associates in honor of his appointment.

Colored stones were still present, but hard times sparked a new taste for semiprecious stones, previously used as fillers in decorative designs. The bracelet made in 1937 for a Hollywood-based French actress, Lili Damita, wife of Errol Flynn at the time, made up of five large rectangular aquamarines and diamonds, is an example. Amethyst,

Long necklace with engraved stones convertible into a pair of bracelets, 1928–29. Platinum, engraved rubies and emeralds, diamonds, black enamel, L. 103 cm Private Collection

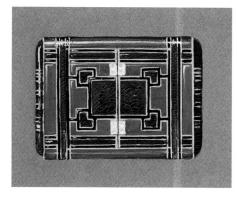
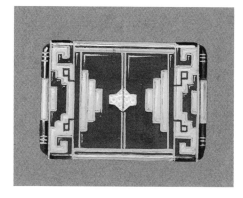
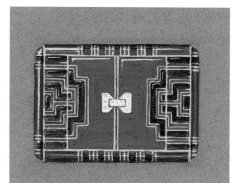

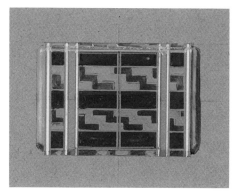
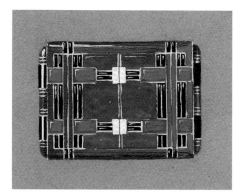
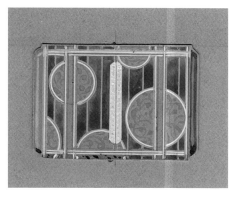
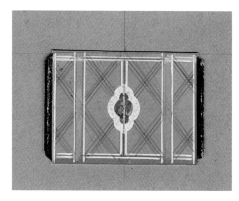
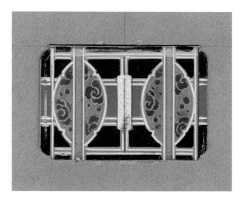
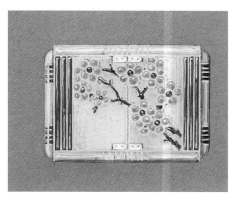
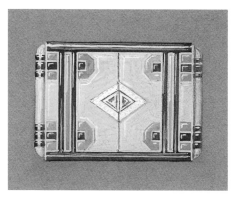
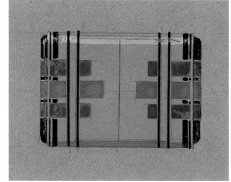

garnet, topaz, coral, and smoky quartz were also fashionable, and their many shades contributed to a more feminine look in jewelry.

In the mid 1930s, economic and social hardship also boosted the popularity of gold, less expensive than platinum. With increasing political threats and the general sense of anxiety, gold was a safe bet to fall back on. The return of gold gave the Chaumet jewelers a new source of inspiration and enabled them to compose powerful, elegantly structured pieces rich in relief, to wear on the wrist or as a clip brooch, which was replacing the classic pin brooch. The overall design was often "step cut" in appearance, with superposed or overlapping levels, in other words, the opposite of the flat surfaces typical of Art Deco. A striking bracelet in gold, diamonds, and rubies perfectly illustrates this multiple-relief style. Dating from around 1940, it was made by Chaumet with the Verger Frères firm, a famous designer of pieces with mechanisms and precious watch casings, and is now in London's Victoria & Albert Museum. Besides the visual effect of its subtly staggered levels, its particularity was that it was closed by pressing together the two separate halves of the bangle, revealing its precious core, three golden discs mounted with caliber-cut rubies standing out from a field of pavé-set diamonds.

After the declaration of war on September 3, 1939, Chaumet's stock was hidden in the countryside. During the war years, with staff and customers called up, a shortage of stones and precious metals considerably limited production, which was nevertheless maintained thanks to a few commissions for work on jewelry brought in by customers. Normal business only resumed on the liberation of France, spawning numerous designs with a patriotic theme, before a new, cheerful, and feminine creativity emerged much later, in the 1950s.

PAGE 354

Handbag watch with a red-and-white enameled pattern, c. 1925.
Gold, diamonds, enamel,
H. 0.6; W. 4.5; D. 3 cm
Chaumet Paris Collection

PAGE 355

Series of designs for handbag watches with enameled patterns, c. 1925.
Graphite pencil, gouache,
H. 16; W. 23.5 cm
Chaumet Paris Collection

ABOVE AND FACING PAGE

Retro-style bangle, Verger Frères for Chaumet, 1935–45.
Gold, platinum, rubies, diamonds, H. 6; W. 5.7; D. 3.2 cm
Victoria and Albert Museum, London

Splendors of the Indies

Alain Stella

For the Parisian jewelers, and their London branches if they had one, the Roaring Twenties were also marked by the tastes of the maharajas. Some of these Indian princes were Francophile, others Anglophile. They traveled widely and were naturally familiar with Western fashions, which they readily embraced. Nevertheless, they remained profoundly attached to their traditions, including an adoration of precious stones, which symbolized the power of the gods from which their own sovereignty derived. In the 1920s, many of them entrusted jewelry pieces and ensembles with French firms—sometimes also providing a mass of precious stones—so that they could be reworked in more modern, lighter designs.

Joseph Chaumet seems to have been the first of the great jewelers to grasp the potential of this market: as early as December 1910, he sent some of his staff to meet with Sayaji Rao Gaekwad III, Maharaja of Baroda. This lover of precious stones—he was fond of wearing a famous diamond, the 128.48 carat Star of the South—appears to have called on the expertise of Joseph Chaumet as a reputed gemologist some time earlier, to appraise the quality of his treasure and to consider remounting his collection of traditional jewelry. Naturally, it was primarily as a jeweler that Chaumet accepted this request, and sent his team to India. His representatives took with them not only jewelry pieces that had been commissioned for the maharani, but also a large number of drawings—crowns, sabers, tableware—that might appeal to the prince. However, this would not be the case, this time, because the prince deemed the pieces unfitting for Indian clothing. Furthermore, the stones could not be assessed because the settings of the scientific instruments had been disturbed during transport. In January 1911, the team set off again, however,

with a commission for a silver desk trim, and the continued patronage of Sayaji Rao. That same year, during several trips to Paris, the maharaja with his wife and nineteen-year-old daughter, Indira, purchased from the jeweler some pieces of traditional Indian inspiration (earrings and a choker), a spectacular pendant watch whose diamond-paved case was set in a ring of crystal bordered with emeralds, and, for the maharani, a platinum and diamond bag. The Baroda family would remain customers of Chaumet until at least the 1930s.

On October 1, 1913, another powerful Indian ruler, Tukoji Rao Holkar III, Maharaja of Indore, was in Paris. He came to number 12, Place Vendôme and asked to see items of jewelry. The sales staff presented a number of wonderful pieces, and the maharaja showed particular interest in a pearl ring and two magnificent and inseparable pear-shaped diamonds of 46.70 and 46.95 carats. These came with a drawing of a very modern design, in which they hung, gracefully staggered, on a flexible necklace cord of diamonds forming a simple, loose knot. The maharaja bought the ring, and said he would pick it up the next day along with the bill. Doubtless he had decided to sleep on it: he was mostly interested in the necklace with the two diamonds, but its price, a little over 231,000 francs, gave him pause.

It was not surprising that the Maharaja of Indore should be drawn to this sumptuous jewel. The two stones were fascinating in themselves, but what pleased him most was the overall style of the necklace, a splendidly modern design. It was another example of Joseph Chaumet's fondness for the pared-down look of what was not yet called Art Deco. And it matched the tastes of the maharaja, who, unlike many of his peers who preferred

The Maharaja of Indore's orders, 1911–13. Invoice book and design project for the pair of pear diamonds known as "the Pears of Indore"

Bill from the Bombay Taj Mahal Hotel during the Chaumet mission to the Indies in 1910–11 Chaumet Paris Collection and Archives

THE "TAJ MAHAL" PALACE HOTEL.

adresse

Maharajah of Indore

303

1934

BERNARD
B DE MONVEL

FACING PAGE

*The Maharaja of
Indore's "Pears of Indore"
necklace*, 1911–13.
Print from gelatin silver
bromide glass negative,
H. 28.5; W. 17.5 cm
Chaumet Paris Collection

ABOVE

Bernard Boutet de Monvel
(1884–1949), *Portrait of
H.R.H. the Maharaja of
Indore*, 1933–34.
Oil on canvas,
H. 180; W. 180 cm
Private Collection

Yeshwant Rao Holkar,
Maharaja of Indore,
wearing the Chaumet
pear diamonds.

the classical French style, had been attracted from an early date to the stylized and abstract forms of modernity. He would later commission the architect and interior designer René Herbst, cofounder of the Union des Artistes Modernes in 1929, to decorate several of his residences.

The next day, the Maharaja of Indore returned to Chaumet. He collected the ring—and purchased the two diamonds as well as the necklace designed for them. He also left a ring with a pear-shaped diamond for Chaumet to reset in a lighter mount. The necklace and ring were sent to him by registered post fifteen days later. The sovereign remained loyal to Chaumet throughout the 1920s, purchasing from the firm various costly pieces with a modern design.

Many other princes and princesses of the Indian Empire frequented the Chaumet salons in Paris or in London during this period, including the Maharaja of Kashmir and the Rana ruler of Nepal, who commissioned a sumptuous traditional headdress adorned with pearls, emeralds, and rubies. Chaumet's Indian customers were not only members of ruling families: they included, for example, Lady Tata, wife of the fabulously wealthy businessman Ratanji Dadabhoy Tata, born Suzanne Brière in France, who was a loyal Chaumet customer in the 1920s.

ABOVE
Study of a crown headdress for a maharaja, c. 1920.
Graphite pencil, gouache, and ink wash, H. 25; W. 26 cm
Chaumet Paris Collection

FACING PAGE
Study for a "Peacock" necklace, c. 1920
Graphite pencil, gouache, and ink wash, H. 35; W. 24 cm
Chaumet Paris Collection

The Trévise Parure: An Example of Disassembly and Transformation

Karine Huguenaud

A loyal clientele is the key to Chaumet's history. The trust placed in the jeweler by grand families was an essential component of enduring relations based on discretion and confidentiality. Thanks to its thorough knowledge of its clients' collections of jewelry, which it supplied, serviced, and then altered from generation to generation and from marriage to marriage, Chaumet became witness to their private moments and major rites of passage. Indeed, one of the roles of a grand jeweler is to repair, alter, and modernize old jewels. One illuminating example is the matching set of jewelry known as the Trévise parure, for it clearly shows the creative process of placing an order, a process involving much communication between client and jeweler. The history of this parure and its successive transformations can be accurately traced thanks to a comparative study of drawings and photographs and various other Chaumet archive documents (visitors' book, ledger of consignments, ledger of stones, and invoice ledger).[1]

On August 25, 1904, the Duchess of Trévise went to Chaumet to order a tiara for the wedding of her daughter, Jeanne, to Hervé Budes, Count of Guébriant, in Paris on October 22. The duchess—wife of the 4th Duke of Trévise, a descendent of Marshal Édouard Mortier, whom Napoleon had named Duke of Trévise in 1808—had brought old family jewels with her. She deposited with Chaumet a series of sapphires-and-diamonds pieces: a pair of stud earrings, a cross, and a brooch. She asked that one of the studs be set as a ring and that the rest be used to make a tiara. Two designs for a tiara were given to her that very day.

She also deposited a sapphire-and-diamond necklace, asking that it be lengthened by adding the ornament from a sapphire ring she also consigned to Chaumet. All these items were photographed, valued, and carefully recorded in the ledger of stones. On August 31 the duchess returned the two proposed designs of the tiara and brought a "coiffure" to serve as a model for the proposed tiara. On September 3 she was shown two drawings, followed by three others on September 8. On September 15 she placed a firm order for a foliate tiara that she wished to see completed by mid-October, several days before the wedding. The final design shows two delicate floral branches of diamonds that meet in the middle, a compositional approach typical of Chaumet's naturalist style during the Belle Époque. The main feature was to be twelve sapphires weighing over sixty carats in total. A model was made, and only after several trials was the tiara executed with the stones from the jewels consigned by the duchess. In keeping with the French tradition of displaying wedding gifts prior to the event itself—usually on the day the marriage contract is signed—the sapphire-and-diamond parure ordered on September 15 was delivered on October 20, two days before the ceremony. The contract was signed the next day. A photo taken the day prior to delivery shows all three pieces of the set: foliate tiara, ring, and altered necklace.

The necklace with its splendid sapphires still exists, but the tiara does not. In late 1945 Count Jean de Guébriant brought it in for another transformation. On December 17, 1945, he ordered a "sapphire and diamond bracelet of silver and chrome-plated gold" along with "two sapphire and diamond clip earrings." Photographed, valued, and disassembled, the old-fashioned tiara of 1904 was transformed into a hinged bracelet with large, chunky shapes, typical of the 1940s vintage style. And that is how it still looks today.

1   Visitors' book, August-September 1904; Ledger of consignments, September 1904; Invoice ledger N (1904–5, p. 166); Invoice ledger Gran-Guy. Negative archives: glass plate negatives no. 2096 (October 19, 1904), no. 19883 (December 17, 1945), no. 21658 (January 22, 1946). Chaumet Archives, Paris. Album of Tiara Designs, 1880–1910, Chaumet Paris Collection.

FACING PAGE

Order placed by the Duchess of Trévise for the "Foliage" tiara, 1904. Invoice book Chaumet Paris Archives

SEPTEM
190

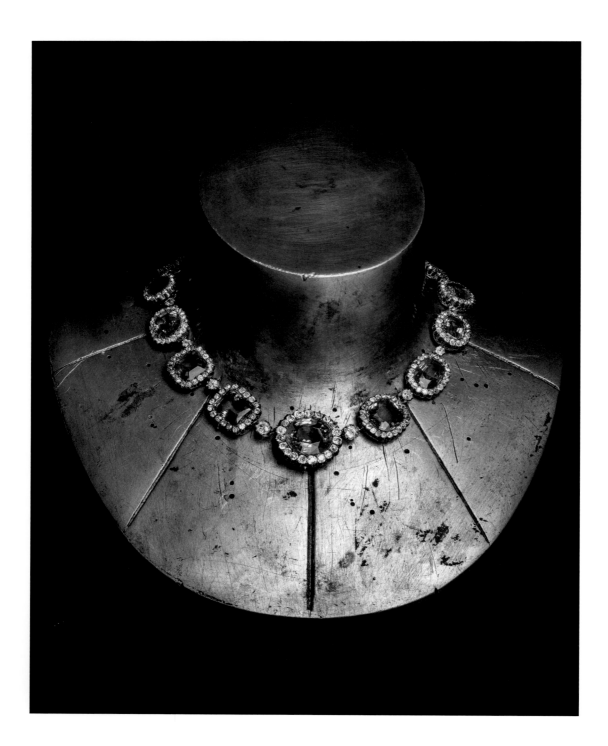

PAGES 366–367
*The "Foliage" tiara
ordered by the Duchess
of Trévise*, 1904.
Original print from gelatin
silver bromide glass
negative, study of the
tiara and guest book
from September 1904
Chaumet Paris Collection
and Archives

LEFT
*Necklace of the Duchess
of Trévise*, 1905.
Silver, gold,
diamonds, sapphires,
H. 2.6; W. 36; D. 1 cm
Private Collection

FACING PAGE
*Bracelet featuring sapphire
cabochons*, 1945.
Silver, gold, diamonds,
sapphires, H. 2.2; W. 17 cm
Private Collection

Theater, Music Hall, and Cinema

Karine Huguenaud and Alain Stella

Since the early nineteenth century, the Chaumet Archives have witnessed the patronage of personalities from the world of the stage, from actresses such as Mademoiselle Mars in the First Empire to the great tragedian Rachel in the July Monarchy, who in 1846 rejected an acrostic bracelet from Fossin that featured the name and portrait of her lover, the Count Alexandre Walewski, illegitimate son of Napoleon and Marie Walewska, because he was going to marry another woman.

In the Belle Époque, Chaumet customers included Réjane, queen of popular theater and a leading contemporary theater actress; Gilda Darthy, who excelled in the classical repertory; and Cécile Sorel of the Comédie Française, who patronized Chaumet to indulge her passion for pearls. Music hall or variety theater and

cinema have made their appearance, too: Caroline Otero, known as La Belle Otero, a famous courtesan whose dance numbers were captured on film in 1898, making her one of the earliest film stars, and the actress and singer Mistinguett, who purchased pearl necklaces in 1913. Some highly glamorous celebrities appear in the archives of the interwar period. The Hungarian-born Dolly Sisters, Jenny and Rosie, dancers who started out at the Ziegfeld Follies and whose flapper style caused a sensation on music hall stages from Broadway to Paris and captured the heart of wealthy magnates. Harry Gordon Selfridge, founder of London's first department store, was smitten and spent a fortune on them. The Heavenly Twins, as they were nicknamed, perfectly embodied the whirlwind Roaring Twenties, which ended with the stock market

crash of 1929. They were frequent customers of Chaumet and owned a jewelry collection estimated at several million dollars. Another international star was Lili Damita, who began her career at the age of fourteen as a ballerina at Paris's Palais Garnier Opera House, and performed at various music hall theaters before becoming the lead dancer at the Casino de Paris. She was a silent film actress in the 1920s, and in 1928 went to Hollywood, where she became a star alongside the greatest actors of the day, Cary Grant, Gary Cooper, Maurice Chevalier, Laurence Olivier, and James Cagney. Lili Damita commissioned pearl necklaces and diamond bracelets from Chaumet, and continued to patronize the firm after her marriage to Errol Flynn in 1935.

The playwright, filmmaker, screenwriter, and actor Sacha Guitry was one of the best-known personalities in France in the first half of the twentieth century. He was a loyal Chaumet customer, purchasing a number of precious waistcoat buttons for himself, as well as a signet ring with a fine sapphire cabochon in 1923. He also acquired numerous items of jewelry from Chaumet for his second wife, the popular actress and singer Yvonne Printemps. In 1924, he gave her a bracelet in a typical Art Deco style, with strongly contrasting forms and colors. The bracelet chain supporting an impressive 111 carat oval emerald cabochon is made up of decreasing-sized trapezoidal links of onyx and a band of diamonds. Flappers often wore sleeveless evening wear and so loved to adorn their bare arms with several bracelets. Guitry was equally generous towards his next wives, Jacqueline Delubac, then Lana Marconi. Marconi gave Alain Decaux the emerald that Guitry wore in a signet ring until the end of his life. Acquired by Chaumet in the 1920s, this emerald would be mounted on the academician's saber that the jeweler made for the historian on his election to the Académie Française in 1980.

ABOVE
Yvonne Printemps wearing Chaumet jewels, including the famous 111-carat emerald cabochon bracelet, 1936.

FACING PAGE
Sacha Guitry wearing his emerald signet ring, Raymond Voinquel (1912–1994), Photo: Studio Harcourt, 1935.

FROM THE 1960S TO THE NEW MILLENNIUM

Béatrice de Plinval

"Octopus" necklace, Robert Lemoine for Chaumet, 1970. Sculpted frosted rock crystal and jasper, diamonds, rubellite H. 24; W. 12 cm Collection of Her Royal Highness Princess of Bourbon-Two Sicilies

—

Part of the wedding basket ordered by Sir Valentine Abdy, 6th Baron of Albyns, for his future wife Mathilde de La Ferté, this necklace representing an octopus symbolises the desire for possession of the newly married couple and is typical of the renewed interest shown after 1968 for iconic creations by surrealist artists such as Salvador Dali, Man Ray or Meret Oppenheim.

Béatrice de Plinval joined Chaumet in 1968 after studying at the École des Beaux-Arts in Tours and the École des Arts Décoratifs in Paris. She witnessed a new creativity being forged at Chaumet by several enlightened and influential artists. Working alongside them, the young designer discovered the world of fine jewelry.

In the course of the year 1968, one day a week, I was allowed to come and learn the technique of jewelry gouache painting under the fine-jewelry designer Gisèle Crevier. She had joined Chaumet in 1959 and had the privilege of working mainly for Jean-Louis Vitse, the firm's head salesman. Madame Crevier was nicknamed "Casque d'Or" (Golden Helmet) after Simone Signoret because of the color of her hair and distinctive chignon, and she mostly designed special orders. With her I practised my skills to get a better grasp of the technique. She had me copy several of her drawings from the 1960s. Her biting sense of humor did not put me off; I respected her, and worked hard. I was able to observe the various personalities and talents of the designers. They were all conscientious, if a tad routine and classical in their approach. But one of them surprised me at our first meeting with his knowledge, whimsy, and sense of humor. He transcended convention, and was determined to give a free rein to his most unusual ideas. His name was René Morin.

The following year, on July 1, 1969, I joined the Chaumet Design Studio. A lot of shared laughter and joie de vivre, as well as ideas in common, soon drew me closer to the man who would become my first master in our craft.

RENÉ MORIN: A NEW VISION

As a student of sculpture at the École des Beaux-Arts in Lyon, René Morin was already fascinated by precious materials, gold, and stones. He attended a jewelry-making school, going on to apprentice at various studios, including that of the Parisian jewelry house of Murat, founded in the nineteenth century. There he studied material treatment and the art of metalwork, executing drawings and models of jewelry pieces and other precious objects. But his whimsical style, creativity, passion, and imagination were detected by one Monsieur Divient, who no doubt realized that this unusual and talented young man should explore new horizons. He advised him to apply to work at Chaumet.

Marcel Chaumet took him on in 1962. At the time, Morin says, the firm was viewed as something of a creative Sleeping Beauty. The year of his arrival, he considered Cartier to be the most creative jewelry maker, but preferred the technique of Van Cleef & Arpels. And so he undertook to breathe new life into Chaumet. He was fascinated by what he found. Nothing had shifted or changed for so many years. Everything was meticulously preserved, with that same concern for the continuation of excellence. Everything could be recreated. In the 1970s, there was little interest in the history of the firm, but for Morin, the time had come to revive the house and restore its legitimacy.

As a talented sculptor, he joined the artistic tradition of Chaumet. In 1965, he created the Unicorn (*Licorne*). He saw this small object as symbolizing a creative turning point. He was inspired by an uncut piece of lapis lazuli featuring the head of a mythical creature. He would use the unicorn theme in a number of works. One of his first precious objects was a clock featuring a lapis lazuli unicorn with an aquamarine-and-diamond-studded mane. It was purchased by King Hassan II of Morocco; a first sign of what the future would hold for the man who would go on to create so many extraordinary pieces for the Kingdom of Morocco.

That same year he created the Minotaur *(Minotaure)* along the same lines as the Unicorn, with variations in the form of a brooch and a bracelet.

In 1968–69, he invented the concept of *or sauvage*, "roughly textured gold." Whether given a mat or highly polished finish, this gold gave the impression of being in the rough. Numerous necklaces, pendants, brooches, bracelets, and rings were executed in this manner and sold at the Arcade, Chaumet's first boutique opened in 1969 and located to the right of the jewelry shop established in 1907. The jewelry shop retained its traditional atmosphere owing to the precious diamond, colored stone, and natural pearl jewelry pieces presented there by the house sales assistants, all male.

Chaumet's first female sales assistants made their appearance at the new Arcade boutique, which had a contemporary decor. They wore a uniform, and, as the magazine *Marie-France* reported in 1973, "You have only to cross the threshold, look at the showcases, where each piece is clearly marked with the price, and a hostess, pretty and smilng as one

"Unicorn" clip,
René Morin for
Chaumet, 1965.
Lapis lazuli, turquoises,
and diamonds,
H. 7.5; W. 5; D. 2.4 cm
Private Collection

FACING PAGE, TOP

Staging for an advertisement for the sets in roughly textured gold, highly polished white gold, and diamonds designed by René Morin in 1970.
Chaumet Archives

FACING PAGE, BOTTOM

Flower set in roughly textured gold and highly polished white gold, 1970.
Chaumet Archives

TOP, LEFT

Design for a naturalistic necklace, René Morin, c. 1975.
Graphite pencil, gouache, ocher chalk highlights, cut-and-pasted paper,
H. 50; L. 32 cm
Chaumet Paris Collection

TOP, RIGHT

Design for a "Flower and panther paw" necklace, René Morin, c. 1975.
Graphite pencil, stump, gouache, and ink wash,
H. 50; L. 32 cm
Chaumet Paris Collection

would expect, is ready to answer questions.… The mood is relaxed, youthful, and designed to put you at your ease."[1]

It was at the Arcade that the highly polished white gold, yellow gold, and diamond pieces of naturalistic inspiration were showcased. René Morin presented five extraordinary, powerful necklaces, all one-off designs.

In 1972, Chaumet created the *Bestiaire Fabuleux* (Fabulous Bestiary) with Baccarat. Using blocks of rough crystal salvaged from the bottom of the melting pots (the residue of cooled crystal after the furnace is turned off), inspired by their diverse, random forms, Morin set about creating a bestiary. That year, more than fifty animals in crystal and vermeil were executed and put on display for several weeks at the Musée de la Chasse et de la Nature in Paris.

I was fortunate to work closely with Morin while these objects were being made. Our drawing tables were replaced by sculpting stands, where we fashioned the most fantastical creatures. Using modeling clay we would shape the identity of the future animal. René would sketch out an idea and then leave me to develop it and make it to his specifications. Once the modeling was completed and approved, the studio would set about making a lost-wax mold.

We shared an interest in animal art. While our predecessors had produced masterly designs inspired by nature, few of these featured mammals. Roebucks and other deer, horses, foxes, bulls, antelopes, and panthers filled the studio.

Credit for this remarkable new and highly original idea of a Fabulous Bestiary must go entirely to René Morin. We, the studio designers, were simply followers. But it taught us much that would later serve each of us as we followed our respective paths.

1   Quoted in Diana Scarisbrick, *Chaumet: Master Jewelers Since 1780* (Paris: Alain de Gourcuff, 1995), p. 304.

The years 1960–70 marked a new turn at Chaumet. Morin's fertile imagination when it came to creating fantastical objects expressed itself in a way that was both powerful and poetic.

The year 1980 saw the launch of the *Pierres d'Or* (Golden Stones) Collection. It was inspired by the ornamental reliefs on keystones over the carriage doors of Parisian mansion houses. René used these motifs in a series of necklaces at the center of which hung a pure gold cabochon, lightly hammered or cracked. The neckband might be a string of pearls, but was more often a braided silk cord of varying colors, onto which the central motif could be threaded. A series of earrings, pendants, and small watches were also created on the same theme.

Morin pursued his creative revolution with his reinterpretation of the Link *(Lien)* Collection in 1980. This symbol of the firm had already appeared in the Belle Époque, in shaped chokers, headbands, and tiaras. The *Lien* Collection showcased at the Arcade boutique was in yellow gold. It featured a simple and charming small ring that was easy to wear, more youthful and accessible, followed by a bracelet and soon afterward a necklace. The Link has proved to be an inexhaustible and enduring theme in Chaumet's collections, a strongly sentimental symbol through the firm's history.

In 1984 Morin presented the *Nouveaux Regards* Collection, made up of twenty-seven fragments of objects from various civilizations—ancient Egypt, Greece, Persia, the Khmer kingdom, Mexico, and the Ashanti kingdom—mounted in gold and set with precious stones. Morin's taste for unusual objects to which he lent a function prompted him to create a series of clocks. The most modern themes and mounts echoed the cutting-edge technology of the time, his beloved "sputnik" style, for example. For a head of state he made the first American space shuttle, "The Space Shuttle Columbia," in gold, an unusual desk holder for a calculator, a thermometer, and a chronometer.

Among the more surprising objects created were ruby-studded ivory ear picks, gold and diamond shoe buckles, a desk table and chairs in tortoiseshell, and trophies for horse races and even camel races.

The Chaumet tradition of executing large cups in hardstone and precious objects since the late eighteenth century was interpreted in the most unusual manner in the 1970s: this exquisite little mouse lacquered in apple green on gold, for example, sitting on a frosted rock crystal base and nibbling at a diamond-studded lump of sugar, which was a clock.

Robert Lemoine (1909–1976): Sculptor of Semiprecious Stones

Béatrice de Plinval

Our collaboration with Robert Lemoine was pivotal. He had worked for Marcel Sandoz, for Cartier in the 1930s, and for Pierre Sterlé, and was an artist who surprised us constantly. René and I regularly visited him at his studio in Enghien-les-Bains outside Paris to give him new work. Every six weeks he came to Place Vendôme. The reason for his visit was naturally to bring us the work we had commissioned; but he would also go to Quai de la Mégisserie to buy a hamster for his boa constrictor, which lived in a glass cage on the cast-iron lid of the stove in his studio. I soon discovered that the six-week interlude was also the amount of time it took the boa to digest the rodent.

Lemoine was a solitary and kindly man who lived for his art. He would forget to keep track of the time spent. What mattered to him was the material he was working with, and how to bring it out in the most sensitive way possible. He excelled in the art of sculpting horses, and in tracing faces such as Pierrot, the first of my dress-clip drawings to be executed. He also sculpted brooches for the *Cartes à Jouer* (Playing Cards) series, the Military Trophy clips, and the *Châteaux* series, to which René kindly asked me to contribute. Lemoine had created brooches depicting Windsor Castle and Sleeping Beauty's castle, and chose to execute two of my drawings, one depicting the Mont Saint-Michel in aquamarine, white gold, and white and yellow *or sauvage* (roughly textured gold), the other the Château de Puységur in tigereye and *or sauvage*.

Robert Lemoine's work is admirable, yet remains little known. Pierre Sterlé and René Morin are indisputably the two designers of the period 1960–80 who fully recognized his talent.

LEFT
"Argine, the queen of clubs" brooch, Pierre Sterlé (1905–1978) for Chaumet, head carved by Robert Lemoine, c. 1965. Gold, malachite, aquamarine, diamonds, H 6.5; W. 8 cm
Chaumet Paris Collection

ABOVE
"Château de Puységur" brooch, Robert Lemoine. Roughly textured gold, white gold, sculpted tigereye
Chaumet Paris Collection

When Pope John XXIII visited Morocco on the invitation of King Hassan II, the King asked us to make his gift for the Pontiff: a gold cross and chain. When the design was presented to him for approval, the King asked for the following words to be engraved on the back of the cross: *Une phrase commune à nos deux religions : "Fils d'Abraham, unissons-nous"* ("A phrase common to both our religions: 'Sons of Abraham, let us unite'").

René Morin's imagination was boundless. And above all, he had a sense of the object. The jewelry pieces he made were imbued with the same originality and forcefulness. He allowed his imagination to run free—a privilege for him, and also for Chaumet. Having the necessary distance and perspective to analyze an era and a style, Morin left his stamp on us. He understood, loved, and interpreted Chaumet with true passion. His work would become a touchstone in jewelry history.

PIERRE STERLÉ (1905–1978): AN UNCLASSIFIABLE JEWELER

One day in 1976, Jacques Chaumet called me into his office. He told me Pierre Sterlé had been appointed as technical adviser, and offered me the job of taking his ideas on board and putting them into practice. When I met the man whom the poet Lucien François described as having "reinvented the art of torturing metal,"[2] I had just turned twenty-eight.

He stood straight as an arrow, had a wonderful smile, amazing blue eyes, and real class. As Viviane Jutheau said in a book she wrote about him in 1990, he was "a pioneering jeweler, atypical, unclassifiable, brilliant."[3]

From 1961, Pierre Sterlé made many of his designs for Chaumet, mostly brooches and earrings. His inventiveness and constant probing of the material bore similarities to the work of René Morin. Sterlé was essentially a jewelry maker. He lacked the strong sculptural approach that René had taught me, but brought more movement, lightness, and femininity.

On his arrival at Chaumet, Pierre Sterlé was smart or tactful enough not to have me draw the themes that he had so brilliantly explored earlier with his designers such as Jacques Desnoues and Yves Poussielgues. I showed him Chaumet from the inside. We talked for hours. He told me about his life. Then I told him about mine, and ventured to show him my work. When he came back the next day, he said to me casually, "Béatrice, now we're a team. You're the white horse and I'm the black horse."

The jewelry pieces we made together speak for themselves. Bronze and gold work in tandem in the *Ginkgo* necklace, the *Arôme* necklace, the pendant disks inspired by Pre-Columbian drawings. Together we made a naturalistic-style necklace featuring an exceptional pairing of Burmese rubies set in a fringe of baguette-cut diamonds. During the production meetings, the studio jewelers would listen to him like a master. He was so good at explaining and courteously imposing his technique.

2   Marguerite de Serval, *Dictionnaire international du bijou* (Paris: Éditions du Regard, 1998), p. 504.

3   Viviane Jutheau, *Sterlé Joaillier Paris* (Paris: Éditions Vecteurs, 1990), n.p.

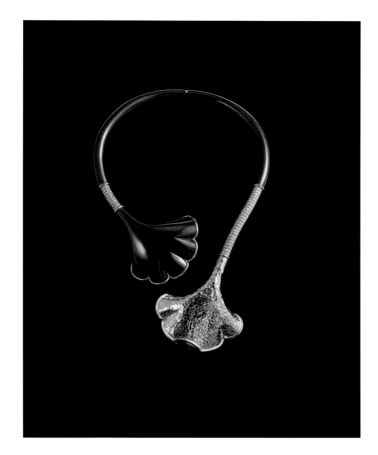

Every Monday, Pierre came in with a new idea he'd picked up here or there: a piece of driftwood from a beach, a grain of wheat, a leaf. Japanese art fascinated him. He loved all poetry. Beyond this inexhaustible source of inspiration, what we all had in common was a passion for drawing inspiration from nature. How often he uttered the word "superb!" For him, detail was that extra touch which could make something good very good, or something very good outstanding.

Pierre Sterlé's work as a jeweler is admirably described by the writer Colette, a friend of his, in her book *The Blue Lantern (Le Fanal bleu)*: "By improving my acquaintance with him, I am able to increase my familiarity with an expansive taste in which I have never indulged. I learn any number of names. I finger the lovely yellow metal, cold at first but quickly warming to the touch, the abettor of so many crimes and wars. More than once, anticipating its eventual recipient, have I held in my hands some gorgeous plaything long promised and awaited with feverish impatience. In the hollow of my hand I have held a precious stone, naked as a slave without a master. I might well have believed it to be a live ember I was smothering, so curiously did its darting red and yellow fires glow within it."[4]

The Dawn of the Twenty-First Century

In an interview by Vincent Toledano published in 1995 in the first issue of the *Chaumet* magazine, Catherine Deneuve, a frequent visitor to the boutique on Place Vendôme, said, "Jewelry is an essential accessory. I love jewelry worn in a casual, undressy way… in fact, I love everything that's romantic," laughing at this turn of phrase.[5] These words summed up the spirit of Chaumet's future collections.

The famous *Anneau de Chaumet* (Chaumet Ring) designed in 1989 by Xavier Rousseau was full-bodied and voluptuous. In yellow gold, pink gold, or white gold, its pink diamond pavé setting transformed it into a precious jewel. A pair of matching earrings completed this elegant ensemble in a simple yet strong style that would characterize the early 1990s.

The year 1997 saw the creation of the *Fidélité* (Fidelity) Collection. Chaumet retained the simplicity typifying the pieces of this decade, while continuing to forge its tradition of the sentimental jewel as a symbol of attachment, as illustrated by the choker or "dog collar" in yellow gold paved with white diamonds, featuring two push-button clasps in yellow gold paved with pink diamonds.

In 2003, Chaumet's artistic director Lionel Giraud chose Stella Tennant as the new face of the firm's advertising campaigns, photographed by Richard Burbridge. She wore the Bourbon-Parma tiara made in 1919, a masterpiece among the heritage collections of the Chaumet museum, and the Class One watch in steel, diamonds, and rubber. The writer and journalist Laurence Benaïm commented on this powerful confrontation through which Chaumet gave new impetus to its story: "The supreme luxury is time, the time we

Coral set: necklace and earrings, Chaumet, 1980. Gold, platinum, coral, and diamonds. Necklace: H. 23.5; W. 19.5; D. 1.8 cm. Earrings: H. 6.2; W. 2; D. 1.8 cm Private Collection

4   Colette, *The Blue Lantern*, trans. Roger Senhouse (New York: Farrar, Straus and Giroux, 1963), p. 153.

5   Vincent Toledano, "Catherine Deneuve—J'adore les bijoux," *Chaumet* 1 (Fall–Winter 1995–96), p. 7.

take, and the time we give. The harmonious juxtaposition of tradition and modernity is echoed in the new Chaumet advertising campaign. An intimate encounter where history complements the future."

After the *Napoléon Amoureux* exhibition opened at Chaumet in September 2004, celebrating the bicentennial of the Consecration of Napoleon and the Coronation of Joséphine, the time had come for Chaumet to pay tribute to the personality, taste, charm, and modernity of Empress Joséphine, one of the firm's earliest patrons. In 2010, Lionel Giraud presented the first Joséphine Collection in the Tiara Room. For the occasion, the Museo Napoleonico in Rome loaned the large portrait of Joséphine commissioned by Emperor Napoleon I from the painter Robert Lefèvre in 1805. Joséphine is shown wearing a court dress embroidered with ears of wheat, a motif that is very much part of Chaumet's identity. Wheat features in the oldest drawings of our collections dating back to the late eighteenth century, and continues to inspire the creative themes of Chaumet's contemporary designs.

The ear of wheat represents the very essence of the house of Chaumet. The firm's founder, Marie-Étienne Nitot, made it his hallmark in 1783. It is also the attribute of Ceres, goddess of agriculture who taught men the art of sowing, cultivating, and harvesting. What better promise of a bountiful future?

LEFT
"Liens" bangle,
Chaumet, 2003.
White gold and diamonds,
H. 4; D. 6.8 (large),
6.2 cm (small)
Chaumet Paris Collection

FACING PAGE
"Ears of wheat"
brooch, 2015.
Gold, diamonds,
H. 12.6; W. 3.7 cm
Chaumet Paris Collection

PRIMARY SOURCES

ARCHIVES NATIONALES, PARIS
IMPERIAL HOUSEHOLD: GRANDS OFFICIERS
DE LA COURONNE (FIRST EMPIRE)
O² 6, 29, 30, 31, 32, 34, 41, 150, 153, 470,
537, 635, 636, 770

CONSULATE AND IMPERIAL SECRETARY OF
STATE (YEAR VIII [1800])
AF/IV 1711/B

ROYAL HOUSEHOLD AND CIVIL LIST
(JULY MONARCHY)
O⁴ 1394 and 1725

INDIVIDUAL AND FAMILY ARCHIVES
300/AP/I/2417 à 2421 (Royal House of
France - Orléans branch)
371/AP/21 (Château de Rosny Collection—
Duke and Duchess of Berry)
400/AP/4, 35, 84, 135 (Napoleon Collection)

PRIVATE PAPERS IN THE PUBLIC DOMAIN
T 299/8 (register)

CENTRAL FILE (MINUTIER CENTRAL)
MC, I/677, VIII/1658, XIV/560, XV/1804,
XXVIII/588, XLVIII/537, LXIX/841,
LXXXIV/441, LXXXVII/1333, 1334, 1363,
1454, 1470 and 1557, XCII/305, XCIII/310,
319 and 326 and 447, XCVII/654 and
XXCIII/305

ARCHIVES DE PARIS, PARIS
D. 31 U³ 51, 129, 2131 ; D. 32 U³ 5 ; D. 32 U⁵ 3 ;
D4B6 22, n° 1110 ; DQ186

CHAUMET ARCHIVES, PARIS
– Visitors' books
– Invoice ledgers (Paris)
– Invoice ledgers (London)
– Correspondence
– Binders of photographs
– Brochures

BIBLIOTHÈQUE THIERS, PARIS
Masson Collection, Ms. 30, 31, 40, 41, 65

DEPARTMENT OF PRINTS & DRAWINGS,
MUSÉE DU LOUVRE, PARIS
Brocard Collection, Picot registers

BIBLIOTHÈQUE MUNICIPALE, GRAY, FRANCE
Ms. 17, 18–20

BIBLIOGRAPHY

Avrillion, Marie-Jeanne-Pierrette. *Mémoires de Mademoiselle Avrillion, première femme de chambre de l'impératrice, sur la vie privée de Joséphine, sa famille et sa cour*, edited by Maurice Dernelle. Paris: Mercure de France, 1969.

Babelon, Ernest. *Catalogue des camées antiques et modernes de la Bibliothèque nationale*. Paris: E. Leroux, 1897, 2 vols.

Babin, Gustave. *Une pléiade de maîtres-joailliers, 1780–1930*. Paris: Imprimerie de Frazier Soye, 1930.

Banville, Théodore de. "Le Palais de la Mode" (January 1850), from *Le sang de la coupe*, in *Poésies complètes de Théodore de Banville*. Paris: Poulet-Malassis et de Broise, 1857.

Bastien, Vincent. "L'orfèvre-joaillier Ange-Joseph Aubert (1736–1785), fournisseur de la reine Marie-Antoinette," *Versalia* 16 (2013), pp. 31–46.

Bazar parisien ou Annuaire raisonné de l'industrie des premiers artistes et fabricans de Paris. Paris, 1821.

Bernard, Martial. "Exposition Internationale Artistique de Saint-Pétersbourg (1901–2)," *Revue de la Bijouterie, Joaillerie, Orfèvrerie* 22 (February 1902).

Boileau, Nicolas. *L'Art poétique*. Paris: Denys Thierry, 1674.

Bouilhet, Henri. *L'Orfèvrerie française aux XVIIIe et XIXe siècle, d'après les documents réunis au Musée centennal de 1900*. Paris: Henri Laurens, 1908–12.

Burty, Philippe. *F.-D. Froment-Meurice, argentier de la Ville, 1802–1855*. Paris: D. Jouaust, 1883.

Cerval, Marguerite de (ed.). *Dictionnaire international du bijou*. Paris: Éditions du Regard, 1998.

Champagny. *Notice sur les objets envoyés à l'exposition des produits de l'industrie rédigées et imprimées sur ordre de M. de Champagny, ministre de l'Intérieur, an 1806*. Paris: Imprimerie Nationale, 1806.

Chaumet, Joseph. *Le rubis: Communication faite aux Chambres Syndicales des Marchands de Diamants et Lapidaires, Joailliers et Bijoutiers, réunies le 21 juin 1904*. Paris: Imprimerie Petit, 1904.

Clary-et-Aldringen, Charles de. *Trois mois à Paris lors du mariage de l'empereur Napoléon Ier et de l'archiduchesse Marie-Louise*. Paris: Librairie Plon, 1914.

Dion-Tenenbaum, Anne. "Le musée du Louvre s'enrichit de la parure d'émeraudes et de diamants de Marie-Louise," *Revue des Musées de France/ Revue du Louvre* 4 (October 2004), pp. 17–18.

——. "Les Parures dans le Tableau de David" in Sylvain Laveissière (ed.), *Le Sacre*. Paris: Musée du Louvre/RMN, 2004, pp. 30–32.

——. "Une parure en or et mosaïque de Marie-Louise donnée par les Amis du Louvre," *Revue du Louvre et des musées de France* 5 (December 2001), pp. 16–17.

——. *Orfèvrerie française du XIXe siècle*. Paris: Somogy, 2011.

Douet, Simon-Pierre. *Tableau des symboles de l'orfèvrerie de Paris*. Paris: Self-published, 1806.

Dumaine, Jacques, *Quai d'Orsay: 1945–1951*. Paris: R. Julliard, 1955.

Dumas, Alexandre. *Henri III et sa cour: drame historique en 5 actes et en prose*. Paris: Vezard, 1933 [3rd ed.].

Ernstyl, Maud. "La Joaillerie française à l'Exposition de 1900," *Revue de la Bijouterie, Joaillerie, Orfèvrerie* 5 (September 1900).

Fontenay, Eugène. *Les Bijoux anciens et modernes*. Paris: Société d'Encouragement pour la Propagation des Livres d'Art, 1887.

Gastinel-Coural, Chantal. "A propos des présents de Napoléon au Pape. Deux tapis de la Savonnerie," *L'Estampille: L'objet d'art* 407 (November 2005), pp. 48–59.

Gaultier, Françoise and Catherine Metzger (eds.), *Trésors antiques, la collection du marquis Campana*. Paris: Musée du Louvre Éditions/ 5 Continents, 2005.

Girardin, Delphine de. *Le vicomte de Launay: Lettre parisiennes*. Paris: Michel Lévy Frères, 1857.

Grandjean, Serge. *Inventaire après décès de l'Impératrice Joséphine à Malmaison*. Paris: RMN, 1964.

Hamy, Ernest Théodore. "L'émeraude du pape Jules II au Museum d'histoire naturelle (1798–1805)," *Bulletin du Museum d'histoire naturelle* II (1896), pp. 48–51.

Héricart de Thury, Louis. *Rapport du jury d'admission des produits de l'industrie du département de la Seine à l'exposition du Louvre*. Paris: C. Ballard, 1819.

Heym, Sabine. "Prachtvolle Kroninsignien für Bayern- aber keine Krönung," in *Bayerns Krone 1806: 200 Jahre Königreich Bayern*, exh. cat., 2006, pp. 37–47 and pp. 248–49.

Huguenaud, Karine. "L'épée consulaire dite Epée du Sacre," *Bulletin de la Société des amis du musée de la Légion d'honneur et des ordres de chevalerie* 17 (2014), pp. 5–14.

Hurel, Roseline and Diana Scarisbrick (eds.), *Chaumet Paris: Two Centuries of Fine Jewellery*, trans Charles Penwarden. Paris: Paris-Musées, 1998.

Inventaire des diamants de la Couronne, perles, pierreries, tableaux, pierres gravées et autres monumens des arts et des sciences existans au Garde-Meuble.... Paris: Imprimerie Nationale, 1791.

Laveissiere, Sylvain (ed.). *Le Sacre*. Paris: Musée du Louvre/RMN, 2004.

La Mésangère, Pierre de. *Collection des maisons de commerce de Paris et intérieurs les mieux décorées*, 1806–28.

Leben, Ulrich. *L'école royale gratuite de dessin de Paris (1767–1815)*. Saint-Remy-en-l'Eau: Éditions Monelle Hayot, 2005.

Leniaud, Jean-Michel. *Saint-Denis de 1760 à nos jours*. Paris: Gallimard-Juliard, 1996.

Lucas, Isabelle. "Itinéraire d'un orfèvre d'exception, Valentin Morel," *L'Estampille-L'objet d'art* 330 (September 2000), pp. 94–103.

——. "Jean-Valentin Morel (1794–1860), un bijoutier parisien à l'époque romantique," *Histoire de l'art* 48 (June 2001), pp. 77–86.

——. *Vie et œuvre de Jean-Valentin Morel (1794–1860), orfèvre-joaillier*, unpublished dissertation for the École du Louvre under the supervision of Daniel Alcouffe, 1999.

Luynes, Honoré d'Albert, Duke of. *Exposition universelle de 1851: Travaux de la commission française sur l'industrie des nations publiés par ordre de l'Empereur. XXIIIe jury, Industrie des métaux précieux par M. le duc de Luynes*. Paris: Imprimerie Impériale, 1854.

Maze-Sencier, Alphonse. *Les fournisseurs de Napoléon Ier et des deux Impératrices*. Paris: Henri Laurens, 1893.

Miel, F., *Essai sur le Salon de 1817*. Paris: L'Imprimerie de Didot le Jeune.

Moléon, Jean-Gabriel-Victor de. *Description des expositions des produits de l'industrie française, faites à Paris depuis leur origine jusqu'à celle de 1819 inclusivement, servant d'introduction aux Annales de l'industrie....* Paris: Bachelier, 1824, 4 vols.

Morel, Bernard. *Les joyaux de la Couronne de France: Les objets du sacre des rois et des reines suivis de l'histoire des joyaux de la Couronne de François Ier à nos jours*. Paris: Albin Michel/Mercator, 1988.

——. *The French Crown Jewels: The Objects of the Coronations of the Kings And Queens of France, Followed by a History of the French Crown Jewels from François I Up to the Present Time*. Antwerp: Fonds Mercator, 1988.

Napoléon III et la reine Victoria. Paris: RMN, 2008.

Nocq, Henry. *Le Poinçon de Paris*. Paris: H. Floury, 1926–31, 4 vols.

Ottomeyer, Hans. *Die Kroninsignien des Königreiches Bayern*. Munich: Schnell und Steiner, 1979.

Pirzio Biroli Stefannelli, Lucia. *La collezione Paoletti: stampi in vetro per impronte di intagli e cammei*. Rome: Gangemi, 2007.

Poiret, Paul. *En habillant l'époque*. Paris: Grasset, 1974 [1930].

Remusat, Claire-Elisabeth-Jeanne Gravier de Vergennes, Countess of. *Mémoire*. Paris: Calmann Lévy, 1880, 3 vols.

Saint-Simon, Fernand de. *La place Vendôme*. Paris: Editions Vendôme, 1982.

Samoyault, Jean-Pierre and Colombe Samoyault-Verlet. *Château de Fontainebleau, Musée Napoléon Ier*. Paris: RMN, 1986.

Sarmant, Thierry and Luce Gaume (eds.). *La Place Vendôme, Art, pouvoir et fortune*, Paris: Action Artistique de la Ville de Paris, 2002.

Scarisbrick, Diana. "An Imperial Parure," *Apollo* (September 2004), pp. 80–83.

———. *Chaumet: Master Jewelers Since 1780*. Paris: Alain de Gourcuff, 1995.

———. *Tiara*. Boston: Museum of Fine Arts, San Francisco/Chronicle Books, 2000.

———. *Timeless Tiaras*. Paris: Assouline, 2002.

Sitwell, Osbert. *Laughter in the Next Room*. London: Macmillan & Co., 1949.

Tuetey, Louis. *Procès-verbaux de la commission temporaire des arts*, Paris: Imprimerie Nationale, 1912–17, 2 vols.

Vever, Henri. *La bijouterie française au XIXe siècle (1800–1900)*. Paris: H. Floury, 1906–8, 3 vols.

Viel-Castel, Horace, Count of. "Conversation," *Le Constitutionnel* (March 19, 1854).

Viruega, Jacqueline. *La bijouterie parisienne du Second Empire à la Première Guerre mondiale*. Paris: L'Harmattan, 2004.

Youssoupoff, Prince Felix. *Avant l'exil 1887–1919*. Paris: Librairie Plon, 1952.

Zeisler, Wilfried. *L'objet d'art et de luxe français en Russie (1881–1917), fournisseurs, clients, collections et influences*. Paris: Mare & Martin, 2014.

EXHIBITIONS

Boston, Museum of Fine Art. *Crowning Glories, Two Centuries of Tiaras*, March 1–June 25, 2000. Catalogue by Pamela J. Russell. Boston: Museum of Fine Arts, 2000.

Colorno (Parma), Palazzo ducale di Colorno. *Maria Luigia donna e sovrana, Una corte europea a Parma (1815–1847)*, May 10–July 26, 1992. Catalogue by Giuseppe Cirillo. Parma: Ugo Guanda, 1992.

Compiègne, Musée National du Palais de Compiègne. *Napoléon III et la reine Victoria, une visite à l'Exposition universelle de 1855*, October 4, 2008–January 18, 2009. Catalogue by Emmanuel Starcky et al. Paris: RMN, 2008.

Compiègne, Musée National du Palais de Compiègne, and Warsaw, Royal Castle. *Napoléon Ier ou la légende des arts, 1800–1815*, April 24–July 27, 2015 (Compiègne), September 11–December 13, 2015 (Warsaw). Catalogue by Emmanuel Starcky et al. Paris: RMN, 2015.

Essen, Villa Hügel/Krupp Foundation and Munich, Kunsthalle. *Paris—Belle Époque 1880–1910*, June 11–November 13, 1994 (Essen), December 15, 1994–February 26, 1995 (Munich). Catalogue by Jean-Marc Léri et al. Recklinghausen: Verlag A. Bongers, 1994.

Fontainebleau, Château de Fontainebleau. *Pie VII face à Napoléon: La tiare dans les serres de l'Aigle. Rome, Paris, Fontainebleau, 1796–1814*, March 28–June 29, 2015. Catalogue edited by Christophe Beyeler. Paris: RMN, 2015.

Kassel, Museumslandschaft Hessen Kassel. *König Lustik!? Jérôme Bonaparte und der Modellstaat Königreich Westphalen*, March 19–June 29, 2008. Catalogue edited by Michael Eissenhauer. München: Hirmer, 2008.

Lisbon, Calouste Gulbenkian Museum. *Art Déco—1925*, October 16, 2009–January 3, 2010. Catalogue by João Carvalho Dias et al. Lisbon: Calouste Gulbenkian Foundation, 2009.

Luxembourg, Musée National d'Histoire et d'Art. *100 Joer Lëtzebuerger Dynastie: Collections et Souvenirs de la Maison Grand-Ducale*, November 30, 1990–January 6, 1991. Catalogue edited by Jean-Claude Muller. Luxembourg: Grand-Duché de Luxembourg, 1990.

Melbourne, National Gallery of Victoria. *Napoleon: Revolution to Empire*, June 2–October 7, 2012. Catalogue edited by Ted Gott and Karine Huguenaud. Melbourne: National Gallery of Victoria, 2012.

Memphis, Tennessee, Convention Center. *Napoleon*, February 2–July 1, 1993. Catalogue by Bernard Chevallier, Jean Tulard and Christophe Pincemaille. Memphis: Lithograph Pub. Co., 1993.

Monaco, Grimaldi Forum. *Moscou, Splendeurs des Romanov*, July 11–September 13, 2009. Catalogue by Brigitte de Montclos et al. Milan/Monaco: Skira/Grimaldi Forum, 2009.

Moscow, State Museums of Moscow Kremlin. *India, Jewels that Enchanted the World*, April 12–July 27, 2014. Catalogue edited by Ekaterina Shcherbi§na. London: Anikst Design, 2014.

Munich, Bayerisches Nationalmuseum. *Pariser Schmuck, vom Zweiten Kaiserreich zur Belle Époque*, November 29, 1989–March 4, 1990. Catalogue by Michael Koch et al. München: Hirmer Verlag, 1989.

New York, Cooper-Hewitt Museum. *"L'art de vivre," Decorative Art and Design, France 1789–1989*, March 27–July 14, 1989. Catalogue by Catherine Arminjon and Yvonne Brunhammer. New York: Vendome Press, 1989.

New York, Metropolitan Museum of Art. *The Age of Napoleon, Costume from Revolution to Empire, 1789–1815*, December 13, 1989–April 15, 1990. Catalogue edited by Katell Le Bourhis. New York: Metropolitan Museum of Art/Harry N. Abrams, 1989.

Paray-Le-Monial, Musée du Hiéron. *Divines Joaillerie: L'art de Joseph Chaumet (1852–1928)*, June 14, 2014–January 4, 2015. Catalogue by Dominique Dendrael, Diana Scarisbrick and Pierre-Yves Chatagnier. City of Paray-Le-Monial, 2014.

Paris, Grand Palais. *Un âge d'or des arts décoratifs 1814–1848*, October 10–December 30, 1991. Catalogue by Laurent de Commines et al. Paris: Impr. J. London, 1991.

Paris, Hôtel de Villemaré. *La place Vendôme. Art, pouvoir et fortune*, January 24–March 2, 2003. Catalogue edited by Thierry Sarmant and Luce Daume. Paris: Action Artistique de la Ville de Paris, 2002.

Paris, Musée Carnavalet. *Chaumet Paris: Two Centuries of Fine Jewellery*, March 25–June 28, 1998. Catalogue edited by Roseline Hurel and Diana Scarisbrick. Paris: Paris Musées, 1998.

Paris, Musée de l'Armée, Hôtel National des Invalides. *Napoléon et l'Europe*, March 27–July 14, 2013. Catalogue edited by Émilie Robbe and François Lagrange. Paris: Musée de l'Armée/Somogy, 2013.

Paris, Musée de la Vie romantique. *Bijoux romantiques, 1820–1850, la parure à l'époque de Georges Sand*, May 3–October 1, 2000. Catalogue by Daniel Marchesseau et al. Paris: Paris-Musées, 2000.

Paris, Musée du Louvre. *Dix siècles de joaillerie française*, May 3–June 3, 1962. Catalogue by Daniel Alcouffe, Bertrand Jestaz and Colombe Verlet. Paris: Musée du Louvre, 1962.

Paris, Musée Galliera, Musée de la Mode de la Ville de Paris. *Japonisme et Mode 1870–1996*, April 17–August 4, 1996. Catalogue by Shuji Takashina et al. Paris: Paris-Musées, 1996.

Paris, Musée Galliera, Musée de la Mode de la Ville de Paris. *Sous l'Empire des Crinolines (1852–1870)*, November 29, 2008–April 26, 2009. Catalogue by Françoise Tétart-Vittu et al. Paris: Paris-Musées, 2008.

Pforzheim, Schmuckmuseum Pforzheim. *Art Déco Schmuck und Accessoires: ein neuer Stil für eine neue Welt*, September 20, 2008–January 11, 2009. Catalogue edited by Cornelie Holzach. Stuttgart: Arnoldsche, 2008.

Pforzheim, Schmuckmuseum Pforzheim. *Himmlisch: Sonne, Mond und Sterne im Schmuck—Heavenly: The Sun, Moon and Stars in Jewellery*, July 8–October 30, 2016, Catalogue edited by Fritz Falk. Stuttgart: Arnoldsche, 2016.

Pforzheim, Schmuckmuseum Pforzheim. *Schaumgeboren und sagenumwoben—Perlen im Schmuck—Angel's Tears or Gems of the Ocean—Pearls in the History of Jewellery*, October 26, 2012–January 27, 2013. Catalogue by Cornelie Holzach and Isabel Schmidt-Mappes. Pforzheim: Schmuckmuseum, 2012.

Stuttgart, Landesmuseum Württemberg. *Das Königreich Württemberg, 1806–1918, Monarchie und Moderne*, September 22, 2006–February 4, 2007. Catalogue by Dieter Langewiesche et al. Ulm: Süddeutsche Verlagsgesellschaft Gesellschaft 2006.

Tokyo, Metropolitan Teien Art Museum, Fukuoka, City Museum, Nagoya, Matzuzakaya Arts Museum and Kyoto, EKI Museum. *Jewelry from Renaissance to Art Deco 1540–1940*, April 24–July 1, 2003 (Tokyo), July 12–August 24, 2003 (Fukuoka), August 30–September 23, 2003 (Nagoya), and October 25–November 30, 2003 (Kyoto). Catalogue by Diana Scarisbricke et al. Fukuoka: Nishinippon Shimbun, 2003.

Tokyo, National Museum, and Osaka, Municipal Museum of Art. *The Splendor of Diamond, 400 Years of Diamond Jewelry in Europe*, October 7–December 21, 2003 (Tokyo), January 9–February 29, 2004 (Osaka). Catalogue by Jan Walgrave et al. Tokyo: APT, International, 2004.

Tokyo, The Bunkamura Museum of Art, Niigata, The Niigata Bandaijima Museum of Art, and Kyoto, The Museum of Kyoto, *Tiara: Dignity and Beauty—The Story of the Tiara*, January 20–March 18, 2007 (Tokyo), April 1–May 9, 2007 (Niigata), June 9–July 22, 2007 (Kyoto). Catalogue by Diana Scarisbrick et al. Tokyo: Nippon Television Network Coop., 2007.

PICTURE CREDITS

t: top, b: bottom, l: left, r: right, c: center

Every effort has been made to identify photographers and copyright holders of the images reproduced in this book. Any errors or omissions referred to the Publisher will be corrected in subsequent printings.

© Chaumet: pp. 14, 18–19, 24l, 30, 32, 37, 60r, 73, 80, 81, 84, 85, 87, 88, 95, 96, 97b, 99, 103, 105t, 108, 115, 124, 125, 127, 129, 148, 149, 155, 156, 161, 162, 164, 168–70, 172, 213, 216, 231, 232, 234, 236–38, 243, 248, 249, 253, 257, 269, 276, 280, 281, 298, 302–4, 309–11, 323c, 328, 334, 335, 339, 346, 347, 350, 355, 360, 362, 363, 370, 378, 380, 381, 384, 389b.

© Chaumet / Bruno Ehrs: front cover and back cover, pp. 4, 5, 8, 11, 20, 22, 116, 131, 134, 136, 139, 143, 181, 184, 202, 205, 208–9, 223–25, 263, 273, 359, 365, 366–69.

© Chaumet / Nils Herrmann: pp. 2, 12, 13, 16, 38, 40, 61, 66, 68, 71, 77, 82, 90l, 92, 100, 106, 109, 113, 118, 123, 138, 140, 147, 153, 157–59l, 165–67, 171, 177, 179, 182, 186, 188, 189, 197–99, 217, 218, 221, 226, 239, 250–52, 282, 284, 287, 288, 290–92, 294–99, 305–8, 312–14, 317, 323t, 325, 326, 336, 337, 340–41, 344–45, 348, 349, 354, 374, 377, 379, 382l, 383, 386–89l, 391–93.

Other images: p. 15: © All rights reserved; p. 21: © Courtesy of Albion Art Jewellery Institute; p. 24r: © All rights reserved; p. 25: © All rights reserved; p. 26: © Époque Fine Jewels, Belgium; pp. 28-29: © Katharina Faerber; p. 33: © Rami Solomon & Kineret Levy Studio, Israël, Musée Lalique, France, Dépôt Shai Bandmann and Ronald Ooi; p. 34: © George Hoyningen-Huene / Condé Nast via Getty Images; p. 42: © Katharina Faerber; p. 44: © RMN-Grand Palais / Gérard Blot; p. 45: © Museo Napoleonico; p. 46: © Musée Carnavalet / Roger-Viollet; p. 48: © All rights reserved; p. 49: © All rights reserved; p. 50: © RMN-Grand Palais (Château de Fontainebleau) / Gérard Blot; p. 51: © All rights reserved; p. 53: © RMN-Grand Palais (musée du Louvre) / Michel Urtado; p. 54: © All rights reserved; p. 57: © Photo12 / Fondation Napoléon; p. 59: © RMN-Grand Palais (musée des châteaux de Malmaison et de Bois-Préau) / André Martin; p. 60l: © All rights reserved; p. 62: © Stéphane Piera / Musée Carnavalet / Roger-Viollet; p. 65: © Archives de la Manufacture, Sèvres, France / Archives Charmet / Bridgeman Images; p. 67: © RMN-Grand Palais (Château de Versailles) / All rights reserved; p. 74: © RMN-Grand Palais (domaine de Compiègne) / Franck Raux; p. 79: © RMN-Grand Palais (Château de Versailles) / Gérard Blot; p. 90r: © All rights reserved; p. 97t: © L'Illustration; p. 102: © All rights reserved; p. 102c: © Bettman /Getty images; p. 105b: © Popperfoto / Getty Images; p. 110: © Janine Niepce-Rapho; p. 111: © All rights reserved; p. 117: © Chaumet / Pénélope Chauvelot; pp. 132–33: © Private Collection / Bridgeman Images; p. 135: © Louvre, Paris, France / Bridgeman Images; p. 141:

© KHM-Museumsverband; p. 144: © All rights reserved; pp. 150–51: © RMN-Grand Palais (domaine de Compiègne) / Agence Bulloz; p. 154: © National Portrait Gallery, London; p. 159r: © Bridgeman Images; p. 160: © Illustrated London News Ltd / Mary Evans; p. 173: © Katharina Faerber; p. 174: © Imagno / Getty Images; p. 175: © All rights reserved; p. 176: © Henry Clarke, Musée Galliera / Adagp, Paris, 2017; p. 190: © Palais Fesch, musée des Beaux-Arts; p. 192: © Bayerische Schlösserverwaltung, Maria Scherf / Rainer Herrmann, München; p. 195: © RMN-Grand Palais / Franck Raux; p. 196: © Victoria and Albert Museum, London; p. 201: © RMN-Grand Palais (musée du Louvre) / Thierry Le Mage; p. 206l: © Sotheby's; p. 206r: © RMN-Grand Palais (musée du Louvre) / Mathieu Rabeau; p. 207: © Foto Alexis Daflos / The Royal Court SWE; p. 210: © RMN-Grand Palais (musée du Louvre) / Jean-Gilles Berizzi; p. 212: © Smithsonian, 2017; p. 215: © RMN-Grand Palais (musée du Louvre) / Hervé Lewandowski; p. 219: © All rights reserved; p. 229: © Photo Les Arts Décoratifs, Paris / Jean Tholance; p. 240: © RMN-Grand Palais (musée du Louvre) / All rights reserved; p. 241: © RMN-Grand Palais (musée du Louvre) / All rights reserved; p. 242: © RMN-Grand Palais (musée d'Orsay) / Adrien Didierjean; p. 244: © Collection Trust / © Her Majesty Queen Elizabeth II 2016; p. 246: © Musée de la Vie Romantique / Roger-Viollet; p. 247: © All rights reserved; p. 254: © The Frick Collection; p. 259: © Schmuckmuseum Pforzheim, Germany; p. 261: © Maison de Balzac / Roger-Viollet; p. 264: © RMN-Grand Palais (musée du Louvre) / All rights reserved; p. 267: © RMN-Grand Palais (musée du Louvre) / Daniel Arnaudet; p. 268: © Musée du Louvre, Dist. RMN-Grand Palais / Martine Beck-Coppola; p. 271: © All rights reserved; p. 274: © RMN-Grand Palais (domaine de Compiègne) / Daniel Arnaudet; p. 275: © RMN-Grand Palais (domaine de Compiègne) / All rights reserved; p. 277: © Chaumet / Olivier Foulon; p. 279: © RMN-Grand Palais (musée des châteaux de Malmaison et de Bois-Préau) / Daniel Arnaudet; p. 301: © Ministère de la Culture - Médiathèque du Patrimoine, Dist. RMN-Grand Palais / Félix Nadar; p. 315: © Ministère de la Culture - Médiathèque du Patrimoine, Dist. RMN-Grand Palais / Félix Nadar; p. 318: © All rights reserved; p. 321: © Imago / Rue des Archives; p. 322: © All rights reserved; p. 323b: © All rights reserved; p. 330: © All rights reserved; p. 333: © The Cecil Beaton Studio Archive at Sotheby's; p. 342: © BnF; p. 351t: © Cour grand-ducale / Vincent Everarts / All rights reserved; p. 351b: © SZ Photo / Bridgeman Images; p. 352: © Katharina Faerber; p. 356: © Victoria and Albert Museum, London; p. 357: © Victoria and Albert Museum, London; p. 361: © Adagp, Paris, 2017; p. 371: © Photo by ullstein bild / ullstein bild via Getty Images; p. 372: © Sasha / Getty Images; p. 373: © akg-images; p. 382r: © All rights reserved.

ACKNOWLEDGMENTS

The Maison Chaumet and the Publisher thank the following for their invaluable contribution to this publication:

H.R.H. The King Karl XVI Gustaf of Sweden

Mr. Kazumi Arikawa, Mr. Philippe Atamian, the General of division Christian Baptiste, Mrs. Laure Barthet, the Duke and the Duchess of Bedford, the descendants of the Countess of Bessborough, Mr. Christophe Beyeler, Mr. Anthony De Bono, H.R.H the Princess of Bourbon-Two Sicilies, Mr. Pierre Branda, Mrs. Catherine Brooks, Mrs. Christelle Brothier, Mrs. Véronique Brumm, Count Jean-Gaspard de Chavagnac, Count Arnaud de Contenson, Mr. Philippe Costamagna, Mr. Laurent Creuzet, Mr. Matthieu Dernis, Mrs. Anne Dion-Tenenbaum, Mr. Vincent Droguet, Mr. Jannic Durand, Mrs. Sabina Eckenfels, Mr. Richard Edgcumbe, Mrs. Lisa Edwards, Mrs. Ida Faerber, Mr. Max Faerber, Mr. and Mrs. Thomas Faerber, Mrs. Sandrine Folpini, Mr. Eric Le Gallais, Mr. Michael Green, Count Hervé de Guébriant, Mrs. Valérie Guillaume, Mr. David Guillet, Mrs. Stéphanie Guyot-Nourry, H.R.H. the Princess of Hanovre, Mr. Felix Harrington, Lady Harrison, Mrs. John Hastings Bass, Mr. Jean-François Hébert, Mrs. Pansy Ho, Mrs. Keiko Horii, Mrs. Muguette Jumeau, Mr. and Mrs. John Kurtz, Mrs. Sabine de La Rochefoucauld, Mrs. Delphine Lannaud, Mrs. Sidonie Laude, Mr. Amaury Lefébure, Mrs. Élodie Lefort, Mr. and Mrs. Joseph de Léotard, Mr. Jean-Luc Martinez, Mrs. Daniela Mascetti, Duke of Rivoli and Prince of Essling Victor-André Masséna, Mrs. Dafna Meitar Nechmad, Mrs. Anne-Sophie Métrau, Mrs. Sara Mittica, Mr. and Mrs. René Morin, Mrs. Sophie Motsch, Mr. Jonathan Norton, Mr. Nicholas Norton, Mr. François d'Orcival, Mrs. Sarah Paronetto, Mr. Alain Pougetoux, Mr. Marco Pupillo, Mrs. Chrystelle Quebriac, Mr. Martin Roth, Mrs. Francesca Sandrini, Mr. and Mrs. Sampiero Sanguinetti, Mr. Emmanuel Sarmeo, Mrs. Diana Scarisbrick, Mrs. Isabel Schmidt-Mappes, Mr. and Mrs. Emmanuel Starcky, Mrs. Carole Treton, Mrs. Élodie Vaysse, Mrs. Robert Valtz, Mrs. Nicole Verschuere, Mrs. Dominique Vitart, the Duchess of Westminster, Mrs. Marjorie Williams, Mr. Haydn Williams, Countess Jérôme de Witt.